THE ROUGH GUIDE

MEXICAN SPANISH

PHRASEBOOK

Compiled by

LEXUS

ROUGH
GUIDES

www.roughguides.com

Credits

Compiled by Lexus with Mike Gonzalez
Lexus Series Editor: Sally Davies
Rough Guides Reference Director: Andrew Lockett
Rough Guides Series Editor: Mark Ellingham

First edition published in 1996.
Reprinted in 1997 and 1998.
Revised in 1999.
This updated edition published in 2006 by
Rough Guides Ltd,
80 Strand, London WC2R 0RL
345 Hudson St, 4th Floor, New York 10014, USA
Email: mail@roughguides.co.uk.

Distributed by the Penguin Group.

Penguin Books Ltd, 80 Strand, London WC2R 0RL
Penguin Putnam, Inc., 375 Hudson Street, NY 10014, USA
Penguin Group (Australia), 250 Camberwell Road, Camberwell,
Victoria 3124, Australia
Penguin Books Canada Ltd, 10 Alcorn Avenue, Toronto,
Ontario, Canada M4V 1E4
Penguin Group (New Zealand), Cnr Rosedale and Airborne Roads,
Albany, Auckland, New Zealand

Typeset in Bembo and Helvetica to an original design by Henry Iles.
Printed in Italy by LegoPrint S.p.A

British Library Cataloguing in Publication Data
A catalogue for this book is available from the British Library.

ISBN 13: 978-1-84353-636-9
ISBN 10: 1-84353-636-6

The publishers and authors have done their best to ensure the accuracy
and currency of all information in The Rough Guide Mexican Spanish
Phrasebook however, they can accept no responsibility for any loss or
inconvenience sustained by any reader using the book.

Online information about Rough Guides can be found at our website www.
roughguides.com

CONTENTS

CONTENTS

Introduction

The Rough Guide Mexican Spanish phrasebook is a highly practical introduction to the contemporary language. Laid out in clear A-Z style, it uses key-word referencing to lead you straight to the words and phrases you want – so if you need to book a room, just look up 'room'. The Rough Guide gets straight to the point in every situation, in bars and shops, on trains and buses, and in hotels and banks.

The main part of the Rough Guide is a double dictionary: English-Spanish then Spanish-English. Before that, there's a section called **Basic Phrases** and to get you involved in two-way communication, the Rough Guide includes, in this new edition, a set of **Scenario** dialogues illustrating questions and responses in key situations such as renting a car and asking directions. You can hear these and then download them free from **www. roughguides.com/phrasebooks** for use on your computer or MP3 player.

Forming the heart of the guide, the **English-Spanish** section gives easy-to-use transliterations of the Spanish words wherever pronunciation might be a problem. Throughout this section, cross-references enable you to pinpoint key facts and phrases, while asterisked words indicate where further information can be found in a section at the end of the book called **How the Language Works**. This section sets out the fundamental rules of the language, with plenty of practical examples. You'll also find here other essentials like numbers, dates, telling the time and basic phrases. In the **Spanish-English** dictionary, we've given you not just the phrases you'll be likely to hear (starting with a selection of slang and colloquialisms) but also many of the signs, labels, instructions and other basic words you may come across in print or in public places.

Near the back of the book too the Rough Guide offers an extensive **Menu Reader**. Consisting of food and drink sections (each starting with a list of essential terms), it's indispensable whether you're eating out, stopping for a quick drink, or browsing through a local food market.

¡buen viaje!
have a good trip!

Basic
Phrases

yes
sí

no
no

OK
bueno
bweno

hello!/hi!
¡hola!
ola

good morning
buenos días
bwenos

good evening
buenas tardes
bwenas

good night
buenas noches
noches

goodbye/see you
hasta luego
asta lwego

please
por favor
fabor

yes please
sí, por favor

thanks, thank you
gracias
gras-yas

no thanks, no thank you
no gracias

thank you very much
muchas gracias
moochas

don't mention it
de nada
deh

how do you do?
¡mucho gusto!
moocho

how are you?
¿cómo le va?
leh

fine, thanks
bien gracias
b-yen gras-yas

nice to meet you
encantado de conocerle
deh konosairleh

excuse me
(to get past) con permiso
(to get attention) ¡por favor!
fabor

(I'm) sorry
disculpe
deeskoolpeh

sorry?/pardon (me)?
(didn't understand) ¿mande?
mandeh

what did you say?
¿qué dijo?
keh deeHo

I see/I understand
entiendo
ent-yendo

I don't understand
no entiendo

do you speak English?
¿habla inglés?
abla

I don't speak Spanish
no hablo español
ablo espan-yol

could you speak more slowly?
¿podría hablar mas lento?
ablar

could you repeat that?
¿puede repetir eso?
pwedeh

could you write it down?
¿puede escribírmelo?

I'd like a ...
quisiera un/una ...
kees-yaira

I'd like to ...
me gustaría ...
meh

can I have ...?
¿me da ...?

how much is it?
¿cuánto vale?
kwanto baleh

cheers!
(toast) ¡salud!
saloo

it is ...
es ...; está ...

where is it?
¿dónde está?
dondeh

where are the ...?
¿dónde están los/las ...?

how far is it to ...?
¿cuánto hay de aquí a ...?
kwanto ī deh akee

is it far?
¿queda lejos?
keda leHos

how long does it take?
¿cuánto dura?
kwanto

at what time ...?
¿a qué hora ...?
keh ora

when is ...?
cuándo es ...?
kwando

9

Scenarios

1. Accommodation

is there an inexpensive hotel you can recommend?
▶ ¿puede recomendarme un hotel que no sea caro?
[pw**e**deh rekomend**a**rmeh oon ot**e**l keh no s**eh**-a k**a**ro]

desgraciadamente parece que todos están llenos ◀
[desgras-y**a**da-menteh par**e**seh keh t**o**dos estan y**e**nos]
I'm sorry, they all seem to be fully booked

can you give me the name of a good middle-range hotel?
▶ ¿me puede dar el nombre de un buen hotel mediano?
[meh pw**e**deh dar el n**o**mbreh deh un bwen ot**e**l med-y**a**no]

déjeme ver ¿prefiere estar en el centro? ◀
[d**e**Hehmeh b**e**r pref-y**e**reh est**a**r en el s**e**ntro]
let me have a look; do you want to be in the centre?

if possible
▶ si es posible
[see es pos**ee**bleh]

¿le importa estar un poco lejos del centro? ◀
[leh eemp**o**rta est**a**r oon p**o**ko l**e**Hos del s**e**ntro]
do you mind being a little way out of town?

not too far out
▶ no demasiado lejos
[no demas-y**a**do l**e**Hos]

where is it on the map?
▶ ¿dónde está en el mapa?
[d**o**ndeh est**a** en el m**a**pa]

can you write the name and address down?
▶ ¿puede anotar el nombre y la dirección?
[pw**e**deh anot**a**r el n**o**mbreh ee la deereks-y**o**n]

I'm looking for a room in a private house
▶ busco un cuarto en una casa particular
[b**oo**sko oon kw**a**rto en **oo**na k**a**sa parteek**oo**lar]

2. Banks

bank account	la cuenta bancaria	[kwenta bankar-ya]
to change money	cambiar dinero	[kamb-yar deenairo]
cheque	el cheque	[chehkeh]
to deposit	depositar	[deposeetar]
dollar	el dólar	[dolar]
peso	el peso	[peso]
pin number	el pin	[peen]
pound	la libra	[leebra]
to withdraw	retirar	[reteerar]

can you change this into pesos?
▶ ¿puede cambiarme esto por pesos?
[pwedeh kamb-yarmeh esto por pesos]

¿cómo quiere el dinero? ◀
[komo k-yaireh el deenairo]
how would you like the money?

small notes
▶ billetes pequeños
[bee-yetes peken-yos]

big notes
▶ billetes grandes
[bee-yetes grandes]

do you have information in English about opening an account?
▶ ¿tiene información en inglés sobre cómo abrir una cuenta?
[t-yeneh eenformas-yon en eengles sobreh komo abreer oona kwenta]

sí ¿qué tipo de cuenta quiere? ◀
[see keh teepo deh kwenta k-yereh]
yes, what sort of account do you want?

I'd like a checking account
▶ quisiera una cuenta corriente
[kees-yaira oona kwenta korr-yenteh]

permítame su pasaporte, por favor ◀
[pairmeetameh soo pasaporteh por fabor]
your passport, please

can I use this card to draw some cash?
▶ ¿puedo sacar dinero con esta tarjeta?
[pwedo sakar deenairo kon esta tarHeta]

tiene que pasar a la caja ◀
[t-yeneh keh pasar ala kaHa]
you have to go to the cashier's desk

I want to transfer this to my account at the Banco de Comercio
▶ quisiera hacer una transferencia a mi cuenta en el Banco de Comercio
[kees-yaira asair oona transferens-ya a mee kwenta en el banko deh komers-yo]

con todo gusto, pero tendremos que cobrarle la llamada ◀
[kon todo goosto pero tendremos keh kobrarleh la yamada]
OK, but we'll have to charge you for the phonecall

14

3. Booking a room

shower	la regadera	[regadera]
telephone in the room	teléfono en el cuarto	[teléfono en el kwarto]
payphone in the lobby	teléfono público	[teléfono poobleeko
	en el vestíbulo	en el besteeboolo]

do you have any rooms?
▶ ¿tiene cuartos libres?
[t-yeneh kwartos leebres]

▶ ¿para cuántas personas?   for one/for two
[para kwantas pairsonas]   ▶ para una/para dos
for how many people?   [para oona/para dos]

                                  sí, tenemos cuartos libres ◀
                                  [see tenemos kwartos leebres]
                                  yes, we have rooms

▶ ¿para cuántas noches?   just for one night
[para kwantas noches]   ▶ sólo para una noche
for how many nights?   [solo para oona nocheh]

how much is it?
▶ ¿cuánto es?
[kwanto es]

---

                90 pesos con baño y 70 sin baño ◀
                [nobenta pesos kon ban-yo ee setenta seen ban-yo]
                90 pesos with bathroom and 70 without bathroom

does that include breakfast?
▶ ¿está incluido el desayuno?
[esta eenkloo-eedo el desa-yoono]

can I see a room with bathroom?
▶ ¿puedo ver un cuarto con baño?
[pwedo bair oon kwarto kon ban-yo]

ok, I'll take it
▶ está bien, lo voy a tomar
[esta b-yen lo boy a tomar]

when do I have to check out?
▶ ¿a qué hora hay que desocupar?
[a keh ora ī keh desokoopar]

is there anywhere I can leave luggage?
▶ ¿tiene dónde dejar el equipaje?
[t-yeneh dondeh deHar el ekeepaHeh]

4. Car hire

automatic	automático	[owtomateeko]
full tank	depósito lleno	[deposeeto yeno]
manual	manual	[manwal]
rented car	el coche alquilado	[kocheh alkeelado]

I'd like to rent a car
▶ quisiera alquilar un coche
[kees-yaira alkeelar oon kocheh]

▶ ¿para cuánto tiempo?   two days
[para kwanto t-yempo]   ▶ dos días
for how long?   [dos dee-as]

I'll take the ...
▶ me llevo el ...
[meh yebo el ...]

is that with unlimited mileage?   sí ◀
▶ ¿es sin límite de kilómetros?   [see]
[es seen leemeeteh deh keelometros]   yes

                        ¿me permite su licencia? por favor ◀
                        [meh pairmeeteh soo leesens-ya por fabor]
                        can I see your driving licence, please?

                                        y su pasaporte ◀
                                        [ee soo pasaporteh]
                                        and your passport

is insurance included?
▶ ¿está incluido el seguro?
[esta eenkl-ooeedo el segooro]

    sí, pero usted tendría que pagar los primeros cien pesos ◀
    [see pairo oosteh tendreea keh pagar los preemairos s-yen pesos]
    yes, but you have to pay the first 100 pesos

         ¿puede dejar una fianza de cien pesos? ◀
         [pwedeh deHar oona fee-ansa deh s-yen pesos]
         can you leave a deposit of 100 pesos?

and if this office is closed, where do I leave the keys?
▶ y si esta oficina está cerrada ¿dónde dejo las llaves?
[ee see esta ofeeseena esta serrada dondeh deHo las yabes]

                        las pone en esa caja ◀
                        [las poneh en esa kaHa]
                        you drop them in that box

16

5. Communications

ADSL modem	el modem ADSL	[modem a-deh-eseh-eleh]
at	arroba	[arroba]
dial-up modem	el modem de	[modem deh
	marcador manual	markador manwal]
dot	punto	[poonto]
Internet	internet	[eentairnet]
mobile (phone)	el celular	[seloolar]
password	la contraseña	[kontrasen-ya]
telephone	el adaptador para	[adaptador para
socket adaptor	el teléfono	el telefono]
wireless	el punto de	[poonto deh akseso
hotspot	acceso inalámbrico	eenalambreeko]

is there an Internet café around here?
▶ ¿hay por aquí un cibercafé?
[ī por akee oon seebairkafeh]

can I send email from here?
▶ ¿puedo mandar emails desde aquí?
[pwedo mandar eemayls desdeh akee]

where's the at sign on the keyboard?
▶ ¿dónde está la arroba en el teclado?
[dondeh esta la arroba en el teklado]

can you switch this to a UK keyboard?
▶ ¿se puede cambiar a teclado británico?
[seh pwedeh kamb-yar a teklado breetaneeko]

can you help me log on?
▶ ¿me puede ayudar a conectarme?
[meh pwedeh a-yoodar a konektarmeh]

I'm not getting a connection, can you help?
▶ no está conectando ¿puede ayudarme?
[no esta konektando pwedeh a-yoodarmeh]

where can I get a top-up card for my mobile?
▶ ¿dónde puedo comprar tarjeta para el celular?
[dondeh pwedo komprar tarHeta para el seloolar]

can you put me through to ...?
▶ ¿puede ponerme con ...?
[pwedeh ponairmeh kon ...]

zero	five
cero	cinco
[sero]	[seenko]
one	six
uno	seis
[oono]	[says]
two	seven
dos	siete
[dos]	[s-yeteh]
three	eight
tres	ocho
[tres]	[ocho]
four	nine
cuatro	nueve
[kwatro]	[nwebeh]

6. Directions

hi, I'm looking for Calle Real
▶ hola, estoy buscando la Calle Real
[**o**la est**oy** boosk**a**ndo la ka-yeh reh-**al**]

disculpe, nunca oí hablar de ella
[deesk**oo**lpeh n**oo**nka o**ee** ablar deh **eh**-ya]
sorry, never heard of it

hi, can you tell me where Calle Real is?
▶ hola, ¿me puede decir dónde queda la
Calle Real?
[**o**la meh pw**e**deh des**ee**r d**o**ndeh k**e**da la ka-yeh reh-**al**]

yo tampoco soy de aquí ◀
[yo tamp**o**ko soy deh ak**ee**]
I'm a stranger here too

hi, Calle
Real, do
you know
where it is?
hola, la
Calle Real,
¿sabe
dónde
queda?
[**o**la la ka-yeh
reh-**al** s**a**beh
d**o**ndeh k**e**da]

where?   which direction?
¿dónde?   ¿por dónde?
[d**o**ndeh]   [por d**o**ndeh]

▶ a la vuelta de la esquina   ▶ entonces es la primera calle a la derecha
[a la bw**e**lta deh la esk**ee**na]   [ent**o**nses es la preem**ai**ra ka-yeh a la der**e**cha]
around the corner   then it's the first street on the right

▶ a la izquierda en el segundo semáforo
[a la eesk-y**ai**rda en el seg**oo**ndo semaforo]
left at the second traffic lights

a la derecha [a la der**e**cha] on the right	calle [ka-yeh] street	justo después [H**oo**sto despw**e**s] just after	todo derecho [**to**do der**e**cho] straight ahead
a la izquierda [a la eesk-y**ai**rda] on the left	cerca [s**ai**rka] near	más allá [mas a-y**a**] further	
allí [a-y**ee**] over there	delante de [del**a**nteh deh] in front of	pasado el... [pas**a**do el...] past the ...	voltee [bolt**eh**-eh] turn off
atrás [atr**a**s] back	en frente de [en fr**e**nteh deh] opposite	siguiente [seeg-y**e**nteh] next	

download these scenarios as MP3s from:

7. Emergencies

accident	el accidente	[akseed**e**nteh]
ambulance	la ambulancia	[amboolans-ya]
consul	el cónsul	[k**o**nsool]
embassy	la embajada	[embaнada]
fire brigade	los bomberos	[bomb**ai**ros]
police	la policía	[poleesee-a]

help!
▶ ¡socorro!
[sok**o**rro]

can you help me?
▶ ¿puede ayudarme?
[pw**e**deh a-yood**a**rmeh]

please come with me! it's really very urgent
▶ ¡por favor, venga conmigo! es realmente urgente
[por fab**o**r b**e**nga konm**ee**go es reh-alm**e**nteh oor**H**enteh]

I've lost (my keys)
▶ perdí (las llaves)
[paird**ee** (las y**a**bes)]

(my car) is not working
▶ (mi carro) no funciona
[(mee k**a**rro) no foons-y**o**na]

(my purse) has been stolen
▶ me robaron (el monedero)
[meh rob**a**ron (el moned**ai**ro)]

I've been mugged
▶ me asaltaron
[meh asalt**a**ron]

¿cómo se llama? ◀
what's your name?
[k**o**mo seh y**a**ma]

¿me permite su pasaporte? ◀
[meh pairm**ee**teh soo pasap**o**rteh]
I need to see your passport

I'm sorry, all my papers have been stolen
▶ disculpe, me robaron todos los documentos
[deesk**oo**lpeh meh rob**a**ron t**o**dos los dok**oo**mentos]

8. Friends

hi, how're you doing?
▶ hola ¿cómo estás?
[ola komo estas]

muy bien ¿y tú? ◀
[mwee b-yen ee too]
OK, and you?

yeah, fine
▶ bien
[b-yen]

not bad
▶ no estoy mal
[no estoy mal]

d'you know Antonio?
▶ ¿conoces a Antonio?
[konoses a anton-yo]

and this is Marta
▶ y ésta es Marta
[ee esta es marta]

si, ya nos conocíamos ◀
[see ya nos konosee-amos]
yeah, we know each other

where do you know each other from?
▶ ¿cómo se conocieron?
[komo seh konos-yeron]

nos conocimos en casa de Gonzalo ◀
[nos konoseemos en kasa deh gonsalo]
we met at Gonzalos's place

that was some party, eh?
▶ estupenda fiesta no
[estoopenda f-yesta no]

▶ fabuloso
[fabooloso]
the best

are you guys coming for a beer?
▶ ¿vienen a tomar una cerveza?
[b-yenen a tomar oona sairbesa]

▶ chido, vamos
[cheedo bamos]
cool, let's go

▶ no. quedé con Lola
[no kedeh kon lola]
no, I'm meeting Lola

see you at Gonzalo's place tonight
▶ nos vemos esta noche en casa de Gonzalo
[nos bemos esta nocheh en kasa deh gonsalo]

hasta luego
[asta lwego]
see you

download these scenarios as MP3s from:

9. Health

I'm not feeling very well
▶ no me siento bien
[no meh s-yento b-yen]

can you get a doctor?
▶ ¿puede llamar a un médico?
[pwedeh yamar a oon medeeko]

¿dónde le duele? ◀
[dondeh leh dweleh]
where does it hurt?

it hurts here
▶ me duele aquí
[meh dweleh akee]

▶ ¿es un dolor constante?
[es oon dolor konstanteh]
is the pain constant?

it's not a constant pain
▶ no es un dolor constante
[no es oon dolor konstanteh]

can I make an appointment?
▶ ¿puedo hacer una cita?
[pwedo aser oona seeta]

can you give me something for ...?
▶ ¿puede darme algo para ...?
[pwedeh darmeh algo para]

yes, I have insurance
▶ sí, tengo seguro
[see tengo segooro]

antibiotics	el antibiótico	[anteeb-yoteeko]
antiseptic ointment	la pomada antiséptica	[pomada anteesepteeka]
cystitis	la cystitis	[seesteeetees]
dentist	el dentista	[denteesta]
diarrhoea	la diarrea	[d-yarreh-a]
doctor	el médico	[medeeko]
hospital	el hospital	[ospeetal]
ill	enfermo	[enfairmo]
medicine	la medicina	[medeeseena]
painkillers	analgésicos	[analHeseekos]
pharmacy	la farmacia	[farmas-ya]
to prescribe	recetar	[resetar]
thrush	las aftas	[aftas]

10. Language difficulties

a few words	unas palabras	[**oo**nas palabras]
interpreter	el intérprete	[een**tair**preteh]
to translate	traducir	[tradoo**seer**]

le rechazaron la tarjeta de crédito ◄
[leh rechas**a**ron la tar**H**eta deh kr**e**deeto]
your credit card has been refused

what, I don't understand; do you speak English?
▶ ¿cómo? no entiendo; ¿habla usted inglés?
[**k**omo no ent-y**e**ndo **a**bla oost**eh** eengl**e**s]

esto no es válido ◄
[**e**sto no es bal**ee**do]
this isn't valid

could you say that again?
▶ ¿puede repetir?
[pw**e**deh repet**ee**r]

slowly
▶ lento
[l**e**nto]

I understand very little Spanish
▶ entiendo muy poco español
[ent-y**e**ndo mwee p**o**ko espan-y**o**l]

I speak Spanish very badly
▶ hablo español muy mal
[**a**blo espan-y**o**l mwee mal]

no puede pagar con esta tarjeta ◄
[no pw**e**deh pagar kon **e**sta tar**H**eta]
you can't use this card to pay

▶ ¿entiende?
[ent-y**e**ndeh]
do you understand?

sorry, no
▶ me temo que no
[meh t**e**mo keh no]

is there someone who speaks English?
▶ ¿hay alguien que hable ingles?
[**i** **a**lg-yen keh **a**bleh eengl**e**s]

oh, now I understand
▶ ah, ahora entiendo
[ah a-**o**ra ent-y**e**ndo]

is that ok now?
▶ ¿ya está bien?
[ya est**a** b-yen]

11. Meeting people

hello
▶ hola
[**o**la]

hola, me llamo Blanca ◀
[**o**la meh y**a**mo bl**a**nka]
hello, my name's Blanca

Graham, from England, Thirsk
▶ soy Graham, de Thirsk, Inglaterra
[soy gr**a**ham deh thirsk eenglat**e**rra]

no lo conozco ¿dónde está? ◀
[no lo kon**o**sko d**o**ndeh est**a**]
don't know it, where is it?

not far from York, in the North; and where are you from?
▶ no lejos de York, en el norte, ¿y de dónde es usted?
[no l**eh**Hos deh york en el n**o**rteh ee deh d**o**ndeh es **oo**steh]

soy de Veracruz; ¿está aquí solo? ◀
[soy deh berakr**oo**s; est**a** ak**ee** s**o**lo]
I'm from Veracruz; here by yourself?

no, I'm with my wife and two kids
▶ no, vengo con mi mujer y mis dos hijos
[no b**e**ngo kon mee moo**H**air ee mees dos **ee**Hos]

what do you do?
▶ ¿a qué se dedica?
[a keh seh ded**ee**ka]

a la informática ◀
[a la eenform**a**teeka]
I'm in computers

me too
▶ yo también
[yo tamb-y**e**n]

here's my wife now
▶ aquí viene mi mujer
[ak**ee** b-y**e**neh mee moo**H**air]

encantada de conocerla ◀
[enkant**a**da deh konos**a**irla]
nice to meet you

12. Post offices

airmail	correo aéreo	[korr**eh**-o a-**ai**ray-o]
post card	la postal	[postal]
post office	Correos	[korr**eh**-os]
stamp	la estampilla	[estamp**ee**ya]

what time does the post office close?
▶ ¿a qué hora cierra Correos?
[a keh **o**ra s-y**e**ra korr**eh**-os]

a las cinco entre semana ◀
[a las s**ee**nko **e**ntreh semana]
five o'clock weekdays

is the post office open on Saturdays?
▶ ¿Correos abre los sábados?
[korr**eh**-os **a**breh los s**a**bados]

hasta mediodía ◀
[**a**sta med-yod**ee**-a]
till midday

I'd like to send this registered to England
▶ quisiera mandar esto certificado a Inglaterra
[kees-y**ai**ra mand**ar** **e**sto sairteefeek**a**do a eenglat**e**rra]

sí, claro, serán 10 pesos ◀
[see kl**a**ro sair**a**n d-y**e**s p**e**sos]
certainly, that will cost 10 pesos

and also two stamps for England, please
▶ y también dos estampillas para Inglaterra, por favor
[ee tamb-y**e**n dos estamp**ee**-yas p**a**ra eenglat**e**rra por fab**o**r]

do you have some airmail stickers?
▶ ¿tiene pegatinas de correo aéreo?
[t-y**e**neh pegat**ee**nas deh korr**eh**-o a-**ai**ray-o]

do you have any mail for me?
▶ ¿tiene correo para mí?
[t-y**e**neh korr**eh**-o para mee]

cartas	letters
lista de correos	poste restante
paquetes	parcels

13. Restaurants

bill	la cuenta	[kwenta]
menu	la carta	[karta]
table	la mesa	[mesa]

can we have a non-smoking table?
▶ ¿nos da una mesa para no fumadores?
[nos da **oo**na **mesa** para no foomad**o**res]

there are two of us
▶ somos dos
[s**o**mos dos]

there are four of us
▶ somos cuatro
[s**o**mos kw**a**tro]

what's this?
▶ ¿qué es esto?
[keh es **e**sto]

es pescado ◀
[es pesk**a**do]
it's fish

es una especialidad de la zona ◀
[es **oo**na espes-yaleed**a** deh la s**o**na]
it's a local speciality

pase y se lo enseño ◀
[p**a**seh ee seh lo ens**e**n-yo]
come inside and I'll show you

we would like two of these, one of these, and one of those
▶ queremos dos de éstos, uno de éstos y uno de aquéllos
[ker**e**mos dos deh **e**stos **oo**no deh **e**stos ee **oo**no deh ak**e**h-yos]

▶ ¿y para beber?
[ee para beb**ai**r]
and to drink?

red wine
▶ vino tinto
[b**ee**no t**ee**nto]

white wine
▶ vino blanco
[b**ee**no bl**a**nko]

a beer and two orange juices
▶ una cerveza y dos jugos de naranja
[**oo**na sairb**e**sa ee dos H**oo**gos deh nar**a**nHa]

some more bread please
▶ un poco más pan, por favor
[oon p**o**ko mas pan por fab**o**r]

▶ ¿cómo estuvo la comida?
[k**o**mo est**oo**bo la kom**ee**da]
how was your meal?

excellent!, very nice!
▶ ¡estupenda! ¡muy buena!
[estoop**e**nda mwee bw**e**na]

▶ ¿algo más?
[**a**lgo mas]
anything else?

just the bill thanks
▶ sólo la cuenta, por favor
[s**o**lo la kw**e**nta por fab**o**r]

14. Shopping

¿en qué puedo servirle? ◀
[en keh pwedo sairbeerleh]
can I help you?

can I just have a look around?
▶ quiero mirar nada más
[k-yairo meerar nada mas]

yes, I'm looking for ...
▶ sí, estoy buscando ...
[see estoy booskando]

how much is this?
▶ ¿cuánto vale esto?
[kwanto baleh esto]

treinta y dos pesos ◀
[traynta ee dos pesos]
thirty-two pesos

OK, I think I'll have to leave it; it's a little too expensive for me
▶ está bien, no me lo llevo; es demasiado caro para mí
[esta b-yen no meh lo yebo es demas-yado karo para mee]

¿y esto? ◀
[ee esto]
how about this?

can I pay by credit card?
▶ ¿puedo pagar con tarjeta de crédito?
[pwedo pagar kon tarHeta deh kredeeto]

it's too big
▶ es demasiado grande
[es demas-yado grandeh]

it's too small
▶ es demasiado pequeño
[es demas-yado peken-yo]

it's for my son – he's about this high
▶ es para mi hijo – es más o menos así de alto
[es para mee eeHo es mas o menos asee deh alto]

▶ ¿va a querer algo más?
[ba a kerair algo mas]
will there be anything else?

that's all thanks
▶ eso es todo, gracias
[eso es todo gras-yas]

make it twenty pesos and I'll take it
▶ si me lo deja en veinte pesos me lo llevo
[see meh lo deHa en baynteh pesos meh lo yebo]

fine, I'll take it
▶ bien, me lo llevo
[b-yen meh lo yebo]

abierto	caja	cambiar	cerrado	rebajas
open	cash desk	to exchange	closed	sale

download these scenarios as MP3s from:

15. Sightseeing

art gallery	la galería de arte	[galairee-a deh arteh]
bus tour	el tour en camión	[toor en kam-yon]
city centre	el centro	[sentro]
closed	cerrado	[serrado]
guide	la guía	[gee-a]
museum	el museo	[mooseh-o]
open	abierto	[ab-yairto]

I'm interested in seeing the old town
▸ quisiera ver el casco antiguo
[kees-yaira bair el kasko anteegwo]

are there guided tours?
▸ ¿hay visitas guiadas?
[i beeseetas gee-adas]

disculpe, está completo ◂
[deekoolpeh esta kompleto]
I'm sorry, it's fully booked

how much would you charge to drive us around for four hours?
▸ ¿cuánto nos cobra por un paseo en carro de cuatro horas?
[kwanto nos kobra por oon paseh-o en karro deh kwatro oras]

can we book tickets for the concert here?
▸ ¿podemos reservar aquí los boletos para el concierto?
[podemos resairbar akee los boletos para el kons-yairto]

▸ si ¿a qué nombre? | ▸ ¿qué tarjeta de crédito?
[see a keh nombreh] | [keh tarHeta deh kredeeto]
yes, in what name? | **which credit card?**

where do we get the tickets?
▸ ¿dónde nos dan los boletos? | recójanlos en la entrada ◂
[dondeh nos dan los boletos] | [rekoHanlos en la entrada]
| **just pick them up at the entrance**

is it open on Sundays? | **how much is it to get in?**
▸ ¿abren los domingos? | ▸ ¿cuánto cuesta la entrada?
[abren los domeengos] | [kwanto kwesta la entrada]

are there reductions for groups of 6?
▸ ¿hay rebaja para grupos de 6?
[i rebaHa para groopos deh says]

that was really impressive!
▸ ¡estuvo impresionante!
[estoobo eempres-yonanteh]

16. Trains

to change trains	hacer correspondencia	[asair korrespondensee-ya]
platform	la vía	[bee-a]
return	el boleto de ida y vuelta	[boleto deh eeda ee bwelta]
single	el boleto de ida	[boleto deh eeda]
station	la estación	[estas-yon]
stop	la parada	[parada]
ticket	el boleto	[boleto]

how much is ...?
▶ ¿cuánto es ...?
[kwanto es]

a single, second class to ...
▶ un boleto de ida, en clase turista a ...
[oon boleto deh eeda en klaseh tooreesta a]

two returns, second class to ...
▶ dos boletos de ida y vuelta, en clase turista a ...
[dos boletos deh eeda ee bwelta en klaseh tooreesta a]

for today	**for tomorrow**	**for next Tuesday**
▶ para hoy	▶ para mañana	▶ para el próximo martes
[para oy]	[para man-yana]	[para el prokseemo martes]

¿quiere reservar el asiento? ◀
[k-yaireh resairbar el as-yento]
do you want to make a seat reservation?

tiene que hacer correspondencia en Córdoba ◀
[t-yeneh keh asair korrespondens-ya en kordoba]
you have to change at Córdoba

what time is the last train to Puebla?
▶ ¿a qué hora es el último tren para Puebla?
[a keh ora es el oolteemo tren para pwebla]

is this seat free?
▶ ¿está libre este asiento?
[esta leebreh esteh as-yento]

excuse me, which station are we at?
▶ disculpe ¿en qué estación estamos?
[deeskoolpeh en keh estas-yon estamos]

is this where I change for Mérida?
▶ ¿es aquí donde tengo que hacer correspondencia para Mérida?
[es akee dondeh tengo keh asair korrespondens-ya para mereeda]

English

→

Spanish

A

a, an* un [oon], una [oona]

about: about 20 unos veinte

it's about 5 o'clock son aproximadamente las cinco [aprokseemadamenteh]

a film about Mexico una película sobre México [sobreh]

above ... arriba de ... [arreeba deh]

abroad en el extranjero [estranHairo]

absolutely! (I agree) ¡claro!

accelerator el acelerador [aselairador]

accept aceptar [aseptar]

accident el accidente [akseedenteh]

there's been an accident hubo un accidente [oobo]

accommodation alojamiento [aloHam-yento]

accurate exacto

ache el dolor

my back aches me duele la espalda [meh dweleh]

across: across the road al otro lado de la calle [ka-yeh]

adapter el adaptador

address la dirección [deereks-yon]

what's your address? ¿cuál es su dirección? [kwal]

address book la libreta de direcciones [deh deereks-yon-es]

admission charge la entrada

adult el adulto [adoolto], la adulta

advance: in advance por adelantado

aeroplane el avión [ab-yon]

after después (de) [despwes (deh)]

after you pase Usted [paseh oosteh]

after lunch después de comer

afternoon la tarde [tardeh]

in the afternoon por la tarde

this afternoon esta tarde

aftershave el aftershave

aftersun cream la crema para después del sol [despwes]

afterwards luego [lwego]

again otra vez [bes]

against contra

age la edad [eda]

ago: a week ago hace una semana [aseh]

an hour ago hace una hora

agree: I agree de acuerdo [deh akwairdo]

AIDS el SIDA [seeda]

air el aire [Ireh]

by air en avión [ab-yon]

air-conditioned con clima artificial [arteefees-yal]

air-conditioning el aire acondicionado [Ireh akondees-yonado]

airmail: by airmail por avión [ab-yon]

airmail envelope el sobre aéreo [sobreh a-Ireh-o]

airplane el avión [ab-yon]

airport el aeropuerto [iropwairto]
to the airport, please al aeropuerto, por favor [fabor]
airport bus el camión del aeropuerto [kam-yon]
aisle seat el asiento de pasillo [as-yento deh pasee-yo]
alarm clock el despertador
alcohol el alcohol [alkol]
alcoholic alcohólico
all: all the boys todos los chicos
  all the girls todas las chicas
  all of it todo
  all of them todos
  that's all, thanks eso es todo, gracias [gras-yas]
allergic: I'm allergic to ... tengo alergia a ... [alairHee-a]
alligator el caimán [kiman]
allowed: is it allowed? ¿se permite? [seh pairmeeteh]
all right! ¡bueno! [bweno]
  I'm all right estoy bien [b-yen]
  are you all right? (fam) ¿estás bien?
  (pol) ¿se encuentra bien? [seh enkwentra]
almond la almendra
almost casi
alone solo
alphabet el alfabeto

a a	g Heh
b beh larga	h acheh
c seh	i ee
ch cheh	j Hota
d deh	k ka

e eh	l eleh
f efeh	m emeh
n eneh	t teh
ñ en-yeh	u oo
o o	v beh cheeka
p peh	w oobeh
q koo	x ekees
r airreh	y ee gr-yega
s eseh	z seta

already ya
also también [tamb-yen]
although aunque [a-oonkeh]
altogether del todo
always siempre [s-yempreh]
am*: I am soy; estoy
a.m.: at seven a.m. a las siete de la mañana [deh la man-yana]
amazing (surprising) increíble [eenkreh-eebleh]
  (very good) extraordinario [estra-ordeenar-yo]
ambulance la ambulancia [amboolans-ya]
  call an ambulance! ¡llame a una ambulancia! [yameh]
America Estados Unidos
American (adj) norteamericano [norteh-amaireekano]
  I'm American (man/woman) soy norteamericano/ norteamericana
among entre [entreh]
amount la cantidad [kanteeda]
  (money) la suma
amp: a 13-amp fuse el fusible de trece amperios [fooseebleh deh – ampairee-os]

and y [ee]
angry enojado [enoHado]
animal el animal
ankle el tobillo [tobee-yo]
anniversary (wedding) el aniversario de boda [aneebairsar-yo deh]
annoy: this man's annoying me este hombre me está molestando [esteh ombreh meh]
annoying molesto
another otro
can we have another room? ¿puede darnos otro cuarto? [pwedeh – kwarto]
another beer, please otra cerveza, por favor [fabor]
antibiotics los antibióticos [anteeb-yoteekos]
antifreeze el anticongelante [anteekonHelanteh]
antihistamines los antihistamínicos [antee-eestameeneekos]
antique: is it an antique? ¿es antiguo? [anteegwo]
antique shop la tienda de antigüedades [t-yenda deh anteegwedad-es]
antiseptic el antiséptico [anteesépteeko]
any: have you got any bread/tomatoes? ¿tiene pan/jitomates? [t-yeneh]
do you have any? ¿tiene?
sorry, I don't have any lo siento, no tengo [s-yento]
anybody cualquiera [kwalk-yaira]
does anybody speak English? ¿habla alguien inglés? [abla alg-yen eeng-les]
there wasn't anybody there (allí) no había nadie [(a-yee) no abee-a nad-yeh]
anything algo
(negative) nada

dialogues

anything else? ¿algo más?
nothing else, thanks nada más, gracias [gras-yas]

would you like anything to drink? ¿quiere algo de beber? [k-yaireh – deh bebair]
I don't want anything, thanks no quiero nada, gracias [k-yairo]

apart from aparte de [aparteh deh]
apartment el departamento, el piso
appendicitis la apendicitis [apendeeseeetees]
appetizer la botana
aperitif el aperitivo [apereeteebo]
apologize: I apologize disculpe [deeskoolpeh]
apology la disculpa
apple la manzana [mansana]
appointment la cita [seeta]

dialogue

good afternoon, sir, how can I help you? buenas tardes, señor, ¿en qué puedo servirle? [bwenas tard-es sen-yor, en keh pwedo sairbeerleh]

I'd like to make an appointment quisiera hacer cita [kees-yaira asair seeta]

what time would you like? ¿a qué hora le conviene? [keh ora leh konb-yeneh]

three o'clock a las tres

I'm afraid that's not possible, is four o'clock all right? lamento que no será posible, ¿está bien a las cuatro? [keh no saira poseebleh – b-yen]

yes, that will be fine sí, está bien

the name was ...? ¿su nombre ...? [nombreh]

apricot el chabacano, el damasco

April abril

are*: we are somos; estamos

you are (fam) eres [air-es]; estás

(pol) es; está

they are son; están

area la zona [sona]

area code el prefijo [prefeeно]

arm el brazo [braso]

arrange: will you arrange it for

us? ¿nos lo organiza Usted? [organeesa oosteh]

arrival la llegada [yegada]

arrive llegar [yegar]

when do we arrive? ¿cuándo llegamos? [kwando yegamos]

has my fax arrived yet? ¿llegó ya mi fax? [yego]

we arrived today llegamos hoy [yegamos oy]

art el arte [arteh]

art gallery la galería de arte [galeree-a deh]

artist (man/woman) el pintor, la pintora

as: as big as tan grande como

as soon as possible lo más pronto posible [poseebleh]

ashtray el cenicero [seneesairo]

ask preguntar

to ask for pedir

I didn't ask for this no pedí esto

could you ask him to ...? ¿puede decirle que ...? [pwedeh deseerleh keh]

asleep: she's asleep está dormida

aspirin la aspirina

asthma el asma

astonishing increíble [eenkreh-eebleh]

at: at the hotel en el hotel

at the station en la estación

at six o'clock a las seis

at Pedro's en casa de Pedro [deh]

athletics el atletismo

Atlantic Ocean el Océano

Atlántico [oseh-ano]
attractive atractivo [atrakteebo]
aubergine la berenjena
[berenHena]
August agosto
aunt la tía
Australia Australia [owstral-ya]
Australian (adj) australiano
I'm Australian (man/woman)
soy australiano/australiana
automatic automático
[owtomateeko]
automatic teller el cajero
automático [kaHairo]
autumn el otoño [oton-yo]
in the autumn en otoño
avenue la avenida [abeneeda]
average (ordinary) mediano
[med-yano]
(not good) regular [regoolar]
on average por término
medio [tairmeeno med-yo]
avocado el aguacate
[agwakateh]
awake: is he awake? ¿está
despierto? [desp-yairto]
away: go away! ¡lárguese!
[largeseh]
he's gone away se ha ido
fuera [seh a eedo fwaira]
is it far away? ¿está lejos?
[leHos]
awful horrible [oreebleh]
axle el eje [eHeh]
Aztec (adj) azteca [asteka]

B

baby el bebé [beh-beh]
baby food la comida de bebé
[deh]
baby's bottle el biberón
[beebairon]
baby-sitter la niñera [neen-
yaira]
back (of body) la espalda
(back part) la parte de atrás
[parteh deh]
at the back en la parte de
atrás
can I have my money back?
¿me devuelve el dinero?
[meh debwelbeh el deenairo]
to come/go back regresar
backache el dolor de espalda
[deh]
bacon el jamón [Hamon], el
tocino [toseeno]
bad malo
a bad headache un fuerte
dolor de cabeza [fwairteh – deh
kabesa]
badly mal
(injured) gravemente
[grabementeh]
bag la bolsa
(handbag) el bolso
(suitcase) la maleta, la petaca
baggage el equipaje
[ekeepaHeh]
baggage check la consigna
[konseegna], la paquetería
[paketairee-a]
baggage claim la recogida

de equipajes [rekoHeeda deh
ekeepaн-es]
bakery la panadería
[panadairee-a]
balcony el balcón
a room with a balcony un
cuarto con balcón [kwarto]
bald calvo [kalbo]
ball (large) la pelota, el balón
(small) la bola
ballet el ballet
banana el plátano
band (musical) la orquesta
[orkesta]
bandage la venda [benda]
Bandaid® la tirita
bandit el bandido
bank (money) el banco
bank account la cuenta
bancaria [kwenta]
bar el bar
a bar of chocolate una barra
de chocolate
[deh chokolateh]
barber's la peluquería
[pelookairee-a]
bargain regatear [regateh-ar]

dialogue

how much is this? ¿a cómo
está?
100 pesos a cien pesos
that's too expensive, how
about 50? es muy caro,
¿me lo deja en cincuenta?
[mwee – deHa]
I'll let you have it for 80
se lo dejo en ochenta [seh

lo deHo]
can't you reduce it a bit
more, to 70 ? ¿me lo
rebaja un poco más, en
setenta? [rebaha]
that's the lowest I'll go es
lo último
OK de acuerdo [deh
akwairdo]

baseball el béisbol [baysbol]
basement el sótano
basket la canasta
(in shop) la cesta [sesta]
bath el baño [ban-yo], la tina
can I have a bath? ¿puedo
bañarme? [pwedo ban-yarmeh]
bathroom el cuarto de baño
[kwarto]
with a private bathroom con
baño privado [preebado]
bath towel la toalla de baño
[to-a-ya deh]
battery la pila
(car) la batería [batairee-a]
bay la bahía [ba-ee-a]
be* ser [sair]; estar
beach la playa [plī-ya]
on the beach en la playa
beach umbrella la sombrilla
[sombree-ya]
beans los frijoles [freeHol-es]
runner beans los ejotes [eHot-
es]
broad beans las habas [abas]
beard la barba
beautiful lindo
because porque [porkeh]
because of ... debido a ...

bed la cama
  I'm going to bed now me voy a acostar ahora [meh boy – a-ora]
bed and breakfast cuarto y desayuno [kwarto ee desī-yoono]
bedroom la recámara
beef la carne de res [karneh deh]
beer la cerveza [sairbesa]
  two beers, please dos cervezas, por favor [fabor]
before antes
begin empezar [empesar]
  when does it begin? ¿cuándo empieza? [kwando emp-yesa]
beginner el/la principiante [preenseep-yanteh]
beginning: at the beginning al principio [preenseep-yo]
behind atrás
  behind me detrás de mí [deh]
beige beige [baysh]
believe creer [kreh-air]
Belize Belice [beleeseh]
below abajo [abaHo]
belt el cinturón [seentooron]
bend (in road) la curva [koorba]
berth (on ship) el camarote [kamaroteh]
beside: beside the ... al lado de la ... [deh]
best el mejor [meHor]
better mejor
  are you feeling better? ¿se siente mejor? [seh s-yenteh]
between entre [entreh]
beyond más allá [a-ya]
bicycle la bicicleta

[beeseekleta]
big grande [grandeh]
  too big demasiado grande [demas-yado]
  it's not big enough no es lo suficientemente grande [soofees-yentementeh]
big game fishing la pesca mayor [mī-yor]
bike la bicicleta [beeseekleta] (motorbike) la moto
bikini el bikini
bill la cuenta [kwenta] (US: banknote) el billete [bee-yeteh]
  could I have the bill, please? me pasa la cuenta, por favor [meh – fabor]
bin el bote de la basura [boteh deh]
bin liners las bolsas de basura
binding (ski) la atadura
bird el pájaro [paHaro]
biro® el bolígrafo
birthday el cumpleaños [koompleh-an-yos]
  happy birthday! ¡feliz cumpleaños! [felees]
biscuit la galleta [ga-yeta]
bit: a little bit un poquito [pokeeto]
  a big bit un pedazo grande [pedaso grandeh]
  a bit of ... un pedazo de ... [deh]
  a bit expensive un poco caro
bite (by insect) la picadura (by dog) la mordedura
bitter (taste etc) amargo

black negro [**neh**-gro]
black coffee el café
  americano [kaf**eh**]
  (strong) el café solo
blanket la cobija [kob**ee**Ha], la
  frazada [fras**a**da]
bleach (for toilet) la lejía [leHee-a]
bless you! ¡Jesús! [Hes**oo**s]
blind ciego [s-**ye**go]
blinds las persianas [pers-**ya**nas]
blister la ampolla [ampo-ya]
blocked (road, pipe) bloqueado
  [blokeh-**a**do]
  (sink) atascado
block (city) la cuadra [**kwa**dra]
  block of flats el edificio de
    departamentos [edeef**ee**s-yo
    deh]
blond güero [gwairo]
blood la sangre [**sa**ngreh]
  high blood pressure la
    tensión alta [tens-**yon**]
blouse la blusa
blow-dry (verb) secar a mano
  I'd like a cut and blow-dry
    quisiera un corte y un
    marcado [kees-**ya**ira oon **ko**rteh
    ee]
blue azul [as**oo**l]
blusher el colorete [kolo**re**teh]
boarding house la pensión
  [pens-**yon**], la hostería
  [ostair**ee**-a]
boarding pass la tarjeta
  de embarque [tar**He**ta deh
  embar**keh**]
boat el barco
body el cuerpo [**kwa**irpo]
boiled egg el huevo pasado

(por agua) [**we**bo pas**a**do por
  agwa]
boiler la caldera [kald**ai**ra]
bone el hueso [**we**so]
bonnet (of car) el capó, el cofre
  [**ko**freh]
book el libro
  (verb) reservar [resair**bar**]
  can I book a seat? ¿puedo
    reservar un asiento? [**pwe**do
    – as-**ye**nto]

dialogue

I'd like to book a table for
two quisiera reservar una
mesa para dos personas
[kees-**ya**ira]
what time would you like
it booked for? ¿para qué
hora la quiere? [keh **o**ra la
k-**ya**ireh]
half past seven las siete y
media
that's fine de acuerdo [deh
akw**ai**rdo]
and your name? ¿y
su nombre …? [ee soo
nombreh]

bookshop, bookstore la
  librería [leebrair**ee**-a]
boot (footwear) la bota
  (of car) la maleta, la cajuela
  [ka**Hwe**la]
border (of country) la frontera
  [front**ai**ra]
bored: I'm bored (said by
  man/woman) estoy aburrido/

aburrida

boring aburrido, pesado

born: I was born in
Manchester nací en
Manchester [nasee]

I was born in 1960 nací en
mil novecientos sesenta

borrow pedir prestado

may I borrow ...? ¿puede
prestarme ...? [pwedeh
prestarmeh]

both los os dos

both... and... tanto ...
como ...

bother: sorry to bother you
siento molestarlo [s-yento]

bottle la botella [boteh-ya], el
frasco

a bottle of house red una
botella de tinto de la casa
[deh]

bottle-opener el abrebotellas
[abreboteh-yas]

bottom (of person) el trasero
[trasairo], el culo

at the bottom of the ... (hill/
road) al pie del/de la ... [p-yeh
del/deh]

(sea) al fondo de ...

box la caja [kaHa]

box office la taquilla [takee-
ya], la boletería [boletairee-a]

boy el chico, el joven [Hoven],
el chavo [chabo]

boyfriend el novio [nob-yo]

bra el brassiere [bras-yair]

bracelet la pulsera [poolsaira]

brake el freno

brandy el coñac [kon-yak]

bread el pan

white bread el pan blanco

brown bread el pan de
centeno [deh senteno]

wholemeal bread el pan
integral [eentegral]

break (verb) romper [rompair]

I've broken the ... rompí el ...

I think I've broken my ... creo
que me he roto el ... [kreh-o
keh meh eh]

break down descomponerse
[deskomponairseh]

I've broken down se me ha
descompuesto el carro [seh
meh a deskompwesto]

breakdown (mechanical) la
descompostura

breakdown service el
servicio de grúa [serbees-yo
deh groo-a]

breakfast el desayuno [desi-
yoono]

break-in: I've had a break-in
entraron en mi casa a robar

breast el pecho

breathe respirar

breeze la brisa

bribe la mordida

bridge (over river) el puente
[pwenteh]

brief breve [brebeh]

briefcase la cartera [kartaira]

bright (light etc) brillante [bree-
yanteh]

bright red rojo vivo [roHo
beebo]

brilliant (idea, person) brillante
[bree-yanteh]

bring traer [tra-**air**]
I'll bring it back later lo devolveré luego [debolbair**eh** lwego]
Britain Gran Bretaña [bretan-ya]
British británico
I'm British (man/woman) soy británico/británica
brochure el folleto [fo-yeto]
broken roto
bronchitis la bronquitis [bronk**ee**tees]
brooch el broche [broch**eh**]
broom la escoba
brother el hermano [air**ma**no]
brother-in-law el cuñado [koon-yado]
brown color café [kaf**eh**]
brown hair el pelo castaño [kastan-yo]
brown eyes los ojos castaños [o**H**os]
bruise el moretón
brush (for hair, cleaning) el cepillo [sepee-yo]
(artist's) el pincel [peensel]
bucket el cubo [k**oo**bo], el balde [bald**eh**]
buffet car el vagón-restaurante [bagon-restowranteh]
buggy (for child) el carrito de niño [deh neen-yo]
building el edificio [edeefees-yo]
bulb (light bulb) el foco
bull el toro
bullfight la corrida
bullring la plaza de toros [plasa deh]

bumper la defensa
bunk la litera [leet**ai**ra]
bureau de change el cambio [kamb-yo], la casa de cambio [deh]
burglary el robo con allanamiento de morada [a-yanam-yento]
burn la quemadura [kemad**oo**ra]
(verb) quemar [kemar]
burnt: this is burnt está quemado [kemado]
burst: a burst pipe la cañería rota [kan-yair**ee**-a]
bus el camión [kam-yon]
(long-distance) el autobús [owtob**oo**s]
what number bus is it to ...? ¿qué número tomo para ...? [keh n**oo**mairo]
when is the next bus to ...? ¿cuándo sale el próximo camión/autobús para ...? [kwando sal**eh**]
what time is the last bus? ¿a qué hora sale el último camión? [keh ora – **oo**lteemo]
could you let me know when we get there? ¿puede avisarme cuando llegamos [pwedeh abeesarmeh kwando yegamos]

dialogue

does this bus go to ...? ¿este camión va a ...? [esteh kam-yon ba]

40

no, you need a number ...
no, tiene que tomar el ...
[t-yeneh keh]

business el negocio [negos-yo]
bus station la central
camionera [sentral kam-
yonaira], la estación de
autobuses [estas-yon deh
owtoboos-es]
bus stop la parada de camión
[kam-yon]
bust el pecho
busy (restaurant etc)
concurrido
I'm busy tomorrow (said by
man/woman) estoy ocupado/
ocupada mañana [man-yana]
but pero [pairo]
butcher's la carnicería
[karneesairee-a]
butter la mantequilla
[mantekee-ya]
button el botón
buy (verb) comprar
where can I buy ...? ¿dónde
puedo comprar ...? [dondeh
pwedo]
buzzard el buitre [bweetreh]
by: by bus/car en camión/
carro
written by ... escrito por ...
by the window junto a la
ventana [Hoonto]
by the sea a orillas del mar
[oree-yas]
by Thursday para el jueves
bye! ¡hasta luego! [asta
lwego]

C

cabbage el repollo [repo-yo]
cabin (on ship) el camarote
[kamaroteh]
cable car el teleférico
[telefaireeko], el funicular
[fooneekoolar]
cactus el cacto
café la cafetería [kafetairee-a]
cagoule el chubasquero
[choobaskairo]
cake el pastel
cake shop la pastelería
[pastelairee-a]
call (verb) llamar [yamar]
(to phone) llamar (por
teléfono)
what's it called? ¿cómo se
llama ? [seh yama]
he/she is called ... se
llama ...
please call the doctor llame
al médico, por favor [yameh
– fabor]
please give me a call at 7.30
a.m. tomorrow por favor,
llámeme mañana a las
siete y media de la mañana
[yamameh man-yana]
please ask him to call me
por favor, dígale que me
llame [deegaleh keh meh yameh]
call back: I'll call back
later regresaré más tarde
[regresareh mas tardeh]
(phone back) volveré a llamar
[bolbaireh a yamar]

call round: I'll call round tomorrow mañana paso
camcorder la videocámara [beedeh-o-kamara]
camera la cámara
camera shop la tienda fotográfica [t-yenda]
camp (verb) acampar
can we camp here? ¿se puede acampar aquí? [seh pwedeh – akee]
camping gas canister la bomba de butano [deh bootano]
campsite el camping
can la lata
a can of beer una lata de cerveza [deh sairbesa]
can*: can you ...? ¿puede ...? [pwedeh]
can I have ...? ¿me da ...? [meh]
I can't ... no puedo ... [pwedo]
Canada el Canadá
Canadian (adj) canadiense [kanad-yenseh]
I'm Canadian soy canadiense
canal el canal
cancel cancelar [kanselar]
candies los dulces [dool-ses]
candle la vela [bela]
canoe la canoa
canoeing el piragüismo [peeragweesmo]
can-opener el abrelatas
canyon el cañón [kan-yon], la cañada [kan-yada]
cap (hat) la gorra
(of bottle) el tapón

car el carro, el auto [owto], el automóvil
by car en carro
caravan la caravana [karabana]
caravan site el camping
carburettor el carburador
card (birthday etc) la tarjeta [tarHeta]
here's my (business) card aquí tiene mi tarjeta (de visita) [akee t-yeneh – deh beeseeta]
cardigan la chamarra
cardphone el teléfono de tarjeta [deh tarHeta]
careful cauteloso [kowteloso]
be careful! ¡cuidado! [kweedado]
caretaker el portero [portairo]
car ferry el ferry, el transbordador de carros [deh]
car hire el alquiler de carros [alkeelair deh]
car park el estacionamiento [estas-yonam-yento]
carpet la alfombra, el tapete [tapeteh]
car rental el alquiler de carros [alkeelair deh]
carriage (of train) el vagón [bagon]
carrier bag la bolsa de plástico [deh]
carrot la zanahoria [sana-or-ya]
carry llevar [yebar]
carry-cot el capazo [kapaso]
carton la caja [kaHa]
carwash el lavado de carros [labado deh]

case (suitcase) la maleta

cash el dinero [deenairo], la plata

to pay (in) cash pagar en efectivo [efekteebo], pagar al contado

will you cash this for me? ¿podría hacerme efectivo un cheque? [asairmeh – chekeh]

cash desk la caja [kaнa]

cash dispenser el cajero automático [kaнairo owtomateeko]

cassette la cassette [kaset]

cassette recorder el cassette

castle el castillo [kastee-yo]

casualty department emergencias [emairнens-yas]

cat el gato

catch (verb) agarrar

where do we catch the bus to ...? ¿dónde se toma el camión para ...? [dondeh seh]

cathedral la catedral

Catholic (adj) católico

cauliflower el coliflor

cave la cueva [kweba]

ceiling el techo

celery el apio [ap-yo]

cellar (for wine) la bodega

cellular phone el teléfono celular [seloolar]

cemetery el cementerio [sementair-yo], el panteón [panteh-on]

centigrade* centígrado [senteegrado]

centimetre* el centímetro [senteemetro]

central central [sentral]

Central America Centroamérica [sentro-amaireeka]

Central American (adj) centroamericano

central heating la calefacción central [kalefaks-yon sentral]

centre el centro [sentro]

how do we get to the city centre? ¿cómo se llega al centro? [seh yega]

cereals los cereales [sereh-al-es]

certainly por supuesto [soopwesto]

certainly not de ninguna manera [deh neengoona manaira]

chair la silla [see-ya]

champagne el champán

change (loose) el suelto [swelto]

(after payment) el vuelto [bwelto]

(verb) cambiar [kamb-yar]

can I change this for ...? ¿puedo cambiar esto por ...? [pwedo]

I don't have any change no tengo suelto

can you give me change for a 1,000 peso note? ¿puede cambiarme un billete de mil? [pwedeh kamb-yarmeh oon bee-yeteh deh meel]

dialogue

do we have to change
(trains)? ¿tenemos que
hacer correspondencia?
[keh aser korrespondens-ya]
yes, change at Xalapa/no
it's a direct train sí, haga
trasbordo en Xalapa/no,
es directo [aga – Halapa]

changed: to get changed
cambiarse [kamb-yarseh]
chapel la capilla [kapee-ya]
charge (verb) cobrar
cheap barato
do you have anything
cheaper? ¿tiene algo más
barato? [t-yeneh]
check (US) el cheque
[chekeh]
(US: bill) la cuenta [kwenta]
check (verb) revisar [rebeesar]
could you check the ...,
please? ¿puede revisar el ...,
por favor? [pwedeh – fabor]
check book el libro de
cheques [deh chek-es]
check-in la facturación
[faktooras-yon]
check in facturar
where do we have to check
in? ¿dónde se factura?
[dondeh seh]
cheek la mejilla [meHee-ya]
cheerio! ¡hasta luego! [asta
lwego]
cheers! (toast) ¡salud! [saloo]
cheese el queso [keso]

cheesecake el pay de queso
[pī deh keso]
chemist's la farmacia
[farmas-ya]
cheque el cheque [chekeh]
do you take cheques?
¿aceptan cheques? [aseptan
chek-es]
cheque book la chequera
[chekaira]
cheque card la tarjeta de
banco [tarHeta deh]
cherry la cereza [sairesa]
(black) la guinda [geenda]
chess el ajedrez [aHed-res]
chest el pecho
chewing gum el chicle
[cheekleh]
chicken el pollo [po-yo], la
gallina [ga-yeena]
chickenpox la varicela
[bareesela]
child (male/female) el niño
[neen-yo], la niña
child minder la niñera [neen-
yaira]
children los niños
children's pool la alberca
infantil [albairka eenfanteel]
children's portion la ración
pequeña (para niños) [ras-yon
peken-ya – neen-yos]
chilli el chile [cheeleh]
chin la barba
china la porcelana [porselana]
Chinese (adj) chino [cheeno]
chips las papas fritas
chocolate el chocolate
[chokolateh]

milk chocolate el chocolate
con leche [lecheh]
plain chocolate el chocolate
negro [neh-gro]
a hot chocolate una taza de
chocolate [tasa deh]
choose elegir [eleHeer],
escoger [eskoHair]
Christian name el nombre de
pila [nombreh deh]
Christmas Navidad [nabeeda]
Christmas Eve Nochebuena
[nocheh-bwena]
merry Christmas! ¡Felices
Pascuas! [felees-es paskwas]
church la iglesia [eegles-ya]
cider la sidra
cigar el puro [pooro]
cigarette el cigarro [seegarro]
cigarette lighter el mechero
[mechairo]
cinema el cine [seeneh]
circle el círculo [seerkoolo]
(in theatre) el anfiteatro
[anfeeteh-atro]
city la ciudad [s-yooda]
city centre el centro de la
ciudad [sentro deh]
clean (adj) limpio [leemp-yo]
can you clean these for me?
¿puede limpiarme estos?
[pwedeh leemp-yarmeh]
cleaning solution (for contact
lenses) el líquido limpiador
para las lentillas [leekeedo
leemp-yador – lentee-yas]
cleansing lotion la crema
limpiadora
clear claro

clever listo
cliff el acantilado
cliff-diving el clavado de
acantilado [deh]
climbing el montañismo
[montan-yeesmo]
cling film el plástico de
envolver [deh embolbair]
clinic la clínica
cloakroom el guardarropa
[gwardarropa]
clock el reloj [reloH]
close (verb) cerrar [serrar]

dialogue

what time do you close?
¿a qué hora cierran? [keh
ora s-yairran]
we close at 8 p.m. on
weekdays and 1.30 p.m.
on Saturdays cerramos a
las ocho de la tarde entre
semana y a la una y media
los sábados [serramos – deh
la tardeh entreh]
do you close for lunch?
¿cierra a mediodía?
[s-yairra]
yes, between 1 and 3.30
p.m. sí, de la una hasta las
tres y media de la tarde
[deh – asta]

closed cerrado [sairrado]
cloth (fabric) la tela
(for cleaning etc) el trapo
clothes la ropa
clothes line la cuerda para

tender [kwairda para tendair]
clothes peg la pinza de la
ropa [peensa deh]
cloud la nube [noobeh]
cloudy nublado
clutch el embrague [embrageh]
coach (bus) el autobús
[owtoboos]
(on train) el vagón [bagon]
coach station la estación de
camiones [estas-yon deh kam-
yon-es]
coach trip la excursión (en
autobús) [eskoors-yon]
coast la costa
on the coast en la costa
coat (long coat) el abrigo
(jacket) el saco
coathanger la percha [paircha]
cockroach la cucaracha
[kookaracha]
cocoa el cacao [kaka-o]
coconut el coco
code (for phoning) el prefijo
[prefeeHo], el código
what's the (dialling) code for
Veracruz? ¿cuál es el prefijo
de Veracruz? [kwal – deh
bairakroos]
coffee el café [kafeh]
two coffees, please dos
cafés, por favor [fabor]
coin la moneda
Coke® la Coca-Cola
cold frío
I'm cold tengo frío
I have a cold tengo resfriado
[resfr-yado]
collapse: he's collapsed se

desmayó [seh desmī-yo]
collar el cuello [kweh-yo]
collect recoger [rekoHair]
I've come to collect ... vine a
recoger ... [beeneh]
collect call la llamada por
cobrar [yamada]
college la Universidad
[ooneebairseeda]
colour el color
do you have this in other
colours? ¿tiene otros
colores? [t-yeneh – kolor-es]
colour film la película en color
comb el peine [payneh]
come venir [beneer]

dialogue

where do you come from?
¿de dónde es? [deh dondeh]
I come from Edinburgh soy
de Edimburgo

come back regresar
I'll come back tomorrow
regreso mañana
come in entrar
come in! ¡pase! [paseh]
comfortable cómodo
compact disc el compact disc
company (business) la
compañía [kompan-yee-a]
compartment (on train) el
compartimento
compass la brújula [brooHoola]
complain quejarse [keh-Harseh]
complaint la queja [keHa]
I have a complaint tengo

queja

completely completamente
[kompletamenteh]

computer la computadora

concert el concierto [kons-
yairto]

concussion la conmoción
cerebral [konmos-yon sairebral]

conditioner (for hair) el
acondicionador de pelo
[akondees-yonador deh]

condom el condón

condor el cóndor

conference el congreso

confirm confirmar

congratulations! ¡felicidades!
[feleeseedad-es]

connecting flight el vuelo de
conexión [bwelo deh koneks-
yon]

connection el enlace [enlaseh]

conscious consciente [kons-
yenteh]

constipation el estreñimiento
[estren-yeem-yento]

consulate el consulado

contact (verb) ponerse en
contacto con [ponairseh]

contact lenses las lentes de
contacto [lent-es deh], las
lentillas [lentee-yas]

contraceptive el
anticonceptivo
[anteekonsepteebo]

convenient a mano
that's not convenient no
conviene [konb-yeneh]

cook (verb) cocinar [koseenar]
not cooked poco hecho

[echo]

cooker el horno [orno]

cookie la galleta [ga-yeta]

cooking utensils los
utensilios de cocina
[ootenseel-yos deh koseena]

cool fresco

cork el corcho

corkscrew el sacacorchos

corner: on the corner en la
esquina [eskeena]
in the corner en el rincón

cornflakes los cornflakes

correct (right) correcto

corridor el pasillo [pasee-yo]

cosmetics los cosméticos

cost (verb) costar, valer [balair]
how much does it cost?
¿cuánto vale? [kwanto baleh]

cot la cuna

cotton el algodón

cotton wool el algodón

couch (sofa) el sofá

couchette la litera [leetaira]

cough la tos

cough medicine la medicina
para la tos [medeeseena]

could: could you ...?
¿podría ...?
could I have ...? ¿quisiera ...?
[kees-yaira]
I couldn't ... no podría ...

country (nation) el país [pa-ees]
(countryside) el campo

countryside el campo

couple (two people) la pareja
[pareHa]
a couple of ... un par de ...
[deh]

courgette la calabacita [kalabaseeta], el calabacín [kalabaseen]

courier el/la guía turístico [gee-a]

course (main course etc) el plato of course por supuesto [soopwesto]

of course not! ¡claro que no! [keh]

cousin (male/female) el primo, la prima

cow la vaca [baka]

crab la jaiba [Hība]

cracker (biscuit) la galleta salada [ga-yeta]

craft shop la tienda de artesanías [t-yenda deh]

crash el accidente [akseedenteh] (verb) chocar I've had a crash tuve un accidente [toobeh]

crazy loco

cream la crema (colour) color crema

creche la guardería infantil [gwardairee-a]

credit card la tarjeta de crédito [tarHeta deh kredeeto]

dialogue

can I pay by credit card? ¿puedo pagar con tarjeta? [pwedo – kon tarHeta] which card do you want to use? ¿qué tarjeta quiere usar? [keh – k-yaireh oosar]

yes, sir sí, señor [sen-yor] what's the number? ¿qué número tiene? [noomairo t-yeneh] and the expiry date? ¿y la fecha de caducidad? [deh kadooseeda]

crisps las patatas fritas (de bolsa)

crockery la loza [losa]

crocodile el caimán [kīman]

crossing (by sea) la travesía [trabesee-a]

crossroads el cruce [krooseh]

crowd la muchedumbre [moocheh-doombreh]

crowded atestado

crown (on tooth) la funda [foonda]

cruise el crucero [kroosairo]

crutches las muletas

cry (verb) llorar [yorar]

Cuban (adj) cubano

cucumber el pepino

cup la taza [tasa] a cup of ..., please una taza de ..., por favor [deh – fabor]

cupboard el armario [armar-yo]

cure la cura [koora]

curly rizado [reesado]

current la corriente [korr-yenteh]

curtains las cortinas

cushion el cojín [koHeen]

custom la costumbre [kostoombreh]

Customs la aduana [adwana]
cut el corte [korteh]
(verb) cortar
I've cut myself me corté [meh korteh]
cutlery los cubiertos [koob-yairtos]
cycling el ciclismo [seekleesmo]
cyclist el/la ciclista [seekleesta]

D

dad el papá
daily cada día [dee-a], todos los días
(adj) diario [d-yar-yo], de cada día [deh]
damage: damaged dañado [dan-yado]
damn! ¡caramba!
damp (adj) húmedo [oomedo]
dance el baile [bīleh]
(verb) bailar [bīlar]
would you like to dance? ¿quiere bailar? [k-yaireh]
dangerous peligroso
Danish danés [dan-es]
dark (adj: colour) oscuro [oskooro]
(hair) moreno
it's getting dark está oscureciendo [oskoores-yendo]
date* la fecha
what's the date today? ¿qué fecha es hoy? [keh – oy]
let's make a date for next Monday quedamos para

el próximo lunes [kedamos – prokseemo]
dates (fruit) los dátiles
daughter la hija [eeHa]
daughter-in-law la nuera [nwaira]
dawn el amanecer [amanesair]
at dawn al amanecer
day el día
the day after el día siguiente [seeg-yenteh]
the day after tomorrow pasado mañana [man-yana]
the day before el día anterior [antair-yor]
the day before yesterday anteayer [anteh-i-yair]
every day todos los días
all day todo el día
in two days' time dentro de dos días [deh]
have a nice day! ¡que pase buen día! [keh paseh bwen]
day trip la excursión [ekskoors-yon]
dead muerto [mwairto]
deaf sordo
deal (business) el negocio [negos-yo]
it's a deal trato hecho [echo]
death la muerte [mwairteh]
decaffeinated coffee el café descafeinado [kafeh deskafay-eenado]
December diciembre [dees-yembreh]
decide decidir [deseedeer]
we haven't decided yet

todavía no hemos decidido [todabee-a no emos deseedeedo]

decision la decisión [deseesyon]

deck (on ship) la cubierta [koobyairta]

deckchair la tumbona

deduct descontar

deep profundo

definitely (certainly) sin duda
definitely not ni hablar [ablar]

degree (qualification) el título

delay la demora
the train was delayed se demoró el tren [seh]

deliberately a propósito

delicatessen la charcutería [charkootairee-a]

delicious delicioso [deleesyoso]

deliver entregar

delivery (of mail) el reparto

Denmark Dinamarca

dental floss el hilo dental [eelo]

dentist el/la dentista

dialogue

it's this one here es ésta de aquí [deh akee]
this one? ¿ésta?
no, that one no, aquélla [akeh-ya]
here? ¿aquí?
yes sí

dentures la dentadura postiza [posteesa]

deodorant el desodorante [desodoranteh]

department el departamento

department store la tienda de departamentos [t-yenda deh]

departure la salida

departure lounge la sala de embarque [deh embarkeh]

depend: it depends depende [dependeh]
it depends when según cuándo [kwando]
it depends on ... depende de ... [deh]

deposit (as security) la fianza [fee-ansa]
(as part payment) el enganche [engancheh]

description la descripción [deskreeps-yon]

desert el desierto [des-yairto]

dessert el postre [postreh]

destination el destino

develop (photos) revelar [rebelar]

dialogue

could you develop these films? ¿puede revelar estos carretes? [pwedeh – karret-es]
when will they be ready? ¿cuándo estarán listos? [kwando]
tomorrow afternoon mañana por la tarde [man-yana – tardeh]
how much is the four-hour service? ¿cuánto es el

50

servicio de cuatro horas?
[kwanto – sairbees-yo deh
kwatro oras]

diabetic (man/woman) el
diabético [dee-abeteeko], la
diabética
  diabetic foods la comida
  para diabéticos
dial (verb) marcar
dialling code el prefijo
[prefeeHo], el código
diamond el diamante
[d-yamanteh]
diaper el pañal [pan-yal]
diarrhoea la diarrea
[d-yarreh-a]
diary (business etc) la agenda
[aHenda]
  (for personal experiences) el
  diario [d-yar-yo]
dictionary el diccionario
[deeks-yonar-yo]
didn't see not
die morir
diesel el gasoil, el diesel [deesel]
diet la dieta [d-yeta]
  I'm on a diet estoy a régimen
  [reHeemen]
  I have to follow a special diet
  tengo que seguir una dieta
  especial [keh segeer – espes-yal]
difference la diferencia
[deefairens-ya]
  what's the difference? ¿cuál
  es la diferencia? [kwal]
different distinto
  this one is different éste es
  distinto [esteh]

  a different table otra mesa
difficult difícil [deefeeseel]
difficulty la dificultad
[deefeekoolta]
dinghy el bote [boteh]
dining room el comedor
dinner (evening) la cena [sena]
  to have dinner cenar [senar]
direct (adj) directo
  is there a direct train? ¿hay
  un tren directo? [ī]
direction la dirección [deereks-
yon], el sentido
  which direction is it? ¿en qué
  dirección está? [keh]
  is it in this direction? ¿es por
  aquí? [akee]
directory enquiries
  información [eenformas-yon]
dirt la suciedad [soos-yeda], la
mugre [moogreh]
dirty sucio [soos-yo]
disabled minusválido
[meenoosbaleedo]
  is there access for the
  disabled? ¿hay acceso para
  minusválidos? [ī akseso]
disappear desaparecer
[desaparesair]
  it's disappeared desapareció
  [desapares-yo]
disappointed decepcionado
[deseps-yonado]
disappointing decepcionante
[deseps-yonanteh]
disaster el desastre [desastreh]
disco la discoteca
discount el descuento
[deskwento]

is there a discount? ¿hay descuento? [ī]

disease la enfermedad [enfairmeda]

disgusting repugnante [repoognanteh]

dish (meal) el plato

dishcloth el trapo de cocina [deh koseena]

disinfectant el desinfectante [deseenfektanteh]

disk (for computer) la disqueta [deesketa]

disposable diapers/nappies los pañales desechables [pan-yal-es desechab-les]

distance la distancia [deestans-ya]

in the distance a lo lejos [leHos]

distilled water el agua destilada [agwa]

district el barrio

disturb molestar, estorbar

diversion (detour) el desvío [desbee-o]

diving board el trampolín

divorced divorciado [deebors-yado]

dizzy: I feel dizzy (said by man/woman) estoy mareado/mareada [mareh-ado]

do hacer [asair]

what shall we do? ¿qué hacemos? [keh asemos]

how do you do it? ¿cómo se hace? [seh aseh]

will you do it for me? ¿me lo puede hacer Usted? [meh lo pwedeh asair oosteh]

dialogues

how do you do? ¿cómo está? [komo]
nice to meet you encantado de conocerle [deh konosairleh]
what do you do? (work) ¿a qué se dedica? [keh seh]
I'm a teacher, and you? soy profesor, ¿y Usted? [ee oosteh]
I'm a student soy estudiante [estood-yanteh]
what are you doing this evening? ¿qué hace esta tarde? [aseh]
we're going out for a drink; do you want to join us? salimos a tomar una copa, ¿nos acompaña? [akompan-ya]

do you want cream? ¿quiere crema? [k-yaireh]
I do, but she doesn't yo sí, pero ella no [pairo eh-ya]

doctor el/la médico
we need a doctor necesitamos un médico [neseseetamos]
please call a doctor por favor, llame a un médico [fabor yameh]

dialogue

where does it hurt?
¿dónde le duele? [**do**ndeh
leh dweleh]

right here justo aquí
[**Hoo**sto a**kee**]

does that hurt now? ¿le
duele ahora? [leh dweleh
a-**o**ra]

yes sí

take this to the chemist's
lleve esto a la farmacia
[**ye**beh – farmas-**ya**]

document el documento
[dok**oo**mento]
dog el perro [**pai**rro]
doll la muñeca [moon-**ye**ka]
domestic flight el vuelo
nacional [**bwe**lo nas-yo**nal**]
donkey el burro [**boo**rro]
don't! ¡no lo haga! [**a**ga]
don't do that! ¡no haga eso!
see not
door la puerta [**pwai**rta]
doorman el portero [por**tai**ro]
double doble [**do**bleh]
double bed la cama
matrimonial [matreemon-**yal**]
double room el cuarto doble
[**kwa**rto **do**bleh]
doughnut la dona
down: **down here** aquí abajo
[a**kee** aba**Ho**]
downwards hacia abajo [**as**-
ya]
put it down over there déjelo
ahí [**deh**-Helo a-**ee**]

it's down there on the right
está ahí a la derecha [dai**re**cha]
it's further down the road está
bajando la calle
[ba**Han**do la ka-**yeh**]
downhill skiing el esquí alpino
[es**kee** al**pee**no]
downmarket (restaurant etc)
popular [popoo**lar**]
downstairs abajo [aba**Ho**]
dozen la docena [do**se**na]
half a dozen media docena
[med-ya]
drain (in sink, road) el desagüe
[des**a**gweh]
draught beer la cerveza de
barril [sair**be**sa deh]
draughty: **it's draughty** hay
corriente [ī korr-**yen**teh]
drawer el cajón [ka**Hon**]
drawing el dibujo [dee**boo**Ho]
dreadful horrible [orr**ee**bleh]
dream el sueño [**swen**-yo]
dress el vestido [bes**tee**do]
dressed: **to get dressed**
vestirse [bes**teer**seh]
dressing (for cut) el vendaje
[ben**da**Heh]
salad dressing el aliño [a**leen**-
yo]
dressing gown la bata
drink (alcoholic) la copa
(non-alcoholic) la bebida
(verb) beber [be**bair**]
a cold drink una bebida fría
can I get you a drink?
¿quiere beber algo?
[k-**yai**reh]
what would you like (to

drink)? ¿qué le apetece beber? [keh leh apeteseh]

no thanks, I don't drink no gracias, no bebo alcohol [gras-yas – alkol]

I'll just have a drink of water sólo agua [agwa]

drinking water agua potable [agwa potableh]

is this drinking water? ¿esto es agua potable?

drive (verb) manejar [maneHar]

we drove here vinimos en carro [beeneemos]

I'll drive you home te llevaré a casa en carro [teh yebareh]

driver (man/woman) el/la chofer [chofair]

driving licence el carnet de chofer [karneh deh chofair]

drop: just a drop, please (of drink) un poquito nada más [pokeeto]

drug la medicina [medeeseena]

drugs (narcotics) la droga

drunk (adj) borracho

drunken driving manejar en estado de embriaguez [maneHar – deh embr-yag-es]

dry (adj) seco

dry-cleaner la tintorería [teentorairee-a]

duck el pato

due: he was due to arrive yesterday tenía que llegar ayer [keh yegar ī-yair]

when is the train due? ¿a qué hora llega el tren? [ora yega]

dull (pain) sordo

(weather) gris [grees]

dummy (baby's) el chupete [choopeteh]

during durante [dooranteh]

dust el polvo [polbo]

dustbin el bote de la basura [boteh deh]

dusty polvoriento [polbor-yento]

duty-free (goods) (los productos) sin impuestos [seen eempwestos]

duty-free shop el duty free

duvet el edredón

E

each cada

how much are they each? ¿a cómo está cada uno?

ear el oído [o-eedo]

earache: I have earache tengo dolor de oídos [deh]

early pronto

early in the morning de madrugada

I called by earlier pasé antes [paseh ant-es]

earring el arete [areteh]

earthquake el temblor

east oriente [or-yenteh]

in the east en el oriente

Easter la Semana Santa

easy fácil [faseel]

eat comer [komair]

we've already eaten, thanks ya comimos, gracias [gras-yas]

eau de toilette el agua de baño [agwa deh ban-yo]

economy class la clase turista [klaseh]

Edinburgh Edimburgo [edeemboorgo]

egg el huevo [webo], el blanquillo [blankee-yo]

eggplant la berenjena [berenHena]

either: either ... or ... o ... o ...
either of them cualquiera de los dos [kwalk-yaira deh]

elastic el elástico

elastic band la gomita

elbow el codo

electric eléctrico

electrical appliances los electrodomésticos

electric fire la estufa eléctrica

electrician el electricista [elektreeseesta]

electricity la electricidad [elektreeseeda]

elevator el ascensor [asensor]

else: something else otra cosa
somewhere else en otra parte [parteh]

dialogue

would you like anything else? ¿algo más?
no, nothing else, thanks nada más, gracias [gras-yas]

embassy la embajada [embaHada]

emergency la emergencia [emairHens-ya]

this is an emergency! ¡es una emergencia!

emergency exit la salida de emergencia [deh]

empty vacío [basee-o]

end el final [feenal]
(verb) terminar [tairmeenar]
at the end of the street al final de la calle [deh la ka-yeh]
when does it end? ¿cuándo termina? [kwando]

engaged (toilet) ocupado
(telephone) comunicando
(to be married) prometido

engine (car) el motor

England Inglaterra [eenglatairra]

English inglés [eeng-les]
I'm English (man/woman) soy inglés/inglesa
do you speak English? ¿habla inglés? [abla]

enjoy disfrutar
to enjoy oneself divertirse [deebairteerseh]

dialogue

how did you like the film? ¿le gustó la película? [leh goosto]
I enjoyed it very much, did you enjoy it? me gustó mucho, ¿le gustó a Usted? [meh – moocho – leh – oosteh]

enjoyable divertido
[deebairt**ee**do]

enlargement (of photo) la
ampliación [ampl-yas-**yon**]

enormous enorme [en**or**meh]

enough bastante [bast**an**teh]
there's not enough no hay
bastante [i]
it's not big enough no es
lo suficientemente grande
[soofees-yentem**en**teh]
that's enough basta

entrance la entrada

envelope el sobre [**so**breh]

epileptic (adj) epiléptico

equipment el equipo
[ek**ee**po]

error el error

especially sobre todo [**so**breh]

essential imprescindible
[eempreseend**ee**bleh]
it is essential that ... es
imprescindible que ... [keh]

Europe Europa [eh-o**oro**pa]

European europeo
[eh-o**oro**peh-o]

even incluso [eenkl**oo**so]
even if ... incluso si ...

evening (early evening) la tarde
[**tar**deh]
(after nightfall) la noche
[**no**cheh]
this evening esta tarde/noche
in the evening por la tarde/
noche

evening meal la cena [**se**na]

eventually finalmente
[feenalm**en**teh], por fin [feen]

ever alguna vez [bes]

dialogue

have you ever been to
Monterrey? ¿estuvo
alguna vez en Monterrey?
[est**oo**bo – montairr**ay**]
yes, I was there two years
ago sí, estuve allí hace dos
años [est**oo**beh a-**yee** **a**seh
– **an**-yos]

every cada

every day todos los días [**dee**-
as]

everyone todos

everything todo

everywhere en todas partes
[**part**-es]

exactly! ¡exactamente!
[eksaktam**en**teh]

exam el examen

example el ejemplo [eH**em**plo]
for example por ejemplo

excellent excelente [eksel**en**teh]
excellent! ¡estupendo!

except excepto [eks**ep**to]

excess baggage el exceso de
equipaje [eks**e**so deh eekeepa**H**eh]

exchange rate el tipo de
cambio [**tee**po deh kamb-yo]

exciting emocionante [emos-
yon**an**teh]

excuse me (to get past) con
permiso
(to get attention) ¡por favor!
[fa**bor**]
(to say sorry) disculpe
[deesk**ool**peh]

exhaust (pipe) el tubo de

escape [**too**bo deh es**ka**peh]

exhausted (tired) ago**ta**do

exhibition la exposición
[eksposees-**yon**]

exit la sa**li**da

where's the nearest exit?
¿cuál es la salida más
cercana? [kwal – sair**ka**na]

expect espe**rar** [espai**rar**]

expensive **ca**ro

experienced con experiencia
[espair-**yens**-ya]

explain expli**car** [esplee**kar**]

can you explain that? ¿puede
explicármelo? [**pwe**deh]

express (mail) urgente
[oor**Hen**teh]

(train) el ex**prés**

extension (phone) extensión
[estens-**yon**], interno
[een**tair**no]

extension 221, please
extensión doscientos
veintiuno, por favor [fa**bor**]

extension lead el alarga**dor**

extra: can we have an extra
one? ¿nos puede dar **o**tro?
[**pwe**deh]

do you charge extra for that?
¿**co**bra **e**xtra **pa**ra **e**sto?

extraordinary extraordinario
[ekstra-ordeen**ar**-yo]

extremely extremadamente
[estremada**men**teh]

eye el **o**jo [**o**Ho]

will you keep an eye on my
suitcase for me? ¿me cuida
la maleta? [meh **kwee**da]

eyebrow pencil el lápiz de

cejas [**la**pees deh **se**Has]

eye drops el colirio [ko**leer**-yo]

eyeglasses las **ga**fas

eyeliner el lápiz de ojos [**la**pees
deh **o**Hos]

eye make-up remover el
desmaquillador de ojos
[desmakee-ya**dor**]

eye shadow la **so**mbra de ojos

F

face la **ca**ra

factory la **fá**brica

Fahrenheit* Fahren**heit**

faint (verb) desma**yar**se [desmī-
yarseh]

she's fainted se desma**yó** [seh
desmī-**yo**]

I feel faint (said by man/woman)
est**oy** mare**a**do/mare**a**da
[mareh-**a**do]

fair la feria [**fair**-ya]

(adj: just) **jus**to [**Hoo**sto]

fairly bas**tan**te [bas**tan**teh]

fake (thing) la imitación
[eemeetas-**yon**]

(adj) falsifi**ca**do

fake fur el piel de imitación
[p-yel]

fall (verb) ca**er**se [ka-**air**seh]

she's had a fall se ca**yó** [seh
kī-**yo**]

fall (US: noun) el otoño [oton-yo]

in the fall en otoño

false **fal**so [**fal**-so]

family la familia [fa**meel**-ya]

famous fa**mo**so

fan (electrical) el ventilador
[benteelad(or)]
(handheld) el abanico
(sports) el/la hincha [eencha]
fan belt la correa del
ventilador [korreh-a del
benteeladdor]
fantastic fantástico
far lejos [lehos]

dialogue

is it far from here? ¿está
lejos de aquí? [deh akee]
no, not very far no, no
muy lejos [mwee]
well how far? bueno, ¿qué
tan lejos? [bweno keh]
it's about 20 kilometres
son unos veinte
kilómetros

fare el pasaje [pasaheh]
farm (large) la hacienda [as-
yenda]
(small) la finca
fashionable de moda [deh]
fast rápido
fat (person) gordo
(on meat) la grasa
father el padre [padreh]
father-in-law el suegro
[swegro]
faucet la llave [la yabeh]
fault el defecto
sorry, it was my fault
disculpe, fue culpa mía
[deeskoolpeh fweh]
it's not my fault no es mi
culpa

faulty defectuoso [defektwoso]
favourite preferido [prefaireedo]
fax el fax
(verb: person) mandar un fax a
(document) mandar por fax
February febrero [febrairo]
feel sentir
I feel hot tengo calor
I feel unwell no me siento
bien [meh s-yento b-yen]
I feel like going for a walk se
me antoja un paseo [seh meh
antoHa]
how are you feeling today?
¿cómo se encuentra hoy?
[enkwentra oy]
I'm feeling better me siento
mejor [mehor]
felt-tip (pen) el rotulador
fence la cerca [sairka]
fender la defensa
ferry el ferry
festival el festival [festeebal],
la fiesta
fetch: I'll fetch him lo pasaré
a recoger [pasareh a
rekohair]
will you come and fetch me
later? ¿vendrás a buscarme
más tarde? [bendras a
booskarmeh mas tardeh]
feverish con fiebre [f-yebreh]
few: a few unos pocos
a few days unos días
fiancé el novio [nob-yo]
fiancée la novia [nob-ya]
field el campo
fight la pelea [peleh-a]

figs los higos [**ee**gos]
fill (verb) llenar [**y**enar]
fill in rellenar [reh-**y**enar]
  do I have to fill this in?
  ¿tengo que rellenar esto?
  [keh]
fill up llenar [**y**enar]
  fill it up, please lleno, por
  favor [**y**eno por fa**bor**]
filling (in cake, sandwich) el
  relleno [reh-**y**eno]
  (in tooth) el empaste [em**pas**teh]
film (movie, for camera) la
  película

dialogue

do you have this kind of
film? ¿tiene películas de
este tipo? [t-**y**eneh – deh
esteh **tee**po]
yes, how many
exposures? sí, ¿de cuántas
fotos? [**kwan**tas]
36 treinta y seis

film processing el revelado
  [rebe**la**do]
filter coffee el café de filtro
  [ka**feh** deh **feel**tro]
filter papers los papeles de
  filtro [pa**pel**-es]
filthy muy sucio [mwee **soos**-
  yo]
find (verb) encontrar
  I can't find it no lo
  encuentro [enk**wen**tro]
  I've found it ya lo encontré
  [enkon**treh**]

find out enterarse [ente**rar**seh]
  could you find out for me?
  ¿me lo puede averiguar?
  [meh lo **pwe**deh abairee**gwar**]
fine (noun) la multa [**mool**ta]
  it's fine today hoy hace buen
  tiempo [oy a**seh** bwen
  t-**yem**po]

dialogues

how are you? ¿cómo estás?
I'm fine, thanks bien,
gracias [b-yen **gras**-yas]

is that OK? ¿va bien así?
[ba]
that's fine, thanks está
bien, gracias

finger el dedo [**de**do]
finish (verb) terminar
  [tairmee**nar**], acabar
  I haven't finished yet no
  he terminado todavía [eh
  tairmee**na**do todabee-a]
  when does it finish? ¿cuándo
  termina? [**kwan**do tair**mee**na]
fire el fuego [**fwe**go]
  (blaze) el incendio [eensend-yo]
  fire! ¡fuego!
  can we light a fire here? ¿se
  puede prender fuego aquí?
  [seh **pwe**deh prend**air** – a**kee**]
  it's on fire está ardiendo [ard-
  yendo]
fire alarm la alarma de
  incendios [deh eensend-yos]
fire brigade los bomberos

[bombairos]

fire escape la salida de incendios [deh eensend-yos]

fire extinguisher el extintor [esteentor]

first primero [preemairo]

I was first (said by man/woman) fui el primero/la primera [fwee]

at first al principio [preenseep-yo]

the first time la primera vez [bes]

first on the left la primera a la izquierda [eesk-yairda]

first aid primeros auxilios [owkseel-yos]

first aid kit el botiquín [boteekeen]

first class (travel etc) de primera (clase) [preemaira (klaseh)]

first floor la primera planta (US) la planta baja [baHa]

first name el nombre de pila [nombreh deh]

fish el pez [pes]
(food) el pescado
(verb) pescar

fishing village el pueblo de pescadores [pweblo deh peskador-es]

fishmonger's la pescadería [peskadairee-a]

fit (attack) el ataque [atakeh]

fit: it doesn't fit me no me viene bien [b-yeneh b-yen]

fitting room el probador

fix (repair) arreglar

(arrange) fijar [feeHar]

can you fix this? ¿puede arreglar esto? [pwedeh]

fizzy con gas

flag la bandera [bandaira]

flannel la manopla

flash (for camera) el flash

flat (noun: apartment) el departamento
(adj) llano [yano]

I've got a flat tyre se me ponchó la llanta [seh meh – yanta]

flavour el sabor

flea la pulga

flight el vuelo [bwelo]

flight number el número de vuelo [noomairo deh]

flippers las aletas

flood la inundación [eenoondas-yon]

floor el piso

florist la florería [florairee-a]

flour la harina [areena]

flower la flor

flu el gripe [greepeh]

fluent: he speaks fluent Spanish domina el español [espan-yol]

fly la mosca
(verb) volar [bolar]

can we fly there? ¿podemos ir en avión? [eer en ab-yon]

fly in llegar en avión [yegar]

fly out irse en avión [eerseh]

fog la niebla [n-yebla]

foggy: it's foggy hay niebla [ī]

folk dancing el baile tradicional [bīleh tradees-yonal]

folk music la música folklórica [**moo**seeka]

follow seguir [seg**ee**r]

follow me sígame [**see**gameh]

food la comida

food poisoning la intoxicación alimenticia [eentokseekas-y**o**n aleement**ee**s-ya]

food shop/store la tienda de alimentos [t-y**e**nda deh], el ultramarinos [ooltramar**ee**nos]

foot* (of person, measurement) el pie [p-yeh]

on foot a pie

football (game) el fútbol (ball) el balón

football match el partido de fútbol

for para, por

do you have something for ...? (headache/diarrhoea etc) ¿tiene algo para ...? [t-yeneh]

dialogues

who's the mole poblano for? ¿para quién es el mole poblano? [k-yen]
that's for me es para mí
and this one? ¿y éste? [ee esteh]
that's for her ése es para ella [eseh – **eh**-ya]

where do I get the bus for Puebla? ¿dónde se toma el autobús para Puebla? [d**o**ndeh seh – pw**e**bla]

the bus for Puebla leaves from the Zócalo el autobús para Puebla sale del Zócalo [saleh del s**o**kalo]

how long have you been here for? ¿cuánto tiempo lleva aquí? [kwanto t-y**e**mpo yeba ak**ee**]
I've been here for two days, how about you? llevo aquí dos días, ¿y Usted? [yebo – ee oosteh]
I've been here for a week llevo aquí una semana

forehead la frente [frenteh]

foreign extranjero [estran**H**airo]

foreigner (man/woman) el extranjero, la extranjera

forest el bosque [b**o**skeh]

forget olvidar [olbeed**a**r]

I forget no me acuerdo [meh akw**ai**rdo]

I've forgotten se me olvidó [seh meh olbeed**o**]

fork el tenedor (in road) la bifurcación [beefoorkas-y**o**n]

form (document) el formulario [formool**a**r-yo]

formal (dress) de etiqueta [deh eteek**e**ta]

fortnight quince días [k**ee**nseh dee-as], la quincena [keens**e**na]

fortunately por suerte [sw**ai**rteh]

forward: could you forward my mail? ¿puede enviarme el correo? [pw**e**deh emb-yarmeh el korr**eh**-o]

forwarding address la nueva dirección [nw**e**ba deereks-y**o**n]

foundation (make-up) la crema base [b**a**seh]

fountain la fuente [fw**e**nteh]

foyer el vestíbulo [besteeb**oo**lo]

fracture la fractura [frakt**oo**ra]

France Francia [frans-ya]

free libre [l**ee**breh]

(no charge) gratuito [gratw**ee**to]

is it free (of charge)? ¿es gratis?

freeway la autopista [owtop**ee**sta]

freezer el congelador [konHelad**o**r]

French francés [frans-**e**s]

French fries las papas fritas

frequent frecuente [frekw**e**nteh]

how frequent is the bus to Monterrey? ¿cada cuánto tiempo hay autobús a Monterrey [k**a**da kw**a**nto t-y**e**mpo ī – montairr**ay**]

fresh fresco

fresh orange el jugo de naranja [H**oo**go de naran**H**a]

Friday viernes [b-y**ai**rn-es]

fridge la refrigeradora [refreeHairad**o**ra]

fried frito

fried egg el huevo frito [w**e**bo]

friend (male/female) el amigo, la amiga

friendly simpático

from de [deh], desde [d**e**sdeh]

when does the next train from Guadalajara arrive?

¿cuándo llega el próximo tren de Guadalajara? [kw**a**ndo yega – deh gwadalaH**a**ra]

from Monday to Friday de lunes a viernes [deh]

from next Thursday a partir del próximo jueves [part**ee**r]

dialogue

> **where are you from?** ¿de dónde es Usted? [d**o**ndeh es oost**e**h]
> **I'm from Los Angeles** soy de Los Angeles [anHel-es]

front la parte delantera [p**a**rteh delant**ai**ra]

in front delante [del**a**nteh]

in front of the hotel delante del hotel

at the front en la parte de delante [deh]

frost la escarcha

frozen congelado [konHel**a**do]

frozen food los congelados

fruit la fruta

fruit juice el jugo de frutas [H**oo**go deh]

fry freír [freh-**ee**r]

frying pan la sartén

full lleno [y**e**no]

it's full of ... está lleno de ... [deh]

I'm full (said by man/woman) estoy lleno/llena

full board pensión completa [pens-y**o**n]

fun: it was fun fue muy

divertido [fweh mwee deebairteedo]

funeral el funeral [foonairal]

funny (strange) raro
(amusing) divertido [deebairteedo]

furniture los muebles [mwebles]

further más allá [a-ya]
it's further down the road está más adelante [adelanteh]

dialogue

how much further is it to Cuernavaca? ¿cuánto falta para Cuernavaca? [kwanto – kwairnabaka]

about 5 kilometres unos cinco kilómetros

fuse el fusible [fooseebleh]
the lights have fused se fundieron los plomos [seh foond-yairon]

fuse box la caja de fusibles [kaHa deh fooseeb-les]

fuse wire el plomo

future el futuro [footooro]
in the future en el futuro

G

gallon* el galón

game (cards etc) el juego [Hwego]
(match) el partido
(meat) la caza [casa]

garage (for fuel) la gasolinera [gasoleenaira]
(for repairs) el taller (de reparaciones) [ta-yair (deh reparas-yon-es)]
(for parking) el garaje [garaHeh], la cochera [kochaira]

garden el jardín [Hardeen]

garlic el ajo [aHo]

gas el gas
(US) la gasolina

gas cylinder (camping gas) la bomba de gas

gasoline la gasolina

gas permeable lenses las lentillas porosas [lentee-yas]

gas station la gasolinera [gasoleenaira]

gate la puerta [pwairta]
(at airport) la puerta de embarque [deh embarkeh]

gay gay

gay bar el bar gay

gearbox la caja de cambios [kaHa deh kamb-yos]

gear lever el cambio

gears la marcha

general general [Heneral]

gents (toilet) el servicio de señores [sairbees-yo deh sen-yor-es]

genuine (antique etc) auténtico [owtenteeko]

German (adj, language) alemán

German measles la rubeola [roobeh-ola]

Germany Alemania [aleman-ya]

get (fetch) traer [tra-air]
will you get me another one,

please? me trae **o**tro, por favor [meh tra-eh – fab**o**r]
how do you get to ...? ¿c**ó**mo se va a ...? [seh ba]
do you know where I can get them? ¿sabe dónde las puedo conseguir? [sab**e**h d**o**ndeh las pw**e**do konseg**ee**r]

dialogue

can I get you a drink? ¿puedo ofrecerle **a**lgo de beber? [pw**e**do ofres**ai**rleh – deh beb**ai**r]
no, I'll get this one – what would you like? no, yo invito – ¿qué se le antoja? [eenb**ee**to keh seh leh ant**o**Ha]
a glass of red wine una c**o**pa de v**i**no tinto [deh]

get back (return) regresar
get in (arrive) llegar [yeg**a**r]
get off bajarse [baHarseh]
where do I get off? ¿d**ó**nde tengo que bajarme? [d**o**ndeh – keh baHarmeh]
get on (to train etc) subirse [soob**ee**rseh]
get out (of car etc) bajarse [baHarseh]
get up (in the morning) levantarse [lebant**a**rseh]
gift el regalo
gift shop la tienda de regalos [t-y**e**nda]
gin la ginebra [Heen**e**bra]
a gin and tonic, please un

gintónic, por favor [Heent**o**neek – fab**o**r]
girl la chica [ch**ee**ka], la joven [H**o**ben], la chava [ch**a**ba]
girlfriend la novia [n**o**b-ya]
give dar
can you give me some change? ¿me da suelto? [meh]
I gave it to him se lo dí (a él) [seh]
will you give this to ...? ¿podría entregarle esto a ...? [entreg**a**rleh]

dialogue

how much do you want for this? ¿cuánto vale **e**sto? [kw**a**nto b**a**leh]
1,000 pesos mil pesos
I'll give you 800 le doy ochocientos [leh]

give back devolver [debolb**ai**r]
glad feliz [fel**ee**s]
glass (material) el vidrio [beedr-yo]
(tumbler) el vaso [b**a**so]
(wine glass) la copa
a glass of wine una copa de vino [deh]
glasses las gafas
gloves los guantes [gw**a**nt-es]
glue el pegamento
go (verb) ir [eer]
we'd like to go to the swimming-pool nos gustaría ir a la alberca
where are you going?

¿adónde va? [adondeh ba]
where does this bus go?
¿adónde va este autobús?
[esteh]
let's go! ¡vamos! [bamos]
she's gone (left) se fue [seh
fweh]
where has he gone? ¿dónde
se ha ido? [dondeh seh a]
I went there last week estuve
la semana pasada [estoobeh]
go away irse [eerseh]
go away! ¡lárguese! [largeh-
seh]
go back (return) regresar
go down (the stairs etc) bajar
[baHar]
go in entrar
go out (in the evening) salir
**do you want to go out
tonight?** ¿quiere salir esta
noche? [k-yaireh – nocheh]
go through pasar por
go up (the stairs etc) subir
goat la cabra
God Dios [d-yos]
goggles las gafas protectoras
gold el oro
golf el golf
golf course el campo de golf
[deh]
good bueno [bweno]
good! ¡muy bien! [mwee
b-yen]
it's no good es inútil
[eenooteel]
goodbye hasta luego [asta
lwego]
good evening buenas tardes

[bwenas tard-es]
Good Friday el Viernes Santo
[b-yairn-es]
good morning buenos días
[bwenos]
good night buenas noches
[bwenas noch-es]
goose el ganso
got: we've got to ... tenemos
que ... [keh]
have you got any apples?
¿tiene manzanas? [t-yeneh]
government el gobierno [gob-
yairno]
gradually poco a poco
grammar la gramática
gram(me) el gramo
granddaughter la nieta [n-yeta]
grandfather el abuelo [abwelo]
grandmother la abuela
[abwela]
grandson el nieto [n-yeto]
grapefruit la toronja [toronHa]
grapefruit juice el jugo de
toronja [Hoogo deh]
grapes las uvas [oobas]
grass el pasto, el césped
[sesped]
grateful agradecido
[agradeseedo]
gravy la salsa
great (excellent) muy bueno
[mwee bweno]
that's great! ¡estupendo!
[estoopendo]
a great success un gran
éxito [ekseeto]
Great Britain Gran Bretaña
[bretan-ya]

greedy gul**o**so
green verde [**bair**deh]
green card (car insurance) la
  tarjeta verde [tar**He**ta]
greengrocer's la fruter**í**a
  [frootair**ee**-a]
grey gris [grees]
grill la parr**i**lla [par**ree**-ya]
grilled a la parr**i**lla, a la
  pl**a**ncha
grocer's (la tienda de)
  abarrotes [(t-y**e**nda deh) abar**ot**-
  es]
ground el p**i**so
  on the ground en el p**i**so
ground floor la pl**a**nta b**a**ja
  [**ba**Ha]
group el gr**u**po
guarantee la garant**í**a
  is it guaranteed? ¿lleva
  garant**í**a? [**ye**va]
Guatemalan (adj)
  guatemalt**e**co [gwatemalt**e**ko]
guest (man/woman) el invit**a**do
  [eembeet**a**do], la invit**a**da
guesthouse la pensi**ó**n [pens-
  yon]
guide el/la gu**í**a [**gee**-a]
guidebook la gu**í**a
guided tour la visita con gu**í**a
  [bees**ee**ta]
guitar la guit**a**rra [geet**a**rra]
Gulf of Mexico el G**o**lfo
gum (in mouth) la enc**í**a
  [ens**ee**-a]
gun la pist**o**la
gym el gimn**a**sio [Heemn**a**s-yo]

H

hair el p**e**lo
hairbrush el cepillo para el
  pelo [sep**ee**-yo]
haircut el corte de pelo
  [**kor**teh deh]
hairdresser's la peluquer**í**a
  [pelookair**ee**-a]
hairdryer el secad**o**r de pelo
  [deh]
hair gel el fijad**o**r (para el
  pelo) [feeHad**or**]
hairgrip la horqu**i**lla [ork**ee**-ya]
hair spray la l**a**ca
half* la mitad [m**ee**ta]
  half an hour media hora
  [med-ya **o**ra]
  half a litre medio litro [med-
  yo]
  about half that
  aproximadamente la mitad
  de eso [aprokseemadam**e**nteh
  – deh]
half board media pensi**ó**n
  [med-ya pens-**yon**]
half fare el medio boleto
  [med-yo], el boleto con
  descuento [desk**w**ento]
half price a mitad del precio
  [m**ee**ta del pres-yo]
ham el jam**ó**n [Ham**on**]
hamburger la hamburguesa
  [amboorg**e**sa]
hammer el martillo [mart**ee**-yo]
hammock la hamaca [am**a**ka]
hand la m**a**no
handbag el b**o**lso

66

handbrake el freno de mano [deh]

handkerchief el pañuelo [pan-ywaylo]

handle (on door) el mango (on suitcase etc) el asa

hand luggage el equipaje de mano [ekeepaH-eh]

hang-gliding el ala delta

hangover la cruda [krooda]
I've got a hangover tengo cruda

happen suceder [soosedair]
what's happening? ¿qué pasa? [keh]
what has happened? ¿qué pasó?

happy contento
I'm not happy about this esto no me convence [meh konbenseh]

harbour el puerto [pwairto]

hard duro [dooro]
(difficult) difícil [deefeeseel]

hard-boiled egg el huevo duro [webo]

hard lenses las lentillas duras [lentee-yas]

hardly apenas
hardly ever casi nunca

hardware shop la ferretería [fairretairee-a], la tlapalería [tlapalairee-a]

hat el sombrero [sombrairo]

hate (verb) odiar [od-yar]

have* tener [tenair]
can I have a ...? ¿me da ...? [meh]
do you have ...? ¿tiene ...? [t-yeneh]
what'll you have? ¿qué va a tomar? [keh ba]
I have to leave now tengo que irme ahora [eermeh a-ora]
do I have to ...? ¿tengo que ...?
can we have some ...? ¿nos pone ...? [poneh]

hayfever la fiebre del heno [f-yebreh del eno]

hazelnut la avellana [abeh-yana]

he* él

head la cabeza [kabesa]

headache el dolor de cabeza [deh], la jaqueca [Hakeka]

headlights las luces de cruce [loos-es de krooseh]

headphones los auriculares [owreekoolar-es]

health food shop la tienda naturista [t-yenda natooreesta]

healthy sano

hear escuchar [eskoochar]

dialogue

can you hear me? ¿me escuchas? [meh eskoochas]
I can't hear you, could you repeat that? no le escucho, ¿podría repetirlo? [leh]

hearing aid el audífono [owdeefono]

heart el corazón [korason]

heart attack el infarto

heat el calor

heater (in room) la estufa
(in car) la calefacción
[kalefaks-yon]

heating la calefacción

heavy pesado

heel (of foot) el talón
(of shoe) el tacón

could you heel these?
¿podría cambiar los tacones?
[kamb-yar – takon-es]

heelbar el zapatero [sapatairo]

height la altura

helicopter el helicóptero

hello! ¡hola! [ola]
(answer on phone) ¡bueno!
[bweno]

helmet el casco

help la ayuda [ī-yooda]
(verb) ayudar [ī-yoodar]

help! ¡socorro!

can you help me? ¿puede
ayudarme? [pwedeh
ī-yoodarmeh]

thank you very much for your
help muchas gracias por su
ayuda [moochas gras-yas]

helpful amable [amableh]

hepatitis la hepatitis
[epateetees]

her*: I haven't seen her no la
he visto [eh beesto]
to her a ella [eh-ya]
with her con ella
for her para ella
that's her ella es
that's her towel ésa es su
toalla

herbal tea el té de hierbas [teh
deh yairbas]

herbs las hierbas

here aquí [akee]
here is/are ... aquí está/
están ...

here you are (offering) aquí
tiene [t-yeneh]

hers* (el) suyo [soo-yo], (la)
suya
that's hers es de ella [deh eh-
ya], es suyo/suya

hey! ¡oiga! [oyga]

hi! (hello) ¡hola! [ola]

hide (verb) esconder [eskondair]

high alto

highchair la silla alta para
bebés [see-ya – beh-bes]

highway (US) la autopista
[owtopeesta]

hill el cerro [sairro]

him*: I haven't seen him no lo
he visto [eh beesto]
to him a él
with him con él
for him para él
that's him él es

hip la cadera [kadaira]

hire (verb) alquilar [alkeelar],
arrendar
for hire de alquiler [deh
alkeelair]
where can I hire a bike?
¿dónde puedo alquilar una
bicicleta? [dondeh pwedo]

his*: it's his car es su carro
that's his eso es de él [deh],
eso es suyo [soo-yo]

history la historia [eestor-ya]

hit (verb) golpear [golpeh-ar]

hitch-hike pedir aventón [abenton], hacer autostop [asair owtostop], pedir ráid [rīd]

hobby el pasatiempo [pasat-yempo]

hold (verb) tener en la mano [tenair]

hole el agujero [agooнairo], el hoyo [oy-o]

holiday las vacaciones [bakas-yon-es]

on holiday de vacaciones [deh]

home la casa

at home (in my house) en casa (in my country) en mi país [pa-ees]

we go home tomorrow regresamos a casa mañana

honest honrado [onrado]

honey la miel [m-yel]

honeymoon la luna de miel [loona deh]

hood (US) el capó, el capote [kapoteh], el cofre [kofreh]

hope la esperanza [espairansa]

I hope so espero que sí [espairo keh]

I hope not espero que no

hopefully it won't rain no lloverá, eso espero [yobaira]

horn (of car) el klaxon

horrible horrible [orreebleh]

horse el caballo [kaba-yo]

horse racing las carreras de caballos [karrairas deh kaba-yos]

horse riding la equitación [ekeetas-yon]

I like horse riding me gusta montar a caballo [meh – kaba-yo]

hospital el hospital [ospeetal]

hospitality la hospitalidad [ospeetaleeda]

thank you for your hospitality gracias por su hospitalidad [gras-yas]

hot caliente [kal-yenteh] (spicy) picante [peekanteh], picoso

I'm hot tengo calor

it's hot today hoy hace calor [oy aseh]

hotel el hotel [otel]

hotel room el cuarto de hotel [kwarto deh otel]

hour la hora [ora]

house la casa

house wine el vino de la casa [beeno deh]

hovercraft el aerodeslizador [a-airodesleesador]

how cómo

how many? ¿cuántos? [kwantos]

how do you do? ¡mucho gusto! [moocho goosto]

dialogues

how are you? ¿cómo le va? [leh ba]

fine, thanks, and you? bien gracias, ¿y Usted? [b-yen gras-yas ee oosteh]

how much is it? ¿cuánto

vale? [kwanto baleh]
1,000 pesos mil pesos
[pesos]
I'll take it me lo quedo
[meh lo kedo]

humid húmedo [oomedo]
humour el humor [oomor]
hungry hambriento [ambr-yento]
I'm hungry tengo hambre
[ambreh]
are you hungry? ¿tiene
hambre? [t-yeneh]
hurry (verb) apurarse
[apoorarseh]
I'm in a hurry tengo prisa
there's no hurry no hay prisa
[i]
hurry up! ¡apúrese!
[apooreseh]
hurt doler [dolair]
it really hurts me duele
mucho [meh dweleh moocho]
husband el marido
hydrofoil la hidroala [eedro-ala]
hypermarket el
hipermercado [eepairmairkado]

I

I yo
ice el hielo [yelo]
with ice con hielo
no ice, thanks sin hielo, por
favor [seen – fabor]
ice cream el helado [elado]
ice-cream cone el cucurucho

[kookooroochoo]
iced coffee el café helado
[kafeh elado]
ice lolly la paleta
idea la idea [eedeh-a]
idiot el/la idiota [eed-yota]
if si
ignition el encendido
[ensendeedo]
ill enfermo [enfairmo]
I feel ill me encuentro mal
[meh enkwentro]
illness la enfermedad
[enfairmeda]
imitation (leather etc) de
imitación [deh eemeetas-yon]
immediately en seguida
[segeeda]
important importante
[eemportanteh]
it's very important es muy
importante [mwee]
it's not important no
tiene importancia [t-yeneh
eemportans-ya]
impossible imposible
[eemposeebleh]
impressive impresionante
[eempres-yonanteh]
improve mejorar [meHorar]
I want to improve my
Spanish quiero mejorar mi
español [k-yairo – espan-yol]
in: it's in the centre está en el
centro
in my car en mi carro
in Xalapa en Xalapa [Halapa]
in two days from now en dos
días más

in five minutes dentro de
cinco minutos [deh]
in May en mayo
in English en inglés [eeng-les]
in Spanish en español [espan-
yol]
is he in? ¿se encuentra? [seh
enkwentra]
inch* la pulgada
include incluir [eenkloo-eer]
does that include meals?
¿están incluídas las
comidas? [eenkloo-eedas]
is that included? ¿está
incluido en el precio?
[eenkloo-eedo en el pres-yo]
inconvenient inoportuno
[eenoportoono]
incredible increíble [eenkreh-
eebleh]
Indian (adj: from India) indio
[eend-yo]
(South American: adj) indígena
[eendeeHena]
(man/woman) el/la indígena
indicator el intermitente
[eentairmeetenteh]
indigestion la indigestión
[eendeeHest-yon]
indoor pool la alberca
cubierta [albairka koob-yairta]
indoors dentro de la casa [deh]
inexpensive económico
infection la infección
[eenfeks-yon]
infectious contagioso [kontaH-
yoso]
inflammation la inflamación
[eenflamas-yon]

informal (occasion, meeting)
informal [eenformal]
(dress) de sport [deh]
information la información
[eenformas-yon]
do you have any information
about ...? ¿tiene
información sobre ... ?
[t-yeneh – sobreh]
information desk la
información
injection la inyección [een-
yeks-yon]
injured herido [ereedo]
she's been injured está
herida
in-laws la familia política
[fameel-ya]
inner tube (for tyre) la cámara
de aire [deh a-eereh]
innocent inocente [eenosenteh]
insect el insecto [eensekto]
insect bite la picadura de
insecto [deh]
do you have anything for
insect bites? ¿tiene algo para
la picadura de
insectos? [t-yeneh]
insect repellent el repelente
de insectos [repelenteh deh]
inside dentro de [deh]
inside the hotel dentro del
hotel
let's sit inside vamos a
sentarnos adentro [bamos]
insist insistir [eenseesteer]
I insist insisto
insomnia el insomnio
[eensomn-yo]

instant coffee el café instantáneo [kaf**eh** eenstantan**e**h-o]

instead: give me that one instead deme ese **o**tro [d**e**meh **e**seh]

instead of ... en lug**a**r de ... [**de**h]

intersection el cruce [kr**oo**seh]

insulin la insulina [eensool**ee**na]

insurance el seguro [seg**oo**ro]

intelligent inteligente [eenteleeH**e**nteh]

interested: I'm interested in ... me inter**e**sa ... [meh eentair**e**sa]

interesting interesante [eenteres**a**nteh]

that's very interesting es muy interesante [mwee]

international internacional [eentairnas-y**o**nal]

interpret actuar de intérprete [actoo-**a**r deh eent**a**irpreteh]

interpreter el/la intérprete

interval (at theatre) el intermedio [eentairm**e**d-yo]

into en

I'm not into ... no me gusta ... [meh g**oo**sta]

introduce presentar

may I introduce ...? le presento a ... [leh]

invitation la invitación [eembeetas-y**o**n]

invite invitar [eembeet**a**r]

Ireland Irlanda [eerl**a**nda]

Irish irlandés [eerland-**e**s]

I'm Irish (man/woman) soy irlandés/irland**e**sa

iron (for ironing) la plancha (metal) el hierro [y**a**irro]

can you iron these for me? ¿puede planch**á**rmelos? [pw**e**deh]

is* es, está

island la isla [**ee**sla]

it ello, lo [**eh**-yo]

it is ... es ...; est**á** ...

is it ...? ¿es ...?; ¿está ... ?

where is it? ¿dónde está? [d**o**ndeh]

it's him es él

it was ... era ... [**a**ira]; est**a**ba ...

Italian (adj) italiano [eetal-y**a**no]

Italy Italia

itch el comezón [komes**o**n]

it itches me pica [meh]

J

jack (for car) el gato

jacket el saco

jam la mermelada [mairmel**a**da]

jammed: it's jammed se atoró [seh]

January enero [en**a**iro]

jar el pote [p**o**teh]

jaw la mandíbula

jazz el jazz

jealous celoso [sel**o**so]

jeans los vaqueros [bak**a**iros]

jellyfish la medusa [med**oo**sa]

jersey el jersey [H**a**irseh]

jetty el muelle [mw**eh**-yeh]

jeweller's shop la joyería [Ho-yair**ee**-a]

jewellery las joyas [Ho-yas]

Jewish judío [Hoodee-o]

job el trabajo [trabaHo], el puesto [pwesto]

jogging el footing
to go jogging hacer footing [asair]

joke el chiste [cheesteh]

journey el viaje [b-yaHeh]
have a good journey! ¡buen viaje! [bwen]

jug la jarra [Harra]
a jug of water una jarra de agua [deh]

juice el jugo [Hoogo]

July julio [Hool-yo]

jump (verb) brincar

jumper el jersey [Hairseh]

jump leads las pinzas (para la batería) [peensas (para la batairee-a)]

junction el cruce [krooseh]

June junio [Hoon-yo]

jungle la selva [selva]

just (only) solamente [solamenteh]
just two sólo dos
just for me sólo para mí
just here aquí mismo [akee meesmo], aquí mero [mairo]
not just now ahora no [a-ora]
we've just arrived acabamos de llegar [deh yegar]

K

kayak el kayak

keep quedarse [kedarseh]

keep the change quédese con el cambio [kedeseh – kamb-yo]
can I keep it? ¿puedo quedármelo? [pwedo kedarmelo]
please keep it por favor, quédeselo [fabor kedeselo]

ketchup el catsup [katsoop]

kettle el hervidor [airbeedor]

key la llave [yabeh]
the key for room 201, please la llave del doscientos uno, por favor [fabor]

keyring el llavero [yabairo]

kidneys los riñones [reen-yon-es]

kill matar

kilo* el kilo

kilometre* el kilómetro
how many kilometres is it to ...? ¿cuántos kilómetros hay a ...? [kwantos – ī]

kind (nice) amable [amableh]
that's very kind es muy amable [mwee]

dialogue

which kind do you want?
¿qué tipo quiere? [keh teepo k-yaireh]
I want this/that kind
quiero este/aquel tipo [k-yairo esteh/akel]

king el rey [ray]

kiosk el quiosco [kee-osko]

kiss el beso

(verb) besarse [besarseh]
kitchen la cocina [koseena]
kitchenette la cocina pequeña [pekwen-ya]
Kleenex® el klínex
knee la rodilla [rodee-ya]
knickers los pantis
knife el cuchillo [koochee-yo]
knock (verb: on door) llamar [yamar]
knock down atropellar [atropeh-yar]
he's been knocked down lo atropellaron [atropeh-yaron]
knock over (object) volcar [bolkar]
(pedestrian) atropellar [atropeh-yar]
know (somebody, a place) conocer [konosair]
(something) saber [sabair]
I don't know no sé [seh]
I didn't know that no lo sabía
do you know where I can find ...? ¿sabe dónde puedo encontrar ...? [sabeh dondeh pwedo]

dialogue

do you know how this works? ¿sabe cómo funciona esto? [foons-yona]
sorry, I don't know lo siento, no sé [s-yento no seh]

L

label la etiqueta [eteeketa]
ladies' room, ladies' (toilet) el servicio de señoras [sairbees-yo deh sen-yoras]
ladies' wear la ropa de señoras
lady la señora [sen-yora]
lager la cerveza clara [sairbesa]
lagoon la laguna
lake el lago
lamb (meat) el cordero [kordairo]
lamp la lámpara
land la tierra [t-yairra]
(verb) aterrizar [aterreesar]
lane (motorway) el carril
(small road) la callejuela [ka-yeh-Hwela]
language el idioma [eed-yoma]
language course el curso de idiomas [koorso deh]
large grande [grandeh]
last último [oolteemo]
last week la semana pasada
last Friday el viernes pasado
last night anoche [anocheh]
what time is the last train to Veracruz? ¿a qué hora es el último tren para Veracruz? [keh ora – bairakroos]
late tarde [tardeh]
sorry I'm late disculpe, me retrasé [deeskoolpeh meh retraseh]
the train was late el tren se demoró
we must go – we'll be late

debemos irnos – llegaremos tarde [eernos – yegaremos]

it's getting late se está haciendo tarde [seh – asyendo]

later más tarde [tardeh]

I'll come back later regresaré más tarde [regresareh]

see you later hasta luego [asta lwego]

later on más tarde

latest lo último [oolteemo]

by Wednesday at the latest para el miércoles a más tardar

Latin America América [amaireeka]

Latin American (adj) americano [amaireekano]

(man) el (latino) americano

(woman) la (latino) americana

laugh (verb) reirse [reh-eerseh]

launderette/laundromat la lavandería automática [labandairee-a owtomateeka]

laundry (clothes) la ropa sucia [soos-ya]

(place) la lavandería [labandairee-a]

lavatory el baño [ban-yo]

law la ley [lay]

lawn el césped [sesped]

lawyer (man/woman) el abogado, la abogada

laxative el laxante [laksanteh]

lazy flojo [floHo]

lead (electrical) el cable [kableh]

lead (verb) llevar [yevar]

where does this lead to?

¿adónde va esto? [adondeh ba]

leaf la hoja [oHa]

leaflet el folleto [fo-yeto]

leak (in roof) la gotera [gotaira]

(gas, water) el escape [eskapeh]

(verb) filtrar [feeltrar]

the roof leaks el tejado tiene goteras [teHado t-yeneh gotairas]

learn aprender [aprendair]

least: not in the least de ninguna manera [deh – manaira]

at least al menos [menos]

leather (fine) la piel [p-yel]

(heavy) el cuero [kwairo]

leave (verb) irse [eerseh]

I am leaving tomorrow me voy mañana [meh]

he left yesterday se fue ayer [seh fweh]

may I leave this here? ¿puedo dejar esto aquí? [pwedo deh-Har esto akee]

I left my coat in the bar dejé el abrigo en el bar [deh-Heh]

dialogue

when does the bus for Taxco leave? ¿cuándo sale el autobús para Taxco? [kwando saleh – tasko]

it leaves at 9 o'clock sale a las nueve

leek el puerro [pwairro]

left izquierda [eesk-yairda]

on the left a la izquierda
to the left hacia la izquierda
[as-yá]
turn left dé vuelta a la
izquierda [deh bwelta]
there's none left no queda
ninguno [keda]
left-handed zurdo [soordo]
left luggage (office) la
consigna [konseegna], la
paquetería [paketairee-a]
leg la pierna [p-yairna]
lemon el limón
lemonade la limonada
lemon tea el té con limón
[teh]
lend prestar
will you lend me your ... ?
¿podría prestarme su ...?
[prestarmeh]
lens (of camera) el objetivo
[obHeteebo]
lesbian la lesbiana [lesb-yana]
less menos
less expensive menos caro
less than 10 menos de diez
[deh]
less than you menos que tú
[keh too]
lesson la lección [leks-yon]
let (allow) dejar [deh-Har]
will you let me know? ¿me
tendrás al corriente? [meh
– korr-yenteh]
I'll let you know le avisaré [leh
abeesareh]
let's go for something to eat
vamos a comer algo [bamos a
komair]

let off: will you let me off
at ...? ¿me deja en...? [meh
deh-Ha]
letter la carta
do you have any letters for
me? ¿tiene cartas para mí?
[t-yeneh]
letterbox el buzón [booson]
lettuce la lechuga [lechooga]
lever la palanca
library la biblioteca [beebl-
yoteka]
licence el permiso
lid la tapa
lie (verb: tell untruth) mentir
lie down acostarse [akostarseh],
echarse [echarseh]
life la vida [beeda]
lifebelt el salvavidas
[salbabeedas]
lifeguard el/la socorrista
life jacket el chaleco
salvavidas [salbabeedas]
lift (in building) el ascensor
[asensor]
could you give me a lift?
¿me podría llevar? [meh
– yebar]
would you like a lift? ¿quiere
que lo lleve? [k-yaireh keh lo
yebeh]
light la luz [loos]
(not heavy) ligero [leeHairo]
do you have a light? (for
cigarette) ¿tiene fuego?
[t-yeneh fwego]
light green verde claro
[bairdeh]
light bulb el foco

I need a new light bulb
necesito un foco nuevo
[neseseeto – nwebo]
lighter (cigarette) el
encendedor [ensendedor]
lightning el relámpago
like (verb) gustar [goostar]
I like it me gusta [meh]
I like going for walks me
gusta pasear
I like you me gustas
I don't like it no me gusta
do you like ...? ¿le gusta ...?
[leh]
I'd like a beer quisiera una
cerveza [kees-yaira]
I'd like to go swimming me
gustaría ir a bañarme
would you like a drink?
¿quiere beber algo? [k-yaireh]
would you like to go for a
walk? ¿quieres dar un paseo?
[k-yair-es]
what's it like? ¿cómo es?
I want one like this quiero
uno como éste [k-yairo – esteh]
lime la lima [leema]
lime cordial el jarabe de lima
[Harabeh deh]
line la línea [leeneh-a]
could you give me an outside
line? ¿puede darme línea?
[pwedeh darmeh]
lips los labios [lab-yos]
lip salve la crema de labios
[deh]
lipstick el lápiz de labios
[lapees]
liqueur el licor

listen oir [o-eer]
litre* el litro
a litre of white wine un litro
de vino blanco [deh]
little chico
just a little, thanks un
poquito, gracias [pokeeto gras-
yas]
a little milk un poco de leche
a little bit more un poquito
más
live (verb) vivir [beebeer]
we live together vivimos
juntos [beebeemos Hoontos]

dialogue

where do you live? ¿dónde
vive? [dondeh
beebeh]
I live in London vivo en
Londres [beebo en lond-res]

lively alegre [alegreh],
animado
liver el hígado [eegado]
lizard la lagartija [lagarteeHa]
loaf el pan
lobby (in hotel) el vestíbulo
[besteeboolo]
lobster la langosta
local local
can you recommend a local
wine/restaurant? ¿puede
recomendarme un vino/un
restaurante local? [pwedeh
rekomendarmeh]
lock la cerradura [sairradoora]
(verb) cerrar [sairrar]

Lo

77

it's locked está cerrado con
llave [sairrado kon yabeh]

lock in dejar encerrado [deh-
Har ensairrado]

lock out: I've locked myself
out he cerrado la puerta con
las llaves dentro [eh sairrado la
pwairta – yab-es]

locker (for luggage etc) la
consigna automática
[konseegna owtomateeka]

lollipop la paleta

London Londres [lond-res]

long largo

how long will it take to fix it?
¿cuánto tiempo tardará en
arreglarlo? [kwanto t-yempo]

how long does it take?
¿cuánto tiempo lleva? [yeba]

a long time mucho tiempo
[moocho]

one day/two days longer un
día/dos días más

long distance call la llamada
de larga distancia [yamada deh
– deestans-ya]

look: I'm just looking, thanks
sólo estoy mirando, gracias
[gras-yas]

you don't look well tienes
cara de enfermo [t-yen-es kara
deh enfairmo]

look out! ¡cuidado!
[kweedado]

can I have a look? ¿me deja
ver? [meh deh-Ha bair]

look after cuidar [kweedar]

look at mirar

look for buscar

I'm looking for ... estoy
buscando ...

look forward to: I'm looking
forward to seeing it tengo
muchas ganas de verlo
[moochas – deh bairlo]

loose (handle etc) suelto [swelto]

lorry el camión [kam-yon], el
tráiler [trīlair]

lose perder [pairdair],
extraviarse [estrab-yarseh]

I've lost my way me extravié
[estrab-yeh]

I'm lost, I want to get to ...
me perdí, quiero ir a ...
[k-yairo eer]

I've lost my bag perdí el
bolso

lost property (office) (la
oficina de) objetos
perdidos [(ofeeseena deh)
obHetos pairdeedos]

lot: a lot, lots mucho, muchos
[moocho]

not a lot no mucho

a lot of people mucha gente

a lot bigger mucho mayor

I like it a lot me gusta mucho
[meh goosta]

lotion la loción [los-yon]

loud fuerte [fwairteh]

lounge (in house, hotel) el salón
(in airport) la sala de espera
[deh espaira]

love el amor
(verb) querer [kairair]

I love Mexico me encanta
México [meh – meHeeko]

lovely encantador

low bajo [baHo]

luck la suerte [swairteh]
 good luck! ¡buena suerte! [bwena]

luggage el equipaje [ekeepaH-eh]

luggage trolley el carrito portaequipajes [porta-ekeepaH-es]

lump (on body) la hinchazón [eenchason]

lunch el almuerzo [almwairso]

lungs los pulmones [poolmon-es]

luxurious (hotel, furnishings) de lujo [deh looHo]

luxury el lujo

M

machine la máquina [makeena]

mad (insane) loco
 (angry) furioso [foor-yoso]

magazine la revista [rebeesta]

maid (in hotel) la camarera [kamaraira]

maiden name el nombre de soltera [nombreh deh soltaira]

mail el correo [korreh-o]
 is there any mail for me? ¿hay correspondencia para mí? [ī korrespondens-ya]
 see post

mailbox el buzón [booson]

main principal [preenseepal]

main course el plato principal

main post office la oficina central de correos [ofeeseena sentral deh korreh-os]

main road (in town) la calle principal [ka-yeh preenseepal]
 (in country) la carretera principal [karretaira]

mains (for water) la llave de paso [yabeh deh]

mains switch (for electricity) el interruptor de la red eléctrica [eentairrooptor deh la reh]

make (brand name) la marca
 (verb) hacer [asair]
 I make it 500 pesos son quinientos pesos en total
 what is it made of? ¿de qué está hecho? [deh keh esta echo]

make-up el maquillaje [makee-yaHeh]

man el hombre [ombreh]

manager el gerente [Hairenteh]
 I'd like to speak to the manager quisiera hablar con el gerente [kees-yaira ablar]

manageress la gerente

manual (car with manual gears) el carro de marchas [deh]

many muchos [moochos]
 not many pocos

map (city plan) el plano
 (road map, geographical) el mapa

March marzo [marso]

margarine la margarina [margareena]

market el mercado [mairkado], el tianguis [t-yangees]

marmalade la mermelada de naranja [mairmelada deh naranHa]

married: I'm married (said by a man/woman) estoy casado/casada

are you married? (to a man/woman) ¿está casado/casada?

mascara el rímel

match (football etc) el partido

matches las cerillas [sairee-yas]

material (fabric) el tejido [teHeedo]

matter: it doesn't matter no importa

what's the matter? ¿qué pasa? [keh]

mattress el colchón

May mayo [mī-yo]

may: may I have another one? ¿me da otro? [meh]

may I come in? ¿se puede? [seh pwedeh]

may I see it? ¿puedo verlo? [pwedo bairlo]

may I sit here? ¿puedo sentarme aqui? [sentarmeh akee]

maybe quizás [keesas]

mayonnaise la mayonesa [mī-yonesa]

me*: that's for me ése es para mí [eseh]

send it to me mándemelo

me too yo también [tamb-yen]

meal la comida

dialogue

did you enjoy your meal? ¿te gustó la comida? [teh goosto]

it was excellent, thank you

estuvo riquísima, gracias [reekeeseema gras-yas]

mean (verb) querer decir [kairair deseer]

what do you mean? ¿qué quiere decir? [keh k-yaireh]

dialogue

what does this word mean? ¿qué significa esta palabra?

it means ... in English significa ... en inglés [eeng-les]

measles el sarampión [sarampyon]

meat la carne [karneh]

mechanic el mecánico

medicine la medicina [medeeseena]

medium (adj: size) medio [med-yo]

medium-dry semi-seco

medium-rare poco hecho [echo]

medium-sized de tamaño medio [taman-yo med-yo]

meet encontrarse [encontrarseh] (for the first time) conocerse [konosairseh]

nice to meet you encantado de conocerle [deh konosairleh]

where shall I meet you? ¿dónde nos vemos? [dondeh nos bemos]

meeting la reunión [reh-oon-yon]

meeting place el lugar de encuentro [loogar deh enkwentro]

melon el melón

men los hombres [omb-res]

mend (clothes) remendar
could you mend this for me? ¿puede arreglarme esto? [pwedeh arreglarmeh]

men's toilet el servicio de hombres [sairbees-yo deh omb-res]

menswear la ropa de hombre [deh ombreh]

mention (verb) mencionar [mens-yonar]
don't mention it de nada [deh]

menu la carta
may I see the menu, please? ¿me deja ver la carta? [meh deh-Ha bair]
see menu reader page 214

message: are there any messages for me? ¿hay algún recado para mí? [ī]
I want to leave a message for ... quisiera dejar un recado para ... [kees-yaira deh-Har]

metal el metal

metre* el metro

Mexican (adj) mexicano [meHeekano]
(man) el mexicano
(woman) la mexicana
the Mexicans los mexicanos

Mexico México [meHeeko]

Mexico City la ciudad de México [s-yooda deh], el Distrito Federal [fedairal], el D.F. [deh efeh]

microwave (oven) el (horno) microondas [(orno) meekro-ondas]

midday el mediodía [med-yodee-a]
at midday a mediodía

middle: in the middle en el centro [sentro]
in the middle of the night en las altas horas de la noche [oras deh la nocheh]
the middle one el de en medio

midnight la medianoche [med-yanocheh]
at midnight a medianoche

might: I might es posible [poseebleh]
I might not go puede que no vaya [pwedeh keh no bī-ya]
I might want to stay another day quizás decida quedarme otro día [keesas deseeda kedarmeh]

migraine la jaqueca [Hakeka]

mild (taste) suave [swabeh]
(weather) templado

mile* la milla [mee-ya]

milk la leche [lecheh]

milkshake el licuado [leekwado]

millimetre* el milímetro

minced meat el picadillo [peekadee-yo]

mind: never mind! ¡no importa!

I've changed my mind cambié de idea [kamb-yeh deh eedeh-a]

dialogue

do you mind if I open the window? ¿le importa que abra la ventana? [leh eemporta keh – bentana]
no, I don't mind no, no me importa [meh]

mine*: it's mine es mío
mineral water el agua mineral [agwa meenairal], el Tehuacán® [teh-wakan]
mint-flavoured con sabor a menta
mints las pastillas de menta [pastee-yas deh]
minute el minuto [meenooto]
in a minute ahorita [a-oreeta]
just a minute un momento
mirror el espejo [espeнo]
Miss Señorita [sen-yoreeta]
miss: I missed the bus perdí el autobús [pairdee]
missing: one of my ... is missing falta uno de mis ... [deh]
there's a suitcase missing falta una maleta
mist la neblina
mistake el error
I think there's a mistake me parece que hay una equivocación [meh pareseh keh

ï oona ekeebokas-yon]
sorry, I've made a mistake perdón, me equivoqué [meh ekeebokeh]
misunderstanding el malentendido
mix-up: sorry, there's been a mix-up perdón hubo una confusión [oobo oona konfoos-yon]
modern moderno [modairno]
modern art gallery la galería de arte moderno [galairee-a deh arteh]
moisturizer la crema hidratante [eedratanteh]
moment: I won't be a moment no me tardo [meh]
monastery el monasterio [monastair-yo]
Monday lunes [loon-es]
money el dinero [deenairo]
month el mes
monument el monumento [monoomento]
(statue) la estatua [estatwa]
moon la luna
moped el ciclomotor [seeklomotor]
more* más
can I have some more water, please? me da más agua, por favor [meh – fabor]
more expensive/interesting más caro/interesante
more than 50 más de cincuenta [deh]
more than that más que eso [keh]

a lot more mucho más
[**moo**cho]

dialogue

> would you like some
> more? ¿quiere más?
> [k-**yai**reh]
> no, no more for me, thanks
> no, para mí no, gracias
> [gras-yas]
> how about you? ¿y Usted?
> [ee oos**teh**]
> I don't want any more,
> thanks nada más, gracias

morning la mañana [man-**yana**]
 this morning esta mañana
 in the morning por la mañana
mosquito el mosquito, el
 zancudo [san**koo**do]
mosquito coil el espiral
 antimosquitos
mosquito net la red
 antimosquitos
mosquito repellent el
 repelente de mosquitos
 [repe**len**teh deh]
most: I like this one most of
 all éste es el que más me
 gusta [**es**teh – keh mas meh
 goosta]
 most of the time la mayor
 parte del tiempo [mī-yor **par**teh
 del t-**yem**po]
 most tourists la mayoría de
 los turistas [mī-yo**ree**-a deh]
mostly generalmente
 [Henairal**men**teh]

mother la madre [**mad**reh]
motorbike la moto
motorboat la (lancha) motora
motorway la autopista
 [owto**pees**ta]
mountain la montaña
 [mon**tan**-ya]
 in the mountains en la sierra
 [s-**yai**ra]
mountaineering el
 montañismo [montan-**yees**mo]
mountain range la sierra
mouse el ratón
moustache el bigote [bee**go**teh]
mouth la boca
mouth ulcer la llaga [**ya**ga]
move: he's moved to another
 room se trasladó a otro
 cuarto [seh – **kwar**to]
 could you move your car?
 ¿podría cambiar de lugar el
 carro? [kamb-yar deh]
 could you move up a little?
 ¿puede correrse un poco?
 [**pwe**deh korr**air**seh]
 where has it moved to?
 ¿adónde se trasladó?
 [a**don**deh seh]
movie la película [pe**lee**koola]
movie theater el cine [**see**neh]
Mr Señor [sen-yor]
Mrs Señora [sen-yora]
Ms Señorita [sen-yo**ree**ta]
much mucho [**moo**cho]
 much better/worse mucho
 mejor/peor [mī-yor/peh-or]
 much hotter mucho más
 caliente [kal-**yen**teh]
 not (very) much no mucho

I don't want very much un poco nada más

mud el barro, el lodo

mug (for drinking) la taza [tasa]

I've been mugged me asaltaron

mum la mamá

mumps las paperas [papairas]

museum el museo [mooseh-o]

mushrooms los champiñones [champeen-yon-es]

music la música [mooseeka]

musician el/la músico [mooseeko]

Muslim (adj) musulmán [moosoolman]

mussels los mejillones [meHee-yon-es]

must: I must tengo que [keh]

I mustn't drink alcohol no debo beber alcohol [bebair alko-ol]

mustard la mostaza [mostasa]

my* mi; (pl) mis

myself: I'll do it myself (said by man/woman) lo haré yo mismo/misma [areh]

by myself (said by man/woman) yo solo/sola

N

nail (finger) la uña [oon-ya]

(metal) el clavo [klabo]

nailbrush el cepillo para las uñas [sepee-yo – oon-yas]

nail varnish el esmalte para uñas [esmalteh]

name el nombre [nombreh]

my name's John me llamo John [meh yamo]

what's your name? ¿cómo se llama? [seh yama], ¿cuál es su nombre? [kwal – nombreh]

what is the name of this street? ¿cómo se llama esta calle?

napkin la servilleta [sairbee-yeta]

nappy el pañal [pan-yal]

narrow (street) estrecho [estrecho]

nasty (person) desagradable [desagradableh]

(weather, accident) malo

national nacional [nas-yonal]

nationality la nacionalidad [nas-yonaleeda]

natural natural [natooral]

nausea la náusea [nowseh-a]

navy (blue) azul marino [asool]

near cerca [sairka]

is it near the city centre? ¿está cerca del centro? [sentro]

do you go near the Zócalo? ¿pasa Usted cerca del Zócalo? [oosteh – socalo]

where is the nearest ...? ¿dónde está el ... más cercano? [dondeh – sairkano]

nearby por aquí cerca [akee]

nearly casi

necessary necesario [nesesar-yo]

neck el cuello [kweh-yo]

necklace el collar [ko-yar]

necktie la corbata

need: I need ... necesito un ...
[neseseeto]
  do I need to pay? ¿necesito
  pagar?
needle la aguja [agooHa]
negative (film) el negativo
[negateeebo]
neither: neither (one) of them
  ninguno (de ellos)
  [neengoono (deh eh-yos)]
  neither ... nor ... ni ... ni ...
nephew el sobrino
net (in sport) la red
Netherlands Los Países Bajos
[pa-ees-es baHos]
network map el mapa
never nunca, jamás [Hamas]

dialogue

have you ever been to
Mérida? ¿ha estado alguna
vez en Merida? [bes]
no, never, I've never been
there no, nunca estuve
[estoobeh]

new nuevo [nwebo]
news (radio, TV etc) las noticias
[notees-yas]
newspaper el periódico [pair-
yodeeko]
newspaper kiosk el puesto de
periódicos [pwesto deh]
New Year el Año Nuevo [an-
yo nwebo]
  Happy New Year! ¡Feliz Año
  Nuevo! [felees]
New Year's Eve Nochevieja

[nocheh-b-yeHa]
New Zealand Nueva Zelanda
[nweba selanda]
New Zealander: I'm a New
Zealander (man/woman) soy
neozelandés/neozelandesa
[neh-o-seland-es]
next próximo
  the next street on the left la
  próxima calle a la izquierda
  [ka-yeh a la eesk-yairda]
  at the next stop en la
  siguiente parada [seeg-yenteh]
  next week la semana que
  viene [keh b-yeneh]
  next to al lado de [deh]
Nicaraguan (adj) nicaraguense
[neekaragwenseh]
nice (food) bueno [bweno]
  (looks, view etc) lindo
  (person) simpático
niece la sobrina
night la noche [nocheh]
  at night de noche [deh], por
  la noche
  good night buenas noches
  [bwenas noch-es]

dialogue

do you have a single room
for one night? ¿tiene un
cuarto individual para una
noche? [t-yeneh oon kwarto
eendeebeedwal]
yes, madam sí, señora
[sen-yora]
how much is it per night?
¿cuánto es la noche?

[kwanto]

it's 3,000 pesos for one night son tres mil pesos la noche

thank you, I'll take it gracias, me la quedo [gras-yas meh la kedo]

nightclub la discoteca [deeskoteka]

nightdress el camisón

night porter el portero [portairo]

no no

I've no change no tengo cambio [kamb-yo]

there's no ... left no queda ... [keda]

no way! ¡ni hablar! [ablar]

oh no! (upset, annoyed) ¡Dios mío! [d-yos]

nobody nadie [nad-yeh]

there's nobody there no hay nadie [i]

noise el ruido [rweedo]

noisy: it's too noisy hay demasiado ruido [i demas-yado]

non-alcoholic sin alcohol [seen alko-ol]

none ninguno

non-smoking compartment no fumadores [foomador-es]

noon el mediodía [med-yodee-a]

no-one nadie [nad-yeh]

nor: nor do I yo tampoco

normal normal [nor-mal]

north norte [norteh]

in the north en el norte

north of Taxco al norte de Taxco [deh tasko]

North America América del norte [amaireeka del norteh]

North American (man) el norteamericano (woman) la norteamericana (adj) norteamericano

northeast nordeste [nordesteh]

northern del norte [norteh]

Northern Ireland Irlanda del Norte [eerlanda del norteh]

northwest noroeste [noro-esteh]

Norway Noruega [norwega]

Norwegian (adj) noruego

nose la nariz [narees]

nosebleed la hemorragia nasal [emorraн-ya]

not* no

no, I'm not hungry no, no tengo hambre [ambreh]

I don't want any, thank you no quiero, gracias [k-yairo gras-yas]

it's not necessary no es necesario [nesesar-yo]

I didn't know that no lo sabía

not that one – this one ése no – éste [eseh – esteh]

note (banknote) el billete [bee-yeteh]

notebook el cuaderno [kwadairno]

notepaper (for letters) el papel de carta [deh]

nothing nada

nothing for me, thanks para mí nada, gracias [gras-yas]

nothing else nada más

novel la novela [nobela]

November noviembre [nob-yembreh]

now ahora [a-ora]

number el número [noomairo]

I've got the wrong number me equivoqué de número [meh ekeebokeh deh]

what is your phone number? ¿cuál es su número de teléfono? [kwal]

number plate la placa

nurse (man/woman) el enfermero [enfairmairo], la enfermera

nursery slope la pista de principiantes [deh preenseep-yant-es]

nut (for bolt) la tuerca [twairka]

nuts las nueces [nwes-es]

O

o'clock: at two o'clock a las dos

occupied (US: toilet etc) ocupado [okoopado]

October octubre [oktoobreh]

odd (strange) extraño [ekstran-yo]

of de [deh]

off (lights) apagado

it's just off calle Corredera está cerca de calle Corredera [sairka deh ka-yeh]

we're off tomorrow nos vamos mañana [bamos]

offensive (language, behaviour) ofensivo [ofenseebo]

office (place of work) la oficina [ofeeseena]

officer (said to policeman) señor oficial [sen-yor ofee-syal]

often a menudo

not often pocas veces [bes-es]

how often are the buses? ¿cada cuándo pasa el camión? [kwando]

oil el aceite [asayteh]

ointment la pomada

OK bueno [bweno]

are you OK? ¿está bien? [b-yen]

is that OK with you? ¿le parece bien? [leh pareseh]

is it OK to ...? ¿se puede ...? [seh pwedeh]

that's OK thanks (it doesn't matter) está bien, gracias [gras-yas]

I'm OK (nothing for me) para mí nada

(I feel OK) me siento bien [meh s-yento]

is this train OK for ...? ¿este tren va a...? [esteh – ba]

I said I'm sorry, OK? ya pedí disculpas ¿okey? [deeskoolpas okay]

old viejo [b-yeHo]

dialogue

how old are you?
¿cuántos años tiene?
[kwantos an-yos t-yeneh]

I'm twenty-five tengo veinticinco años
and you? ¿y Usted? [ee oosteh]

old-fashioned pasado de moda [deh]
old town (old part of town) el barrio antiguo [barr-yo anteegwo]
in the old town en el barrio antiguo
olive la aceituna [asaytoona], la oliva [oleeba]
black/green olives las aceitunas negras/verdes [baird-es]
olive oil el aceite de oliva [asayteh deh oleeba]
omelette la tortilla de huevo [tortee-ya deh webo]
on en
on the street/beach en la calle/playa
is it on this road? ¿está en esta calle?
on the plane en el avión
on Saturday el sábado
on television en la tele
I haven't got it on me no lo traigo [trīgo]
this one's on me (drink) ésta me toca a mí [meh]
the light wasn't on la luz no estaba prendida
what's on tonight? ¿qué ponen esta noche? [keh]
once (one time) una vez [bes]

at once (immediately) en seguida [segeeda]
one* uno [oono], una
the white one el blanco, la blanca
one-way: a one-way ticket to ... un boleto de ida para ... [deh eeda]
onion la cebolla [sebo-ya]
only sólo
only one sólo uno
it's only 6 o'clock son sólo las seis
I've only just got here acabo de llegar [deh yegar]
on/off switch el interruptor [eentairrooptor]
open (adj) abierto [ab-yairto] (verb) abrir [abreer]
when do you open? ¿a qué hora abre? [keh ora abreh]
I can't get it open no puedo abrirlo [pwedo]
in the open air al aire libre [īreh leebreh]
opening times el horario [orar-yo]
open ticket el boleto abierto [ab-yairto]
opera la ópera
operation (medical) la operación [opairas-yon]
operator (telephone: man/woman) el operador, la operadora
opposite: the opposite direction el sentido contrario
the bar opposite el bar de enfrente [deh enfrenteh]

opposite my hotel enfrente de mi hotel

optician el óptico

or o

orange (fruit) la naranja [naranнa]

(colour) (color) naranja

orange juice (fresh) el jugo de naranja [Hoogo deh]

(fizzy, diluted) el refresco de naranja

orchestra la orquesta [orkesta]

order: can we order now? (in restaurant) ¿podemos pedir ya?

I've already ordered, thanks ya pedí, gracias [gras-yas]

I didn't order this no pedí esto

out of order averiado [abair-yado], fuera de servicio [fwaira deh sairbees-yo]

ordinary corriente [korr-yenteh]

other otro

the other one el otro

the other day el otro día

I'm waiting for the others estoy esperando a los demás

do you have any others? ¿tiene otros? [t-yeneh]

otherwise de otra manera [deh – manaira]

our* nuestro [nwestro], nuestra; (pl) nuestros, nuestras

ours* (el) nuestro, (la) nuestra

out: he's out no está

three kilometres out of town a tres kilómetros de la ciudad

outdoors fuera de casa [fwaira deh]

outside ... fuera de ...

can we sit outside? ¿podemos sentarnos fuera?

oven el horno [orno]

over: over here por aquí [akee]

over there por allá [a-ya]

over 500 más de quinientos [deh]

it's over se acabó [seh]

overcharge: you've overcharged me me cobró de más [meh – deh]

overcoat el abrigo

overlook: I'd like a room overlooking the courtyard quiero un cuarto que da al patio [k-yairo oon kwarto keh da]

overnight (travel) toda la noche [nocheh]

overtake adelantarse a [adelantarseh]

owe: how much do I owe you? ¿cuánto le debo? [kwanto leh]

own: my own ... mi propio ... [prop-yo]

are you on your own? (to a man/woman) ¿está solo/sola?

I'm on my own (said by man/woman) estoy solo/sola

owner (man/woman) el propietario [prop-yetar-yo], la propietaria

P

Pacific Ocean el Océano
Pacífico [oseh-ano]
pack: a pack of ... un
paquete de ... [paketeh deh]
(verb) hacer las maletas [asair]
a pack of cigarettes una
cajetilla de cigarros [kaнetee-
ya deh seegarros]
package (parcel) el paquete
[paketeh]
package holiday el paquete
packed lunch la bolsa con la
comida
packet: a packet of cigarettes
una cajetilla de cigarros
[kaнetee-ya deh seegarros]
padlock el candado
page (of book) la página
[paнeena]
could you page Mr ...?
¿podría llamar al Señor ...
(por altavoz)? [yamar – altabos]
pain el dolor
I have a pain here me duele
aquí [meh dweleh akee]
painful doloroso
painkillers los analgésicos
[analнeseekos]
paint la pintura
painting el cuadro [kwadro]
pair: a pair of ... un par de ...
[deh]
Pakistani (adj) paquistaní
[pakeestanee]
palace el palacio [palas-yo]
pale pálido

pale blue azul claro [asool]
pan la olla [o-ya]
panties (underwear: women's) las
bragas, los pantis
pants (underwear: men's) los
calzones [kalson-es]
(women's) las bragas
(US: trousers) los pantalones
[pantalon-es]
pantyhose las pantimedias
[panteemed-yas]
paper el papel
(newspaper) el periódico [pair-
yodeeko]
a piece of paper un pedazo
de papel [pedaso deh]
paper handkerchiefs los
klínex®
parcel el paquete [paketeh]
pardon (me)? (didn't understand/
hear) ¿mande? [mandeh]
parents: my parents mis
padres [pad-res]
parents-in-law los suegros
[swegros]
park el parque [parkeh]
(verb) estacionar [estas-
yonar]
can I park here? ¿puedo
estacionarme aquí? [pwedo
estas-yonarmeh akee]
parking lot el
estacionamiento [estas-yonam-
yento]
part la parte [parteh]
partner (boyfriend, girlfriend etc) el
compañero [kompan-yairo], la
compañera
party (group) el grupo [grupo]

(political) el partido
(celebration) la fiesta

pass (in mountains) el paso

passenger (man/woman) el pasajero [pasaHairo], la pasajera

passport el pasaporte [pasaporteh]

past*: in the past antiguamente [anteegwamenteh]

just past the information office justo después de la oficina de información [Hoosto despwes deh]

path el camino

pattern el dibujo [deebooHo]

pavement la acera [asaira]
on the pavement en la acera

pavement café el café terraza [kafeh terrasa]

pay (verb) pagar
can I pay, please? me pasa la cuenta, por favor [meh – kwenta por fabor]
it's already paid for ya está pagado

dialogue

pay phone el teléfono público [poobleeko], la caseta telefónica

peaceful tranquilo [trankeelo]

peach el durazno [doorasno]

peanuts los cacahuates [kakawat-es]

pear la pera [paira]

peas los chícharos [cheecharos]

peculiar extraño [ekstran-yo]

pedestrian crossing el paso de peatones [peh-aton-es]

pedestrian precinct la calle peatonal [ka-yeh peh-atonal]

peg (for washing) la pinza [peensa]
(for tent) la estaca

pen la pluma [plooma]

pencil el lápiz [lapees]

penfriend (male/female) el amigo/la amiga por correspondencia [korrespondens-ya]

penicillin la penicilina [peneeseeleena]

penknife la navaja [nabaHa]

pensioner el jubilado [Hoobeelado], la jubilada

people la gente [Henteh]
the other people in the hotel los otros huéspedes en el hotel [wesped-es]
too many people demasiada gente [demas-yada]

pepper (spice) la pimienta [peem-yenta]
(vegetable) el pimiento

peppermint (sweet) el dulce de menta [doolseh deh]

per: per night por noche
[nocheh]
how much per day? ¿cuánto
es por día? [kwanto]
per cent por ciento [s-yento]
perfect perfecto [pairfekto]
perfume el perfume
[pairfoomeh]
perhaps quizás [keesas]
perhaps not quizás no
period (of time) el período
[pairee-odo]
(menstruation) la regla
perm la permanente
[pairmanenteh]
permit el permiso [pairmeeso]
person la persona [pairsona]
personal stereo el walkman®
[wolkman]
Peruvian (adj) peruano [peroo-
ano]
petrol la gasolina
petrol can la lata de gasolina
[deh]
petrol station la gasolinera
[gasoleeneira]
pharmacy la farmacia [far-
mas-ya]
phone el teléfono
(verb) llamar por teléfono
[yamar]
phone book la guía
telefónica [gee-a]
phone box la caseta
telefónica
phonecard la tarjeta de
teléfono [tarHeta deh]
phone number el número de
teléfono [noomairo deh]

photo la foto
excuse me, could you take a
photo of us? ¿le importaría
sacarnos una foto? [leh]
phrasebook el libro de frases
[deh fras-es]
piano el piano [p-yano]
pickpocket el/la carterista
[kartaireesta]
pick up: will you come and
pick me up? ¿pasarás a
recogerme? [rekoHairmeh]
picnic el picnic
picture el cuadro [kwadro]
pie (meat) la empanada
(fruit) la tarta
piece el pedazo [pedaso]
a piece of ... un pedazo de ...
[deh]
pig el chancho, el cerdo
[sairdo]
pill la píldora
I'm on the pill estoy
tomando la píldora
pillow la almohada [almo-ada]
pillow case la funda (de
almohada) [foonda (deh)]
pin el alfiler [alfeelair]
pineapple la piña [peen-ya]
pineapple juice el jugo de
piña [Hoogo deh]
pink rosa
pipe (for smoking) la pipa
[peepa]
(for water) el tubo [toobo]
pipe cleaners los limpiapipas
[leemp-yapeepas]
pity: it's a pity! ¡qué pena!
[keh]

pizza la pizza

place el lugar [loogar]

 at your place en tu casa

 at his place en su casa

plain el llano [yano]

 (not patterned) liso

plane el avión [ab-yon]

 by plane en avión

plant la planta

plaster cast la escayola [eski-yola]

plasters las tiritas

plastic plástico

 (credit cards) las tarjetas de crédito [tarHetas deh kredeeto]

plastic bag la bolsa de plástico

plate el plato

platform la vía [bee-a]

 which platform is it for Puebla, please? ¿de qué vía sale el tren para Puebla, por favor? [deh keh bee-a saleh – pwebla por fabor]

play (in theatre) la obra

 (verb) jugar [Hoogar]

 (instrument) tocar

playground el patio de recreo [pat-yo deh rekreh-o]

pleasant agradable [agradableh]

please por favor [fabor]

 yes please sí, por favor

 could you please ...? ¿podría hacer el favor de ...? [asair – deh]

 please don't no, por favor

pleased: pleased to meet you (said by man/woman) encantado/encantada de

conocerle [deh konosairleh]

pleasure: my pleasure es un gusto [goosto]

plenty: plenty of ... mucho ... [moocho]

 there's plenty of time tenemos mucho tiempo [t-yempo]

 that's plenty, thanks es suficiente, gracias [soofees-yenteh gras-yas]

pliers los alicates [aleekat-es]

plug (electrical) el enchufe [enchoofeh]

 (for car) la bujía [booHee-a]

 (in sink) el tapón

plumber el plomero [plomairo]

p.m. de la tarde [deh la tardeh]

poached egg el huevo escalfado [webo]

pocket el bolsillo [bolsee-yo]

point: two point five dos coma cinco

 there's no point no vale la pena [baleh]

points (in car) los platinos

poisonous venenoso [benenoso]

police la policía [poleesee-a]

 call the police! ¡llame a la policía! [yameh]

policeman el (agente de) policía [aHenteh deh]

police station la comisaría de policía

policewoman la policía

polish el betún [betoon]

polite educado [edookado]

polluted contaminado

pony el poney

pool (for swimming) la alberca [albairka]

poor (not rich) pobre [pobreh]
(quality) de baja calidad [deh baHa kaleeda]

pop music la música pop [mooseeka]

pop singer el/la cantante de música pop [kantanteh deh]

population la población [poblas-yon]

pork la carne de chancho [karneh deh chancho]

port (for boats) el puerto [pwairto]
(drink) el Oporto

porter (in hotel) el portero [portairo]

portrait el retrato

posh (restaurant) de lujo [deh looHo]

possible posible [poseebleh]
is it possible to ...? ¿es posible ...?
as ... as possible lo más ... posible

post (mail) el correo [korreh-o]
(verb) echar al correo
could you post this for me? ¿podría echarme esto al correo? [echarmeh]

postbox el buzón [booson]

postcard la postal [pos-tal]

postcode el código postal

poster el póster [postair], el cartel

poste restante la lista de Correos [leesta deh korreh-os]

post office el correo [korreh-o]

potato la papa

potato chips (US) las patatas fritas (de bolsa) [deh]

pots and pans los cacharros de cocina [deh koseena], las ollas [o-yas]

pottery (objects) la cerámica [sairameeka]

pound* (money, weight) la libra

power cut el apagón

power point la toma de corriente [deh korr-yenteh]

practise: I want to practise my Spanish quiero practicar el español [k-yairo – espan-yol]

prawns las gambas

prefer: I prefer ... prefiero ... [pref-yairo]

pregnant embarazada [embarasada]

prescription (for chemist) la receta [reseta]

present (gift) el regalo

president (of country) el/la presidente [preseedenteh]

pretty lindo
it's pretty expensive es bastante caro [bastanteh]

price el precio [pres-yo]

priest el sacerdote [sasairdoteh]

prime minister (man/woman) el primer ministro [preemair], la primera ministra

printed matter los impresos

priority (in driving) la preferencia [prefairens-ya]

prison la cárcel [karsel]

private privado [preebado],

particular [parteekoolar]
private bathroom el baño
privado [ban-yo]
probably probablemente
[probableh-menteh]
problem el problema
no problem! ¡con mucho
gusto! [moocho goosto]
program(me) el programa
promise: I promise lo prometo
pronounce: how is this
pronounced? ¿cómo se
pronuncia esto? [seh pronoons-
ya]
properly (repaired, locked etc)
bien [b-yen]
protection factor (of suntan
lotion) el factor de
protección [deh proteks-yon]
Protestant (adj) protestante
[protestanteh]
public convenience los
servicios públicos [sairbees-
yos poobleekos]
public holiday el día feriado
[dee-a fer-yado]
pudding (dessert) el postre
[postreh]
pull jalar [Halar]
pullover el suéter [swetair]
puncture la ponchadura
purple morado
purse (for money) el
monedero [monedairo]
(US: handbag) el bolso
push empujar [empoo-Har]
pushchair la sillita de ruedas
[see-yeeta deh rwedas]
put poner [ponair]

where can I put ...? ¿dónde
pongo ...? [dondeh]
could you put us up for the
night? ¿podría alojarnos esta
noche? [aloHarnos – nocheh]
pyjamas el pijama [peeHama]
pyramid la pirámide
[peerameedeh]

Q

quality la calidad [kaleeda]
(personal) la cualidad
[kwaleeda]
quarantine la cuarentena
[kwarentena]
quarter la cuarta parte [kwarta
parteh]
quayside: on the quayside en
el muelle [mweh-yeh]
question la pregunta
[pregoonta]
queue la cola
quick rápido [rapeedo]
that was quick sí que ha sido
rápido [keh a]
what's the quickest way
there? ¿cuál es el camino
más directo? [kwal – deerekto]
fancy a quick drink? ¿se te
antoja una copa? [seh teh
antoHa]
quickly rápidamente
[rapeedamenteh]
quiet (place, hotel) tranquilo
[trankeelo]
(person) callado [ka-yado]
quiet! ¡cállese! [ka-yeseh]

quite (fairly) bastante [bastanteh]
(very) muy [mwee]
that's quite right eso es
cierto [s-yairto]
quite a lot bastante

R

rabbit el conejo [koneHo]
race (for runners, cars) la
carrera [karraira]
racket (tennis etc) la raqueta
[raketa]
radiator (of car, in room) el
radiador [rad-yador]
radio la radio [rad-yo]
on the radio por radio
raft la balsa
rail: by rail en tren
railway el ferrocarril
rain la lluvia [yoob-ya]
in the rain bajo la lluvia
[baHo]
it's raining está lloviendo
[yob-yendo]
raincoat el impermeable
[eempairmeh-ableh]
rape la violación [b-yolas-yon]
rare (uncommon) poco común
(steak) (muy) poco hecho
[mwee – echo]
rash (on skin) la erupción
cutánea [airoops-yon kootaneh-a]
raspberry la frambuesa
[frambwesa]
rat la rata
rate (for changing money) el tipo
de cambio [teepo deh kamb-yo]

rather: it's rather good es
bastante bueno [bastanteh
bweno]
I'd rather ... prefiero ... [pref-
yairo]
razor la maquinilla de afeitar
[makeenee-ya deh afaytar]
(electric) la máquina de afeitar
eléctrica [makeena]
razor blades las hojas de
afeitar [oHas]
read leer [leh-air]
ready preparado
are you ready? (to man/woman)
¿estás listo/lista?
I'm not ready yet (said by man/
woman) aún no estoy listo/
lista [a-oon]

dialogue

when will it be ready?
¿cuándo estará listo?
[kwando]
it should be ready in a
couple of days estará listo
en un par de días

real verdadero [bairdadairo],
auténtico [owtenteeko]
really realmente [reh-almenteh]
that's really great eso es
estupendo
really? (doubt) ¿no puede ser?
[pwedeh sair]
(polite interest) ¿de veras? [deh
bairas]
rear lights las calaveras
[kalabairas]

rearview mirror el (espejo) retrovisor [espeHo retrobeesor]
reasonable (prices etc) modesto
receipt el recibo [reseebo]
recently recientemente [resyentementeh], recién [res-yen]
reception la recepción [resepsyon]
 at reception en la recepción
reception desk la recepción
receptionist el/la recepcionista [reseps-yoneesta]
recognize reconocer [rekonosair]
recommend: could you recommend ...? ¿puede Usted recomendar ...? [pwedeh oosteh]
record (music) el disco [deesko]
red rojo [roHo]
 red wine el vino tinto [beeno teento]
refund la devolución [debeloosyon]
 can I have a refund? ¿puede devolverme el dinero? [pwedeh debolbairmeh el deenairo]
region la zona [sona], la región [reH-yon]
registered: by registered mail por correo certificado [korreH-o sairteefeekado]
registration number el número de placa [noomairo deh]
relatives los parientes [par-yent-es]
religion la religión [releeH-yon]
remember: I don't remember

no recuerdo [rekwairdo]
I remember recuerdo
do you remember? ¿recuerda?
rent (for apartment etc) la renta, el arriendo [arr-yendo]
 (verb) rentar, arrendar, alquilar [alkeelar]
 to/for rent se alquila [seh alkeela]
rented car el carro rentado
repair (verb) arreglar
 can you repair it? ¿puede arreglarlo? [pwedeh]
repeat repetir
 could you repeat that? ¿puede repetir eso? [pwedeh]
reservation la reservación [resairbas-yon]
 I'd like to make a reservation quisiera hacer reservación [kees-yaira asair]

dialogue

I have a reservation tengo cuarto reservado [kwarto resairbado]
yes sir, what name please? sí, señor, ¿a nombre de quién, por favor? [sen-yor a nombreh deh k-yen por fabor]

reserve reservar [resairbar]

dialogue

can I reserve a table for tonight? ¿puedo reservar una mesa para esta noche?

[pwedo – nocheh]
yes madam, for how many people? sí, señora, ¿para cuántos? [sen-yora – kwantos]
for two para dos
and for what time? ¿y para qué hora? [ee para keh ora]
for eight o'clock para las ocho
and could I have your name please? ¿me deja su nombre, por favor? [meh deh-Ha soo nombreh por fabor]
see alphabet for spelling

rest: I need a rest necesito un descanso [neseseeto]
the rest of the group el resto del grupo [groopo]
restaurant el restaurante [restowranteh]
restaurant car el coche-comedor [kocheh komedor]
rest room el baño [ban-yo], los servicios [sairbees-yos]
see toilet
retired: I'm retired estoy jubilado/jubilada [Hoobeelado]
return (ticket) el boleto de ida y vuelta [deh eeda ee bwelta]
see ticket
reverse charge call la llamada por cobrar [yamada]
reverse gear la marcha atrás
revolting asqueroso [askairoso]
rib la costilla [kostee-ya]
rice el arroz [arros]
rich rico [reeko]

ridiculous ridículo [reedeekoolo]
right (correct) correcto
(not left) derecho
you were right tenía razón [rason]
that's right es cierto [s-yairto]
this can't be right esto no puede ser [pwedeh sair]
right! ¡bueno! [bweno]
is this the right road for ...? ¿es éste el camino para ...? [esteh]
on the right a la derecha
turn right dé vuelta a la derecha [deh bwelta]
right-hand drive con el volante a la derecha [bolanteh]
ring (on finger) el anillo [anee-yo]
I'll ring you te llamaré [teh yamareh]
ring back volver a llamar [bolbair a yamar]
ripe (fruit) maduro
rip-off: it's a rip-off es una estafa
rip-off prices los precios exagerados [pres-yos eksaHairados]
risky arriesgado [arr-yesgado]
river el río
road la carretera [karretaira]
is this the road for ...? ¿es ésta la carretera para ...?
down the road calle abajo [ka-yeh abaHo]
road accident el accidente de tránsito [akseedenteh deh]

road map el mapa de carreteras

roadsign la señal de tráfico [sen-yal deh]

rob: I've been robbed! ¡me robaron! [meh]

rock la roca

(music) el rock

on the rocks (with ice) con hielo [yelo]

rodeo la charreada [charreh-ada]

roll (bread) el bolillo [bolee-yo]

roof el tejado [teHado]

roof rack la baca

room el cuarto [kwarto]

in my room en mi cuarto

room service el servicio de cuarto [sairbees-yo deh]

rope la cuerda [kwairda]

rosé (wine) el vino rosado [beeno]

roughly (approximately) approximadamente [–menteh]

round: it's my round me toca [meh]

roundabout (for traffic) la glorieta [glor-yeta]

round trip ticket el boleto de ida y vuelta [deh eeda ee bwelta]

see ticket

route la ruta [roota]

what's the best route? ¿cuál es la mejor ruta? [kwal es la meHor]

rubber (material) el hule [ooleh]

(eraser) la goma de borrar

rubber band la gomita

rubbish (waste) la basura

(poor quality goods) las porquerías [porkairee-as]

rubbish! (nonsense) ¡babosadas!

rucksack la mochila

rude grosero [grosairo]

rug (mat) la alfombra, el tapete [tapeteh]

(blanket) la cobija [kobeeHa], la manta, la frazada [frasada]

ruins las ruinas [rweenas]

rum el ron

rum and Coke® la cuba (de ron)

run (verb: person) correr [korrair]

how often do the buses run? ¿cada cuánto pasan los camiones? [kwanto]

I've run out of money se me acabó el dinero [seh meh – deenairo]

rush hour la hora pico [ora]

S

sad triste [treesteh]

saddle (for horse) la silla de montar [see-ya deh]

(on bike) el sillín [see-yeen]

safe seguro [segooro]

safety pin el seguro

sail la vela [bela]

sailboard el windsurf

sailboarding el windsurf

salad la ensalada

salad dressing el aliño para la ensalada [aleen-yo]

sale: for sale se vende [seh bendeh]

salmon el salmón [sal-mon]

salt la sal

same: the same el mismo, la misma

the same as this igual a éste [eegwal a esteh]

the same again, please otro igual, por favor [fabor]

it's all the same to me me da igual [meh]

sand la arena [areh-na]

sandals los guaraches [warach-es]

sandwich el sandwich [sandweech], la torta

sanitary napkin/towel la compresa

sardines las sardinas

Saturday sábado

sauce la salsa

saucepan la cacerola [kaserola]

saucer el platillo [platee-yo]

sauna la sauna [sowna]

sausage la salchicha

say: how do you say ... in Spanish? ¿cómo se dice ... en español? [seh deeseh en espan-yol]

what did he say? ¿qué dijo? [keh deeHo]

I said ... dije ... [deeHeh]

he said ... dijo ...

could you say that again? ¿podría repetirlo?

scarf (for neck) la bufanda (for head) el pañuelo [pan-ywelo]

scenery el paisaje [pīsaHeh]

schedule (US) el horario [orar-yo]

scheduled flight el vuelo regular [bwelo regoolar]

school la escuela [eskwela]

scissors: a pair of scissors las tijeras [teeHairas]

scotch el whisky

Scotch tape® el scotch, el Durex®

Scotland Escocia [eskos-ya]

Scottish escocés [eskos-es]

I'm Scottish (man/woman) soy escocés/escocesa [eskoses-a]

scrambled eggs los huevos revueltos [webos rebweltos]

scratch el rasguño [rasgoon-yo]

scream chillar [chee-yar]

screw el tornillo [tornee-yo]

screwdriver el destornillador [destornee-yador]

sea el mar

by the sea junto al mar [Hoonto]

seafood los mariscos

seafood restaurant la marisquería [mareeskairee-a]

seafront el paseo marítimo [paseh-o mareeteemo]

on the seafront en la playa [plī-ya]

seagull la gaviota [gab-yota]

search for (verb) buscar

seashell la concha marina

seasick: I feel seasick (said by man/woman) estoy mareado/mareada [mareh-ado]

I get seasick me mareo [meh

Sa

mar**eh**-o]

seaside: by the seaside en la playa [pl**ī**-ya]

seat el asiento [as-y**e**nto]
is this seat taken? ¿está ocupado este asiento? [**e**steh]

seat belt el cinturón de seguridad [seentoor**o**n deh segoor**ee**da]

sea urchin el erizo de mar [air**ee**so]

seaweed el **a**lga

secluded apartado

second (adj) seg**u**ndo
(of time) el seg**u**ndo
just a second! ¡un moment**i**to!

second class (travel) de segunda clase [seg**oo**nda kl**a**seh]

secondhand usado [oos**a**do]

see ver [bair]
can I see? ¿puedo ver? [pw**e**do]
have you seen ...? ¿ha visto ...? [a b**e**esto]
I saw him this morning lo vi esta mañana [bee]
see you! ¡hasta luego! [**a**sta lw**e**go]
I see (I understand) entiendo [ent-y**e**ndo]

self-service autoservicio [owtosairb**e**es-yo]

sell vender [bend**a**ir]
do you sell ...? ¿vende ...? [b**e**ndeh]

Sellotape® el scotch®, el Durex®

send enviar [emb-y**a**r], mandar
I want to send this to England quiero enviar esto a Inglaterra [k-y**a**iro]

senior citizen el jubilado, [Hoobeel**a**do], la jubilada

separate separado
a separate room un cuarto aparte [apart**eh**]

separated: I'm separated (said by man/woman) est**oy** separado/separada

separately (pay, travel) por separado

September septiembre [set-y**e**mbreh]

septic s**é**ptico

serious serio [s**a**ir-yo]
(illness) grave [gr**a**beh]

service charge el servicio [sairb**ee**s-yo]

service station la estación de servicio [estas-y**o**n deh]

serviette la servilleta [sairbee-y**e**ta]

set menu el menú [men**oo**], la comida corrida

several varios [b**a**r-yos]

sew coser [kos**a**ir]
could you sew this back on? ¿podría coserme esto? [kos**a**irmeh]

sex el s**e**xo

sexy s**e**xy

shade: in the shade a la s**o**mbra

shallow (water) p**o**co prof**u**ndo

shame: what a shame! ¡qué pena! [keh]

shampoo el champú
a shampoo and set un lavado y marcado [labado ee]
share (verb) compartir
sharp (knife) afilado
(taste) ácido [aseedo]
(pain) agudo
shattered (very tired) agotado
shaver la máquina de afeitar [makeena deh afaytar]
shaving foam la espuma de afeitar
shaving point el enchufe (para la máquina de afeitar) [enchoofeh – makeena]
shawl el rebozo [reboso]
she* ella [eh-ya]
is she here? ¿está (ella) aquí? [akee]
sheet (for bed) la sábana
shelf la estantería [estantairee-a]
shellfish los mariscos
sherry el jerez [Her-es]
ship el barco
by ship en barco
shirt la camisa
shit! ¡mierda! [m-yairda]
shock el susto
I got an electric shock me dio un choque eléctrico [meh – chokeh]
shock-absorber el amortiguador [amorteegwador]
shocking chocante [chokanteh]
shoes los zapatos [sapatos]
a pair of shoes un par de zapatos [deh]
shoelaces las agujetas [a-ooHetas]
shoe polish el betún
shoe repairer's la zapatería [sapatairee-a]
shop la tienda [t-yenda]
shopping: I'm going shopping voy de compras [boy deh]
shopping centre el centro comercial [sentro komairs-yal]
shop window el escaparate [eskaparateh]
shore la orilla [oree-ya]
short (time, journey) corto
(person) bajo [baHo]
it's only a short distance queda bastante cerca [keda bastanteh sairka]
shortcut el atajo [ataHo]
shorts los pantalones cortos [pantalon-es]
should: what should I do? ¿que hago? [keh ago]
he shouldn't be long no debe tardar [debeh]
you should have told me me lo hubieras dicho [meh oob-yairas]
shoulder el hombro [ombro]
shout (verb) gritar
show (in theatre) el espectáculo [espektakoolo]
could you show me? ¿me lo enseña? [meh lo ensen-ya]
shower (in bathroom) la regadera [regadaira]
(of rain) el chubasco [choobasko]
with shower con baño [ban-yo]

shower gel el gel de baño [Hel deh]

shut (verb) cerrar [sairrar]

when do you shut? ¿a qué
hora cierran? [keh ora s-
yairran]

when do they shut? ¿a qué
hora cierran?

they're shut está cerrado
[sairrado]

I've shut myself out cerré y
dejé la llave dentro [sairreh ee
deh-Heh la yabeh]

shut up! ¡cállese! [ka-yeseh]

shutter (on camera) el
obturador
(on window) la contraventana
[kontrabentana]

shy tímido [teemeedo]

sick (ill) enfermo [enfairmo]

I'm going to be sick (vomit)
voy a devolver [boy a
debolbair]

side el lado

the other side of town al otro
lado de la ciudad [deh la
s-yooda]

sidelights los pilotos, las
calaveras [kalabairas]

side salad la ensalada aparte
[aparteh]

side street la callejuela [ka-
yeh-Hwela]

sidewalk la banqueta [banketa]

sight: the sights of ... los
lugares de interés de ...
[loogar-es deh entair-es]

sightseeing: we're going
sightseeing vamos a hacer

un recorrido turístico [bamos
a asair oon]

sightseeing tour el recorrido
turístico

sign (notice) el letrero [letrairo]
(roadsign) la señal de tráfico
[sen-yal deh]

signal: he didn't give a signal
no hizo ninguna señal [eeso]

signature la firma [feerma]

signpost el letrero [letrairo]

silence el silencio [seelens-yo]

silk la seda

silly tonto

silver la plata

silver foil el papel de
aluminio [aloomeen-yo]

similar parecido [pareseedo]

simple (easy) sencillo [sensee-
yo]

since: since yesterday desde
ayer [desdeh ī-yair]

since we got here desde que
llegamos aquí [keh yegamos
akee]

sing cantar

singer el/la cantante
[kantanteh]

single: a single to ... un
boleto de ida para ... [deh
eeda oon]

I'm single (said by man/woman)
soy soltero/soltera [soltairo]

single bed la cama
individual [eendeebeedwal]

single room el cuarto
individual [kwarto]

single ticket el boleto de ida
[deh eeda]

sink (in kitchen) el fregadero [fregadairo]

sister la hermana [airmana]

sister-in-law la cuñada [koonyada]

sit: can I sit here? ¿puedo sentarme aquí? [pwedo sentarmeh akee]

is anyone sitting here? ¿está ocupado este asiento? [esteh as-yento]

sit down sentarse [sentarseh]

sit down! ¡siéntese! [s-yenteseh]

size el tamaño [taman-yo]
(of clothes) la talla [ta-ya]

skin la piel [p-yel]

skin-diving el buceo [booseh-o]

skinny flaco

skirt la falda

sky el cielo [s-yelo]

sleep (verb) dormir

did you sleep well? ¿dormiste bien? [dormeesteh b-yen]

I need a good sleep necesito dormir bien [neseseeto]

sleeper (on train) el coche-cama [kocheh kama]

sleeping bag la bolsa de dormir [deh]

sleeping car el coche-cama [kocheh-kama]

sleeping pill la pastilla para dormir [pastee-ya]

sleepy: I'm feeling sleepy tengo sueño [swen-yo]

sleeve la manga

slide (photographic) la

diapositiva [d-yaposeeteeba]

slip (under dress) la funda [foonda]

slippery resbaladizo [resbaladeeso]

slow lento

slow down! ¡cálmese! [kalmeseh]

slowly: could you say it slowly? ¿podría decirlo despacio? [deseerlo despas-yo]

very slowly muy lento [mwee]

small chico

smell: it smells! (smells bad) ¡apesta!

smile (verb) sonreír [sonreh-eer]

smoke el humo [oomo]

do you mind if I smoke? ¿le importa que fume? [leh – keh foomeh]

I don't smoke no fumo

do you smoke? ¿fuma?

snack la comida ligera [leeHaira]

snake la culebra, la víbora [beebora]

sneeze (verb) estornudar

snorkel el tubo de buceo [toobo deh booseh-o]

snow la nieve [n-yebeh]

it's snowing está nevando [nebando]

so: it's so good es tan bueno [bweno]

not so fast no tan de prisa [deh preesa]

so am I yo también [tamb-yen]

so do I yo también

so-so más o menos

soaking solution (for contact lenses) el líquido preservador [leekeedo presairbador]

soap el jabón [Habon]

soap powder el jabón en polvo [em polbo]

sober sobrio [sobr-yo]

sock el calcetín [kalseteen]

socket (electrical) el enchufe [enchoofeh]

soda (water) la soda

sofa el sofá

soft (material etc) suave [swabeh]

soft-boiled egg el huevo pasado por agua [webo – agwa]

soft drink el refresco

soft lenses las lentes blandas [lent-es]

sole (of shoe, of foot) la suela [swela]

could you put new soles on these? ¿podría cambiarles las suelas? [kamb-yarl-es]

some: can I have some water? ¿me da agua? [meh]

can I have some rolls? ¿me da unos bolillos?

can I have some? ¿me da unos?

somebody, someone alguien [alg-yen]

something algo

something to drink algo de beber [deh bebair]

sometimes a veces [bes-es]

somewhere en alguna parte [parteh]

son el hijo [eeHo]

song la canción [kans-yon]

son-in-law el yerno [yairno]

soon dentro de poco [deh]

I'll be back soon no me tardo [meh]

as soon as possible lo antes posible [ant-es poseebleh]

sore: it's sore me duele [meh dweleh]

sore throat el dolor de garganta [deh]

sorry: (I'm) sorry disculpe [deeskoolpeh]

sorry? (didn't understand) ¿mande? [mandeh]

sort: what sort of ...? ¿qué clase de ...? [keh klaseh deh]

soup la sopa

sour (taste) ácido [aseedo]

south el sur [soor]

in the south al sur

South Africa Sudáfrica

South African (adj) sudafricano

I'm South African (man/woman) soy sudafricano/sudafricana

South America América del Sur [amaireeka]

South American (adj) sudamericano

(man/woman) el sudamericano, la sudamericana

southeast el sudeste [sood-esteh]

southwest el sudoeste [soodo-esteh]

souvenir el recuerdo [rekwairdo]

Spain España [espan-ya]
Spaniard (man/woman) el
 español [espan-yo], la
 española
Spanish español
spanner la llave inglesa [yabeh]
spare parts los repuestos
 [repwestos], las refacciones
 [refaks-yon-es]
spare tyre la llanta de
 repuesto [yanta deh]
sparkplug la bujía [booHee-a]
speak hablar [ablar]
 do you speak English?
 ¿habla inglés? [abla eeng-les]
 I don't speak ... no hablo ...
 [ablo]

dialogue

 can I speak to Pablo?
 ¿puedo hablar con Pablo?
 [pwedo]
 who's calling? ¿quién le
 llama? [k-yen leh yama]
 it's Patricia soy Patricia
 I'm sorry, he's not in, can I
 take a message? lo
 siento, no está, ¿quiere
 dejar recado? [s-yento –
 k-yaireh deh-Har]
 no thanks, I'll call back
 later no gracias, llamaré
 más tarde [gras-yas yamareh
 mas tardeh]
 please tell him I called
 por favor, dígale que
 llamé [fabor deegaleh keh
 yameh]

speciality la especialidad
 [espes-yaleeda]
spectacles las gafas
speed la velocidad
 [beloseeda]
speed limit el límite de
 velocidad [leemeeteh deh]
speedometer el velocímetro
 [beloseemetro]
spell: how do you spell it?
 ¿cómo se escribe? [seh
 eskreebeh]
 see alphabet
spend gastar
spider la araña [aran-ya]
spin-dryer la secadora
splinter la astilla [astee-ya]
spoke (in wheel) el radio [rad-
 yo]
spoon la cuchara
sport el deporte [deporteh]
sprain: I've sprained my ... me
 torcí el ... [meh torsee]
spring (season) la primavera
 [preemabaira]
 (of car, seat) el resorte
 [resorteh]
square (in town) la plaza
 [plasa]
 main square el zócalo
 [sokalo]
stairs la escalera [eskalaira]
stale (bread) duro
 (food) pasado
stall: the engine keeps stalling
 el motor se para cada rato
 [seh]
stamp la estampilla [estampee-
 ya], el timbre [teembreh]

dialogue

a stamp for England, please **u**na estampilla **pa**ra Inglat**e**rra, por favor [fabor]

what are you sending? ¿qué es lo que envía? [keh – emb**ee**-a]

this postcard **e**sta postal

standby el vuelo standby [bw**e**lo]

star la estrella [estr**eh**-ya]
(in film) el/la protagon**i**sta

start el princ**i**pio [preens**ee**p-yo]
(verb) comenzar [komens**a**r]
when does it start? ¿cuándo comienza? [kw**a**ndo com-y**e**nsa]
the car won't start el c**a**rro no arr**a**nca

starter (of car) el mot**o**r de arr**a**nque [arr**a**nkeh]
(food) la entr**a**da

starving: I'm starving me mu**e**ro de h**a**mbre [meh mw**a**iro deh **a**mbreh]

state (country) el est**a**do
the States (USA) los Est**a**dos Un**i**dos [oon**ee**dos]

station la estaci**ó**n de ferrocarr**i**l [estas-y**o**n deh fairrokarr**ee**l]

statue la est**a**tua [est**a**twa]

stay: where are you staying? ¿d**ó**nde est**á** aloj**a**do? [d**o**ndeh – alo**H**ado]

I'm staying at ... (said by man/

woman) estoy aloj**a**do/aloj**a**da en ...

I'd like to stay another two nights me gustar**í**a quedarme dos n**o**ches m**á**s [meh – ked**a**rmeh – n**o**ch-es]

steak el fil**e**te [feel**e**teh]

steal rob**a**r
my bag has been stolen me rob**a**ron el b**o**lso [meh]

steep (hill) empin**a**do, escarp**a**do

steering la direcci**ó**n [deereks-y**o**n]

step: on the steps en las escal**e**ras [eskal**a**iras]

stereo el est**é**reo [est**a**ireh-o]

sterling la l**i**bra esterl**i**na [est**a**irl**ee**na]

steward (on plane) el auxil**i**ar de vu**e**lo [owks**ee**l-y**a**r deh bw**e**lo]

stewardess la azaf**a**ta [asaf**a**ta]

sticking plaster la tir**i**ta

still: I'm still waiting s**i**go esper**a**ndo
is he still there? ¿sigue ah**í**? [s**ee**geh a-**ee**]
keep still! ¡qu**é**dese qui**e**to! [k**e**deseh k-y**e**to]

sting: I've been stung **a**lgo me ha pic**a**do [meh a]

stockings las m**e**dias [med-yas]

stomach el est**ó**mago

stomach ache el dol**o**r de est**ó**mago [deh]

stone (rock) la pi**e**dra [p-y**e**dra]

stop (verb) par**a**r
please, stop here (to taxi driver

etc) pare aquí, por favor [pareh akee por fabor]

do you stop near ...? ¿para cerca de ...? [sairka deh]

stop doing that! ¡deje de hacer eso! [deh-Heh deh asair]

stopover la escala

storm la tormenta

straight: it's straight ahead todo recto

a straight whisky un whisky solo

straightaway en seguida [segeeda]

strange (odd) extraño [estran-yo]

stranger (man/woman) el forastero [forastairo], la forastera

I'm a stranger here no soy de aquí [deh akee]

strap la correa [korreh-a]

strawberry la fresa, la frutilla [frootee-ya]

stream el arroyo [arro-yo]

street la calle [ka-yeh]

on the street en la calle

streetmap el plano de la ciudad [deh la s-yooda]

string la cuerda [kwairda]

strong fuerte [fwairteh]

stuck atascar

the key's stuck la llave se atascó [yabeh seh]

student el/la estudiante [estood-yanteh]

subway (US) el metro

suburb el suburbio [sooboorb-yo]

suddenly de repente [deh

repenteh]

suede el ante [anteh]

sugar el azúcar [asookar]

suit el traje [traHeh]

it doesn't suit me (jacket etc) no me queda bien [meh keda b-yen]

it suits you te queda muy bien [teh – mwee]

suitcase la maleta

summer el verano [bairano]

in the summer en verano

sun el sol

in the sun al sol

out of the sun a la sombra

sunbathe tomar el sol

sunblock (cream) la crema protectora, el filtro solar

sunburn la quemadura de sol [kemadoora deh]

sunburnt quemado [kemado]

Sunday domingo

sunglasses las gafas de sol [deh]

sun lounger la tumbona

sunny: it's sunny hace sol [aseh]

sunroof (in car) el techo corredizo [korredeeso]

sunset la puesta del sol [pwesta]

sunshade la sombrilla [sombree-ya]

sunshine la luz del sol [loos]

sunstroke la insolación [eensolas-yon]

suntan el bronceado [bronseh-ado]

suntan lotion la loción

bronceadora [los-yon bronseh-adora]

suntanned bronceado [bronseh-ado]

suntan oil el aceite bronceador [asayteh]

super fabuloso

supermarket el supermercado [soopairmairkado]

supper la cena [sena]

supplement (extra charge) el suplemento [sooplemento]

sure: are you sure? ¿está seguro?

sure! ¡por supuesto! [soopwesto]

surfboard la tabla de surf [deh soorf]

surfing el surfing

surname el apellido [apeh-yeedo]

swearword la grosería [grosairee-a]

sweater el suéter [swetair]

sweatshirt la sudadera [soodadaira]

Sweden Suecia [swes-ya]

Swedish (adj) sueco [sweko]

sweet (dessert) el postre [postreh]

(adj: taste) dulce [doolseh]

sweetcorn el elote [eloteh]

sweets los dulces [dools-es]

swelling el hinchazón [eenchason]

swim (verb) bañarse [ban-yarseh]

I'm going for a swim voy a bañarme [boy a ban-yarmeh]

let's go for a swim vamos a bañarnos [bamos a ban-yarnos]

swimming costume el traje de baño [traHeh deh ban-yo]

swimming pool la alberca [albairka]

swimming trunks el traje de baño [traHeh deh ban-yo]

switch el interruptor [eentairrooptor]

switch off apagar

switch on prender [prendair]

swollen hinchado [eenchado]

T

table la mesa

a table for two una mesa para dos

tablecloth el mantel

table tennis el ping-pong

table wine el vino de mesa [beeno deh]

tailback (of traffic) la caravana de carros [karabana deh]

tailor el sastre [sastreh]

take (lead) tomar

(accept) aceptar [aseptar]

can you take me to the airport? ¿me lleva al aeropuerto? [meh yeba al iropwairto]

do you take credit cards? ¿acepta tarjetas de crédito? [asepta tarHetas deh kredeeto]

fine, I'll take it me llevo éste [meh yebo esteh]

can I take this? (leaflet etc)

¿puedo llevarme esto? [pwedo yebarmeh]

how long does it take? ¿cuánto tarda? [kwanto]

it takes three hours tarda tres horas [oras]

is this seat taken? ¿está ocupado este asiento? [esteh as-yento]

a hamburger to take away una hamburguesa para llevar [yebar]

can you take a little off here? (to hairdresser) ¿puede quitarme un poco de aquí? [pwedeh keetarmeh – deh akee]

talcum powder el talco

talk (verb) platicar

tall alto

tampons los tampones [tampon-es]

tan el bronceado [bronseh-ado]

to get a tan broncearse [bronseh-arseh]

tank (in car) el depósito [deposeeto]

tap la llave [yabeh]

tape (for cassette) la cinta [seenta]

(sticky) la cinta adhesiva [adeseeba]

tape measure la cinta métrica

tape recorder la grabadora

taste el sabor

can I taste it? ¿puedo probarlo? [pwedo]

taxi el taxi, el colectivo [kolekteebo]

will you get me a taxi? ¿me

consigue un taxi? [meh konseegeh]

where can I find a taxi? ¿dónde encuentro un taxi? [dondeh enkwentro]

dialogue

to the airport/to the Sol Hotel please al aeropuerto/al hotel Sol, por favor [iropwairto/al otel – fabor]

how much will it be? ¿cuánto va a ser? [kwanto ba a sair]

1,000 pesos mil pesos

that's fine, right here, thanks está bien aquí mismo, gracias [b-yen akee meesmo gras-yas]

taxi-driver el/la taxista

taxi rank la parada de taxis [deh]

tea (drink) el té [teh]

tea for one/two please un té/dos tés, por favor [fabor]

teabags las bolsas de té [deh]

teach: could you teach me? ¿podría enseñarme? [ensen-yarmeh]

teacher (primary: man/woman) el maestro [ma-estro], la maestra (secondary) el profesor, la profesora

team el equipo [ekeepo]

teaspoon la cucharita

tea towel el trapo de cocina

[deh koseena]
teenager el/la adolescente [adolesenteh]
telephone el teléfono
see phone
television la televisión [telebees-yon]
tell: could you tell him ...? ¿podría decirle ...? [deseerleh]
temperature (weather) la temperatura [tempairatoora] (fever) la fiebre [f-yebreh]
temple el templo
tennis el tenis
tennis ball la pelota de tenis [deh]
tennis court la cancha de tenis
tennis racket la raqueta de tenis [raketa]
tent la tienda de campaña [t-yenda deh kampan-ya] la carpa
term (at university, school) el trimestre [treemestreh]
terminus (rail) la terminal [tairmeenal]
terrible malísimo
terrific fabuloso [fabooloso]
text (message) el mensaje (de texto) [mensaHeh]
than* que [keh]
smaller than más pequeño que [peken-yo]
thanks, thank you gracias [gras-yas]
thank you very much muchas gracias [moochas]
thanks for the lift gracias por traerme [tra-airmeh]
no thanks no gracias

dialogue

thanks gracias
that's OK, don't mention it
no hay de qué [i deh keh]

that: that man ese hombre [eseh ombreh]
that woman esa mujer [mooHair]
that one ése [eseh]
I hope that ... espero que ... [espairo keh]
that's nice (clothes, souvenir etc) qué lindo
is that ...? ¿es ése ...?
that's it (that's right) eso es
the* el, la; (pl) los, las
theatre el teatro [teh-atro]
their* su; (pl) sus [soos]
theirs* su, sus; (pl) suyos [soo-yos], suyas; de ellos [deh eh-yos], de ellas
them* (things) los, las (people) les
for them para ellos/ellas [eh-yos/eh-yas]
with them con ellos/ellas
I gave it to them se lo di a ellos/ellas [seh]
who? – them ¿quiénes? – ellos/ellas [k-yen-es]
then luego [lwego]
there allí [a-yee]
over there allá [a-ya]
up there allá arriba
is/are there ...? ¿hay ...? [i]
there is/are ... hay ...
there you are (giving something)

111

aquí tiene [akee t-yeneh]
thermometer el termómetro
[tairmometro]
Thermos® flask el termo
[tairmo]
these: these men estos
hombres
these women estas mujeres
can I have these? ¿me puedo
llevar éstos? [meh pwedo yebar]
they* (male) ellos [eh-yos]
(female) ellas [eh-yas]
thick grueso [groo-eso]
(stupid) bruto
thief (man/woman) el ladrón, la
ladrona
thigh el muslo
thin flaco
thing la cosa
my things mis cosas [mees]
think pensar
(believe) creer [kreh-air]
I think so creo que sí [kreh-o
keh]
I don't think so no creo
I'll think about it lo pensaré
[pensareh]
third party insurance el seguro
contra terceros
[tairsairos]
thirsty: I'm thirsty tengo sed
[seh]
this: this man este hombre
[esteh]
this woman esta mujer
this one éste/ésta [esteh]
this is my wife le presento a
mi mujer [leh]
is this ...? ¿es éste/ésta ...?

those: those men aquellos
hombres [akeh-yos]
those women aquellas
mujeres [akeh-yas]
which ones? – those ¿cuáles?
– aquéllos/aquéllas [kwal-es]
thread el hilo [eelo]
throat la garganta
throat pastilles las pastillas
para la garganta [pastee-yas]
through a través de [trav-es deh]
does it go through ...? (train,
bus) ¿pasa por ...?
throw (verb) echar, aventar
[abentar]
throw away (verb) tirar, botar
thumb el pulgar
thunderstorm la tormenta
Thursday jueves [Hweb-es]
ticket el boleto

dialogue

a return to Tijuana un
boleto de ida y vuelta a
Tijuana [deh eeda ee bwelta a
teeHwana]
coming back when?
¿cuándo piensa regresar?
[kwando p-yensa]
today/next Tuesday hoy/el
martes que viene [oy/el
mart-es keh b-yeneh]
that will be 2,000 pesos
son dos mil pesos

ticket office (bus, rail) la
taquilla [takee-ya], la
boletería [boletairee-a]

tide la marea [mareh-a]

tie (necktie) la corbata

tight (clothes etc) ajustado [aHoostado]

it's too tight me viene estrecho [meh b-yeneh]

tights las pantimedias [panteemed-yas]

till la caja [kaHa]

time* el tiempo [t-yempo]

what's the time? ¿qué hora es? [keh ora]

this time esta vez [bes]

last time la última vez [oolteema]

next time la próxima vez

four times cuatro veces [bes-es]

timetable el horario [orar-yo]

tin (can) la lata, el bote [boteh]

tinfoil el papel de aluminio [aloomeen-yo]

tin-opener el abrelatas

tiny minúsculo [meenooskoolo]

tip (to waiter etc) la propina

tired cansado

I'm tired (said by a man/woman) estoy cansado/cansada

tissues los klínex®

to: to Puebla/London a Puebla/Londres

to Mexico/England a México/Inglaterra

to the post office a la oficina de Correos

toast (bread) la tostada

today hoy [oy]

toe el dedo del pie [p-yeh]

together juntos [Hoontos]

we're together (in shop etc) estamos juntos

can we pay together? ¿podemos pagar todo junto, por favor? [fabor]

toilet el baño [ban-yo], los servicios [sairbees-yos]

where is the toilet? ¿dónde están los servicios? [dondeh]

I have to go to the toilet tengo que ir al baño [keh]

toilet paper el papel higiénico [eeH-yeneeko]

tomato el jitomate [Heetomateh]

tomato juice el jugo de jitomate [Hoogo deh]

tomato ketchup el catsup

tomorrow mañana [man-yana]

tomorrow morning mañana por la mañana

the day after tomorrow pasado mañana

toner (for skin) el tonificador facial [fas-yal]

tongue la lengua [lengwa]

tonic (water) la tónica

tonight esta noche [nocheh]

tonsillitis las anginas [anHeenas]

too (excessively) demasiado [demas-yado]

(also) también [tamb-yen]

too hot demasiado caliente [kal-yenteh]

too much demasiado

me too yo también

tooth el diente [d-yenteh], la muela [mwela]

toothache el dolor de muelas [deh]

toothbrush el cepillo de dientes [seepee-yo deh d-yent-es]

toothpaste la pasta de dientes

top: on top of ... encima de ... [enseema deh], arriba de

at the top en la parte de arriba [parteh]

at the top of ... en la parte más alta de ...

top floor el último piso [oolteemo]

topless topless

torch la linterna [leentairna]

total el total [tot-al]

tour la excursión [eskoors-yon]

is there a tour of ...? ¿hay recorrido de ...? [ï – deh]

tour guide el/la guía turístico [gee-a]

tourist el/la turista

tourist information office la oficina de información turística [ofeeseena deh eenformas-yon]

tour operator la agencia de viajes [aHens-ya deh b-yaH-es]

towards hacia [as-ya]

towel la toalla [to-a-ya]

town la ciudad [s-yooda]

in town en el centro [sentro]

just out of town a la salida de la ciudad

town centre el centro de la ciudad [sentro deh la s-yooda]

town hall el ayuntamiento [ï-yoontam-yento]

toy el juguete [Hoogeteh]

track (US) la vía [bee-a]

tracksuit el chandal

traditional tradicional [tradees-yonal]

traffic el tránsito, la circulación [seerkoolas-yon]

traffic jam el embotellamiento [emboteh-yam-yento]

traffic lights el semáforo

trailer (for carrying tent etc) el remolque [remolkeh] (US: caravan) la caravana [karabana]

trailer park el camping

train el tren

by train en tren

dialogue

is this the train for ...? ¿es éste el tren para ...? [esteh] sure sí, exacto no, you want that platform there no, tiene que ir a aquella vía [t-yeneh keh eer a akeh-ya bee-a]

trainers (shoes) los tráiner [trïnair]

train station la estación de ferrocarril [estas-yon deh fairokareel]

tram el tranvía [trambee-a]

translate traducir [tradooseer]

could you translate that? ¿podría traducir eso?

translation la traducción [tradooks-yon]

translator (man/woman) el
traductor, la traductora

trashcan el bote de la basura
[boteh deh]

travel (verb) viajar [b-yaHar]

we're travelling around
andamos de paseo [deh paseh-o]

travel agent's la agencia de
viajes [aHens-ya deh b-yaHes-]

traveller's cheque el cheque
de viajero [chekeh deh
b-yaHairo]

tray la bandeja [bandeHa]

tree el árbol

tremendous tremendo

trendy de moda [deh]

trim: just a trim please (to
hairdresser) córtemelo sólo un
poco, por favor [fabor]

trip (excursion) la excursión
[eskoors-yon]

I'd like to go on a trip to ...
me gustaría hacer una
excursión a ... [meh – asair]

trolley el carrito

trouble problemas [problemas]

I'm having trouble with ...
tengo problemas con ...

sorry to trouble you disculpe
la molestia [deeskoolpeh]

trousers los pantalones
[pantalon-es]

true cierto [s-yairto]

that's not true no es cierto

trunk (US) la cajuela [kaHwela]

trunks (swimming) el traje de
baño [traHeh deh ban-yo]

try (verb) intentar

can I try it? ¿puedo

intentarlo yo? [pwedo]

try on: can I try it on? ¿puedo
probármelo?

T-shirt la camiseta, la playera
[plī-yaira]

Tuesday martes [mart-es]

tuna el bonito

tunnel el túnel [toonel]

turn: turn left/right tuerce a la
izquierda/derecha [twairseh]

turn off: where do I turn off?
¿dónde doy vuelta? [dondeh
doy bwelta]

can you turn the heating off?
¿puede apagar la
calefacción? [pwedeh –kalefaks-
yon]

turn on: can you turn the
heating on? ¿puede poner la
calefacción? [ponair]

turning (in road) el desvío
[desbee-o]

TV la tele [teleh]

tweezers las pinzas [peensas]

twice dos veces [bes-es]

twice as much el doble
[dobleh]

twin beds las camas gemelas
[Hemelas]

twin room el cuarto con dos
camas [kwarto]

twist: I've twisted my ankle
me torcí el tobillo [meh torsee
el tobee-yo]

type el tipo [teepo]

a different type of ... otro
tipo de ... [deh]

typical típico [teepeeko]

tyre la llanta [yanta]

U

ugly feo [**feh**-o]

UK el Reino Unido [**ray**no oo**nee**edo]

ulcer la úlcera [**oo**lsaira]

umbrella el paraguas [**parag**was]

uncle el tío

unconscious inconsciente [eenkons-**yen**teh]

under (in position) debajo de [deba**ho** deh]

(less than) menos de

underdone (meat) poco hecho [**echo**]

underground (railway) el metro

underpants los calzones [kals**on**-es]

understand: I understand lo entiendo [ent-**yen**do]

I don't understand no entiendo

do you understand? ¿entiende Usted? [ent-**yen**deh oos**teh**]

unemployed desempleado [desempleh-**ado**]

unfashionable fuera de moda [**fwai**ra deh]

United States los Estados Unidos [oo**nee**dos]

university la universidad [ooneebairs**eeda**]

unleaded petrol la gasolina sin plomo [seen]

unlimited mileage sin límite de kilometraje [**lee**meeteh deh keelometra**Heh**]

unlock abrir [a**breer**]

unpack deshacer las maletas [desa**sair**]

until hasta que [**asta** keh]

unusual poco común [kom**oon**]

up arriba

up there allá arriba [a-**ya**]

he's not up yet (not out of bed) todavía no se ha levantado [todab**ee**-a no seh a lebant**ado**]

what's up? (what's wrong?) ¿qué pasa? [keh]

upmarket (restaurant, hotel etc) de lujo [deh **loo**Ho]

upset stomach el mal del estómago

upside down al revés [reb-**es**], boca abajo [aba**Ho**]

upstairs arriba

urgent urgente [oor**Hen**teh]

Uruguayan (adj) uruguayo [ooroogw**ī**-yo]

us*: with us con nosotros/ nosotras

for us para nosotros/nosotras

USA EE.UU., Estados Unidos [oo**nee**dos]

use (verb) emplear [empleh-**ar**]

may I use ...? ¿me permite ...? [meh per**mee**teh]

useful útil [**oo**teel]

usual de costumbre [deh kost**oom**breh]

the usual (drink etc) lo de siempre [s-**yem**preh]

V

vacancy: do you have any vacancies? (hotel) ¿tiene cuartos libres? [t-yeneh kwartos leeb-res]

vacation las vacaciones [bakas-yon-es]

vaccination la vacuna [bakoona]

vacuum cleaner la aspiradora

valid (ticket etc) válido [baleedo]
how long is it valid for? ¿hasta cuándo tiene validez? [asta kwando t-yeneh baleed-es]

valley el valle [ba-yeh]

valuable (adj) valioso [bal-yoso]
can I leave my valuables here? ¿puedo dejar aquí mis objetos de valor? [pwedo deh-Har akee mees obHetos deh balor]

value el valor

van la camioneta [kam-yoneta]

vanilla vainilla [bīnee-ya]
a vanilla ice cream un helado de vainilla [elado deh]

vary: it varies depende [dependeh]

vase el florero [florairo]

veal la ternera [tairnaira]

vegetables las verduras [bairdooras]

vegetarian (man/woman) el vegetariano [beHetar-yano], la vegetariana

vending machine la máquina vendedora [makeena bendedora]

Venezuelan (adj) venezolano [benesolano]

very muy [mwee]
very little for me muy poquito para mí [pokeeto]
I like it very much me gusta mucho [meh goosta moocho]

vest (under shirt) la camiseta

via por

video el video [beedeh-o]

view la vista [beesta]

villa el chalet [chaleh]

village el pueblo [pweblo]

vinegar el vinagre [beenagreh]

vineyard el viñedo [been-yedo]

visa la visa

visit (verb) visitar [beeseetar]
I'd like to visit Guanajuato me gustaría conocer Guanajuato [konosair gwanaHwato]

vital: it's vital that ... es imprescindible que ... [eempreseendeebleh keh]

vodka el vodka [bodka]

voice la voz [bos]

volcano el volcán [bolkan]

voltage el voltaje [boltaHeh]

vomit vomitar [bomeetar]

vulture el zopilote [sopeeloteh]

W

waist la cintura [seentoora]

waistcoat el chaleco

wait esperar [espairar]
wait for me espéreme [espairemeh]
don't wait for me no me

espere [meh espaireh]
can I wait until my wife/
partner gets here? ¿puedo
esperar hasta que llegue mi
mujer/compañero? [pwedo
– asta keh yegeh]
can you do it while I wait?
¿puede hacerlo ahora
mismo? [pwedeh asairlo a-ora]
could you wait here for me?
¿puede esperarme aquí?
[espairarmeh akee]

waiter el mesero [mesairo]
waiter! ¡señor! [sen-yor]
waitress la mesera [mesaira]
waitress! ¡señorita! [sen-
yoreeta]

wake: can you wake me up at
5.30? ¿podría despertarme
a las cinco y media?
[despairtarmeh]

wake-up call la llamada para
despertar [yamada]

Wales Gales [gal-es]
walk: is it a long walk? ¿se
tarda mucho caminando?
[seh – moocho]
it's only a short walk está
cerca [sairka]
I'll walk iré caminando
[eereh]
I'm going for a walk voy a
dar una vuelta [boy – bwelta]

Walkman® el walkman®
[wolkman]

wall (inside) la pared [pareh]
(outside) el muro

wallet la cartera [kartaira]

wander: I like just wandering

around me gusta caminar sin
rumbo fijo [meh goosta – seen
roombo feeHo]

want: I want a ... quiero un/
una ... [k-yairo]
I don't want ... no quiero
ninguno/ninguna ...
I want to go home quiero
irme a casa [eermeh]
I don't want to no quiero
he wants to ... quiere ...
[k-yaireh]
what do you want? ¿qué
quiere? [keh]

ward (in hospital) el pabellón
[pabeh-yon]

warm caliente [kal-yenteh]
I'm very warm tengo mucho
calor [moocho]

was*: it was ... era ... [aira];
estaba ...

wash (verb) lavar [labar]
can you wash these? ¿puede
lavar estos? [pwedeh]

washer (for bolt etc) el
fregadero [fregadairo]

washhand basin el lavabo
[lababo]

washing (clothes) la ropa sucia
[soos-ya]

washing machine la lavadora
[labadora]

washing powder el
detergente [detairHenteh]

washing-up liquid el
(detergente) lavavajillas
[lababaHee-yas]

wasp la avispa [abeespa]

watch (wristwatch) el reloj

[reloH]

will you watch my things for
me? ¿puede cuidarme mis
cosas? [pwedeh kweedarmeh
mees]

watch out! ¡cuidado!
[kweedado]

watch strap la correa [korreh-a]

water el agua [agwa]

may I have some water? ¿me
da un poco de agua? [meh
– deh]

waterproof (adj) impermeable
[eempairmeh-ableh]

waterskiing el esquí acuático
[eskee akwateeko]

wave (in sea) la ola

way: it's this way es por aquí
[akee]

it's that way es por allí [a-yee]

is it a long way to ...? ¿queda
lejos ...? [keda leh-Hos]

no way! ¡de ninguna
manera! [deh – manaira]

dialogue

could you tell me the
way to ...? podría
indicarme el camino a ...?
[eendeekarmeh]

go straight on until you
reach the traffic lights
siga recto hasta llegar al
semáforo [asta yegar]

turn left tuerce a la
izquierda [twairseh]

take the first on the right
tome la primera a la

derecha [tomeh]
see where

we* nosotros, nosotras

weak débil

weather el tiempo [t-yempo]

dialogue

what's the weather going
to be like? ¿qué tiempo va
a hacer? [keh – ba a asair]

it's going to be fine va a
hacer bueno [bweno]

it's going to rain va a llover
[yobair]

it'll brighten up later
despejará más tarde [despeh-
Hara mas tardeh]

wedding la boda

wedding ring el anillo de
casado [anee-yo]

Wednesday miércoles
[m-yairkol-es]

week la semana

a week (from) today dentro
de una semana [deh]

a week (from) tomorrow
dentro de una semana a
partir de mañana [man-yana]

weekend el fin de semana
[feen deh]

at the weekend el fin de
semana

weight el peso

weird extraño [ekstran-yo]

weirdo: he's a weirdo es un
tipo raro [teepo]

welcome: welcome to ...
bienvenido a ...
[b-yenben**ee**do]

you're welcome (don't mention it) no hay de qué [ī deh keh]

well: I don't feel well no me siento bien [meh s-**ye**nto b-yen]

she's not well no se siente bien [seh s-**ye**nteh]

you speak English very well habla inglés muy bien [**a**bla eeng-les mwee]

well done! ¡bravo! [**bra**bo]

this one as well éste también [**es**teh tamb-yen]

well well! (surprise) ¡ándale, pues! [**a**ndaleh pwes]

dialogue

how are you? ¿cómo le va? [leh ba]

very well, thanks muy bien, gracias [mwee b-yen **gra**s-yas]

– and you? – ¿y Usted? [ee oost**eh**]

well-done (meat) bien hecho [b-yen **e**cho]

Welsh galés [gal-es]

I'm Welsh (man/woman) soy galés/gal**e**sa

were*: we were est**á**bamos; éramos [**ai**ramos]

you were estaban; eran [**ai**ran]

they were estaban; eran

west el oeste [o-**e**steh], el occidente [oksee**de**nteh]

in the west en el oeste

West Indian (adj) antillano [antee-**ya**no]

wet mojado [mo**H**ado]

what? ¿qué? [keh]

what's that? ¿qué es eso?

what should I do? ¿qué hago? [**a**-go]

what a view! ¡qué vista!

what number bus is it? ¿qué número de camión es ese? [**noo**mairo deh – **e**seh]

wheel la rueda [**rwe**da]

wheelchair la silla de ruedas [**see**-ya deh **rwe**das]

when? ¿cuándo? [**kwa**ndo]

when we get back cuando regresamos

when's the train/ferry? ¿cuándo es el tren/ferry?

where? ¿dónde? [**do**ndeh]

I don't know where it is no sé dónde est**á** [seh]

dialogue

where is the cathedral? ¿dónde está la catedral?

it's over there está por ahí [a-ee]

could you show me where it is on the map? ¿puede enseñarme en el mapa dónde está? [pw**e**deh ensen-**ya**rmeh]

it's just here está aquí

mero [akee mairo]
see way

which: which bus? ¿qué
camión? [keh]

dialogue

which one? ¿cuál? [kwal]
that one ese [eseh]
this one? ¿éste? [esteh]
no, that one no, aquél
[akel]

while: while I'm here ya que
estoy aquí [keh estoy akee]
whisky el whisky
white blanco
white wine el vino blanco
[beeno]
who? ¿quién? [k-yen]
who is it? ¿quién es?
the man who ... el hombre
que... [keh]
whole: the whole week toda
la semana
the whole lot todo
whose: whose is this? ¿de
quién es esto? [deh k-yen]
why? ¿por qué? [keh]
why not? ¿por qué no?
wide ancho
wife la mujer [mooHair], la
esposa
will*: will you do it for me?
¿puede hacer esto por mí?
[pwedeh asair]
wind el viento [b-yento]
window (of house) la ventana

[bentana]
(of ticket office, vehicle) la
ventanilla [bentanee-ya]
near the window cerca de la
ventana [sairka deh]
in the window (of shop) en el
escaparate [eskaparateh]
window seat el asiento junto
a la ventana [as-yento Hoonto a
la bentana]
windscreen el parabrisas
windscreen wiper el
limpiaparabrisas [leemp-ya-
parabreesas]
windsurfing el windsurf
windy: it's very windy hace
mucho viento [aseh moocho
b-yento]
wine el vino [beeno]
can we have some more
wine? ¿podría traernos más
vino? [tra-airnos]
wine list la lista de vinos
[leesta deh beenos]
winter el invierno [eemb-
yairno]
in the winter en invierno
winter holiday las vacaciones
de invierno
[bakas-yon-es deh]
wire el alambre [alambreh]
(electric) el cable eléctrico
[kableh]
wish: best wishes saludos
with con
I'm staying with ... estoy en
casa de ... [deh]
without sin [seen]
witness el/la testigo [testeego]

121

will you be a witness for me? ¿acepta ser mi testigo? [asepta sair]

woman la mujer [mooнair]

wonderful estupendo [estoopendo]

won't*: it won't start no arranca

wood (material) la madera [madaira]

woods (forest) el bosque [boskeh]

wool la lana

word la palabra

work el trabajo [trabaнo]
it's not working no funciona [foons-yona]
I work in ... trabajo en ...

world el mundo [moondo]

worry: I'm worried (said by man/ woman) estoy preocupado/preocupada [preh-okoopado]

worse: it's worse es peor [peh-or]

worst el peor

worth: is it worth a visit? ¿vale la pena visitarlo? [baleh – beeseetarlo]

would: would you give this to ...? ¿le puede dar esto a ...? [leh pwedeh]

wrap: could you wrap it up? ¿me lo envuelve? [meh lo embwelbeh]

wrapping paper el papel de envolver [deh embolbair]

wrist la muñeca [moon-yeka]

write escribir [eskreebeer]

could you write it down? ¿puede escribírmelo? [pwedeh]

how do you write it? ¿cómo se escribe? [seh eskreebeh]

writing paper el papel de escribir

wrong: it's the wrong key no es ésa la llave [yabeh]
this is the wrong train éste no es el tren [esteh]
the bill's wrong la cuenta está equivocada [kwenta – ekeebokada]
sorry, wrong number perdone, me equivoqué de número [pairdoneh meh ekeebokeh deh noomairo]
there's something wrong with ... le pasa algo a ... [leh]
what's wrong? ¿qué pasa? [keh]

X

X-ray la radiografía [radyografee-a]

Y

yacht el yate [yateh]

yard* (courtyard) el patio

year el año [an-yo]

yellow amarillo [amaree-yo]

yes sí

yesterday ayer [i-yair]
yesterday morning ayer por

la mañana [man-yana]
the day before yesterday
anteayer [anteh-ī-yair]
yet

dialogue

is it here yet? ¿está aquí
ya? [akee]
no, not yet no, todavía no
[todabee-a]
you'll have to wait a little
longer yet tendrá que
esperar un poquito más
[keh espairar oon pokeeto]

yobbo el hampón [ampon]
yoghurt el yogur [yogoor]
you* (fam, sing) tú [too]
(pol, sing) Usted [oosteh]
(pol, pl) Ustedes [oosted-es]
this is for you esto es para
tí/Usted
with you contigo/con
Usted
young joven [Hoben]
your* (fam, sing) tu; (pl) tus
[toos]
(pol, sing) su; (pl) sus [soos]
yours* (fam, sing) tuyo [too-yo],
tuya
(pol, sing) suyo [soo-yo],
suya; de Usted [deh
oosteh]
youth hostel el albergue
juvenil [albairgeh Hoobeneel]

Z

zero cero [sairo]
zip el cierre [s-yairreh]
could you put a new zip in?
¿podría cambiar el cierre?
[kamb-yar]
zip code el código postal
[pos-tal]
zoo el zoo(lógico) [zo(loHeeko)]

Spanish

→

English

Colloquial Spanish

The following are words you might well hear. Some of them you wouldn't ever want to use and you shouldn't be tempted to use any of the stronger ones unless you are sure of your audience.

¡ándale pues! [**a**ndaleh pwes] go on then!, OK!

¡bien! [b-yen] good!

cabrón **m** bastard

¡carajo! [kara**H**o] Christ!, shit!

chingar to fuck

¡chinga tu madre! fuck off!

coger [ko**H**air] to fuck

¡Dios mío! [d-yos m**ee**-o] my God!

¿dónde carajos? [d**o**ndeh] where in hell?

¡está padre! it's great!

¡hijo de la chingada! [**ee**Ho] son of a bitch!

¡híjole! [**ee**Holeh] hell!, damn!

joder [Hod**air**] to screw up

¡lárguese! [l**a**rgeseh] go away!

¡lo jodiste! [Hod**ee**steh] you screwed up!

¡mamón! idiot!

mano pal, buddy

marica **m**, maricón **m** queer

mariposa **f** butterfly; fairy, pansy

me pega la gana I feel like it

me vale (madre) [m**a**dreh] I don't give a shit

¡mierda! [m-y**ai**rda] shit!

¡ni modo! well, what can you do?

no le hace [leh **a**seh] don't worry about it

¡oiga! [**oy**ga] listen here!; excuse me!

¡órale! [**o**raleh] go on then!, get on with it!

pinche [p**ee**ncheh] bloody, lousy

pocho Americanized (used to refer to Americanized Mexican)

¡qué chingadera! [keh cheengad**ai**ra] what a fuck-up!

¡qué desmadre! [keh desm**a**dreh] what a mess!

¿qué húbole? [keh **oo**boleh] how's it going?

¡qué va! [ba] no way!

un chingo de [deh] loads of

A

a to; at; per; from
abajo [abaнo] downstairs; down below
abarrotes: tienda de abarrotes f [t-yenda deh abarrot-es] grocer's, dry goods store
abierto [ab-yairto] open
abierto de ... a ... open from ... to ...
abierto las 24 horas del día open 24 hours
abogada f, abogado m lawyer
abonos mpl season tickets
aborrezco [aborresko] I hate
ábrase aquí open here
ábrase en caso de emergencia open in case of emergency
abrazo m [abraso] embrace
abrebotellas m [abreboteh-yas] bottle-opener
abrelatas m tin-opener
abrigo m coat
abrigo de pieles [deh p-yel-es] fur coat
abril m April
abrir to open
abróchense los cinturones fasten your seatbelts
abuela f [abwela] grandmother
abuelo m grandfather
abuelos mpl grandparents
aburrido boring; bored
aburrirse [aboorreerseh] to be bored; to get bored
acabar to finish
  acabo de ... [deh] I have just ...
acantilado m cliff
acceso a ... access to ...
acceso a la vía to the trains
acceso playa to the beach
accidente m [akseedenteh] accident
  tener un accidente [tenair] to have an accident
accidente de carro [deh] car accident
accidente de montaña [montan-ya] mountaineering accident
accidente de tránsito road accident
accidente en cadena [kadena] pile-up
acelerador m [aselairador] accelerator, gas pedal
acelerar [aselairar] to accelerate
acento m [asento] accent
aceptar [aseptar] to accept
acera f [asaira] pavement, sidewalk
acerca de [asairka deh] about, concerning
acero m [asairo] steel
acetona f [asetona] nail polish remover
ácido (m) [aseedo] sour; acid
acompañar [akompan-yar] to accompany
  le acompaño en el sentimiento my condolences
acondicionador de pelo m [akondees-yonador deh] hair conditioner
aconsejar [akonseh-нar] to advise

acordarse [akordarseh] to remember

acostar to put to bed; to lay down

acostarse [akostarseh] to lie down; to go to bed

al acostarse when you go to bed

actriz f [aktrees] actress

acuerdo m [akwairdo] agreement

estoy de acuerdo [deh] I agree

de acuerdo OK

adaptador m adaptor

adelantado: por adelantado [adelantado] in advance

adelantarse a [–arseh] to overtake

además de [deh] besides, as well as

adentro inside

adolescente m/f [adolesenteh] teenager

aduana f [adwana] Customs

aduanero m [adwanairo] Customs office

aerodeslizador m [a-airo-desleesador] hovercraft

aerolínea f [a-airoleeneh-a] airline

aeropuerto m [a-airopwairto] airport

afeitarse [afaytarseh] to shave

aficionada f [afees-yonada], aficionado m [afees-yonado] fan, enthusiast

afortunadamente [–menteh] fortunately

afueras fpl [afwairas] suburbs

agarrar to hold, to grasp; to catch; to take

agencia f [aHens-ya] agency

agencia de viajes [deh b-yaH-es] travel agency

agenda f [aHenda] diary

agítese antes de usar(se) shake before use

agosto m August

agradable [agradableh] pleasant

agradar to please

agradecer [agradesair] to thank

agradecido [agradeseedo] grateful

agradezco [agradesko] I thank

agresivo [agreseebo] aggressive

agricultor m farmer

agua f [agwa] water

agua de colonia [deh kolon-ya] eau de toilette

aguantar: no aguanto ... [agwanto] I can't stand ...

agua potable [potableh] drinking water

águila ratonera f [ageela] buzzard

aguja f [agooHa] needle

agujero m [agooHairo] hole

agujetas fpl [agooHetas] shoelaces

ahora [a-ora] now

ahorita [a-oreeta] right away; soon; just a moment ago

aire m [īreh] air

aire acondicionado [akondees-yonado] air-conditioning

ajedrez m [aHed-res] chess

ajustado [aHoostado] tight

ala f wing

alambre m [alambreh] wire

alambre de púa [deh poo-a] barbed wire

alarma f alarm

dar la señal de alarma [sen-yal deh] to raise the alarm

alberca f [albairka] swimming pool

albergue juvenil [albairgeh Hoobeneel] youth hostel

alcoba f bedroom; sleeping compartment

alcohómetro m Breathalyzer®

alegre [alegreh] happy

alegro: me alegro I'm pleased; I'm pleased to hear it

alemán German

Alemania f [aleman-ya] Germany

alérgico a [alairHeeko] allergic to

aletas fpl flippers

alfiler m [alfeelair] pin

alfombra f rug, carpet

algo something

algodón m cotton; cotton wool, absorbent cotton

algo más something else

alguien [alg-yen] somebody; anybody

algún some; any

alguno someone; anyone; one; any one

alianza f [al-yansa] wedding ring

alimentos mpl groceries, foodstuffs

allá: más allá [a-ya] further (on)

allí [a-yee] there

almacén m [almasen] department store; warehouse

almohada f [almo-ada] pillow

almuerzo m [almwairso] lunch

alojamiento m [aloHam-yento] accommodation

alojamiento y desayuno [desi-yoono] bed and breakfast

alpinismo m mountaineering

alquilar [alkeelar] to rent; to hire

alquiler m [alkeelair] rental

alquiler de barcos boat hire

alquiler de bicicletas [beeseekletas] cycle hire

alquiler de carros car rental

alquiler de esquís [eskees] water-ski hire

alquiler de tablas surfboard hire

alquileres rentals

alrededor (de) [deh] around

alta costura f haute couture, high fashion

alto (m) stop sign; high; tall

¡alto! stop!

en lo alto at the top

altura f altitude; height

altura máxima maximum headroom

aluminio m aluminium

amable [amableh] kind; si fuera tan amable [fwaira] if you wouldn't mind

amamantar to breastfeed

amanecer m [amanesair] sunrise, daybreak

¿cómo amaneciste? how did you sleep?

amargo bitter

amarillo [amar**ee**-yo] yellow

ambos both

ambulancia f [amboo**la**ns-ya] ambulance

América f [amai**ree**ka] Latin America

América del Norte [**no**rteh] North America

América del Sur South America

americana (f), americano (m) Latin American

amiga f friend, amigo m friend

amor m love

hacer el amor [as**air**] to make love

amortiguador m [amorteegwa**do**r] shock-absorber

amperio m [amp**air**-yo] amp

ampliación f [amplee-as-y**o**n] enlargement

amplio broad; loose-fitting

ampolla f [amp**o**-ya] blister

analgésico m [anal**H**e**see**ko] painkiller

análisis clínicos mpl clinical tests

anaranjado [anaran**H**a**do**] orange (colour)

ancho (m) width, breadth; wide; loose

anchura f width, breadth

¡ándale pues! [**a**ndaleh pwes] go on then!, OK!

andaluz [andal**oos**] Andalusian

andar to walk; to move; to work

andinismo m mountaineering

anémico anaemic

anestesia f [anestes-ya] anaesthetic

anfiteatro m [anfeeteh-**a**tro] amphitheatre

Angeles Verdes mpl [**a**ngel-es ba**i**rd-es] breakdown service

angina (de pecho) f [an**H**e**e**na] angina

anginas fpl tonsillitis

anillo m [an**ee**-yo] ring

anoche [an**o**cheh] last night

anochecer m [anoches**air**] nightfall, dusk

anochece [anoch**e**seh] it's getting dark

ante m [**a**nteh] suede

anteayer [anteh-ī-y**air**] the day before yesterday

antepasado m ancestor

antes de [**a**nt-es deh] before

antes de entrar dejen salir let passengers off first

antes de que [keh] before

anticipo m [ant**ee**s**ee**po] advance

anticonceptivo m [anteekonsept**ee**bo] contraceptive

anticongelante m [anteekon**H**e**la**nteh] antifreeze

anticuado [antee**kwa**do] out of date

anticuario m [anteek**war**-yo] antiques dealer

antigüedades: una tienda de antigüedades [t-y**e**nda deh anteegwe**da**d-es] an antique shop

antiguo [ant**ee**gwo] old; ancient

antihistamínico **m** [antee-eestameeneeko] antihistamine

Antillas **fpl** [antee-yas] the West Indies

antipático unpleasant, nasty

anulado cancelled

anular to cancel

añadir [an-yadeer] to add

año **m** [an-yo] year

Año Nuevo **m** [nwebo] New Year

  día de Año Nuevo **m** [dee-a deh] New Year's Day

  ¡feliz Año Nuevo! [felees] Happy New Year!

apagar to switch off

apagón **m** power cut

apague el motor switch off your engine

apague las luces switch off your lights

aparato **m** device

aparatos electrodomésticos electrical appliances

aparecer [aparesair] to appear

aparezco [aparesko] I appear

apasionante [apas-yonanteh] thrilling

apellido **m** [apeh-yeedo] surname

apenado sorry; embarrassed, shy

apenarse [–arseh] to be ashamed, to be embarrassed

apenas scarcely

  apenas ... (cuando) [kwando] hardly ... when

  son las seis apenas it's only just six o'clock

apetecer: me apetece [meh apeteseh] I feel like

apetito **m** appetite

apodo **m** nickname

apoplejía **f** [apopleнee-a] stroke; fit

aprender [aprendair] to learn

aprensivo [aprenseebo] fearful, apprehensive

apriete botón para cruzar press button to cross

aprovechar [aprobechar] to take advantage of

  ¡que aproveche! [keh aprobecheh] enjoy your meal!

aproximadamente [–menteh] about

apto para mayores de 14 años y menores acompañados authorized for those over 14 and young people accompanied by an adult

apto para mayores de 18 años for adults only

apto para todos los públicos suitable for all

apurado in a hurry

apurarse [–arseh] to rush, to hurry

  ¡apúrate! [apoorateh] hurry up!

aquel [akel] that

aquél that (one)

aquella [akeh-ya] that

aquélla that (one)

aquellas [akeh-yas] those

aquéllas those (ones)

aquellos [akeh-yos] those

aquéllos those (ones)

aquí [akee] here

aquí tiene [t-yeneh] here you
  are

araña f [aran-ya] spider

arañazo m [aran-yaso] scratch

árbol m tree

ardor de estómago m [deh]
  heartburn

área de servicios m [areh-a
  deh serbees-yos] service area,
  motorway services

arena f [areh-na] sand

aretes mpl [aret-es] earrings

argentino (m) [arHenteeno]
  Argentine; Argentinian

armario m cupboard

armería f [armairee-a]
  gunsmith's

aro m ring

arqueología f [arkeh-oloHee-a]
  archaeology

arrancar to pull out, to tear
  out; to start up

arranque m [arrankeh] ignition

arreglar to mend; to sort out,
  to arrange

arrendar [arrendar] to rent; to
  hire

  se arrienda to rent, for hire

arriba up; upstairs; on top

arroyo m stream

arte m [arteh] art

artesanía f crafts

artículos de artesanía mpl [deh]
  arts and crafts

artículos de boda wedding
  presents

artículos de deporte [deporteh]
  sports goods

artículos de limpieza [leemp-

yesa] household cleaning
  products

artículos de piel [p-yel] leather
  goods

artículos de playa [plī-ya]
  beachwear

artículos de viaje [b-yaHeh]
  travel goods

artículos escolares [eskolar-es]
  schoolwear

artículos para el bebé [beh-beh]
  babywear

artista m/f artist

artritis f arthritis

ascensor m [asensor] lift,
  elevator

asegurar to insure

aseos mpl [aseh-os] toilets, rest
  rooms

así like this; like that

asiento m [as-yento] seat

así que so (that)

asma m asthma

aspiradora f vacuum cleaner

asqueroso [askairoso]
  disgusting

astigmático long-sighted

asustado afraid

asustar to frighten

atacar to attack

atajo m [ataHo] shortcut

ataque m [atakeh] attack

ataque al corazón [korason]
  heart attack

atención [atens-yon] please note

¡atención! take care!, caution!

atención al tren beware of
  trains

ateo [ateh-o] atheist

aterrizaje m landing

aterrizaje forzado emergency landing

aterrizar [atairreesar] to land

atletismo m athletics

atorado stuck

atorarse [atorarseh] to get stuck

atracar to assault; to hold up

atracciones turísticas fpl [atraks-yon-es] tourist attractions

atraco a mano armada m armed robbery, hold-up

atractivo [atrakteebo] attractive

atrás at the back; behind

¡atrás! get back!

la parte de atrás [parteh deh] the back

está más atrás it's further back

años atrás [an-yos] years ago

atrasado late

atraso m delay

atravesar [atrabesar] to cross

atravieso [atrab-yeso] I cross

atreverse [atrebairseh] to dare

atropellar [atropeh-yar] to knock down

atroz [atros] dreadful

audífono m [owdeefono] hearing aid

aun [own] even

aún [a-oon] still; yet

aunque [ownkeh] although

auto m [owto] car

autobús m [owtoboos] coach, long-distance bus

auto-estopista m/f [owto-estopeesta] hitch-hiker

automóvil m [owtomobeel] car

autopista f [owtopeesta] motorway, freeway, highway

autopista de cuota [deh kwota] toll motorway/highway

auto-servicio m [owto-sairbees-yo] self-service

autostop: hacer autostop [asair owtostop] to hitchhike

autovía f [owtobee-a] slow, local train

avenida f [abeneeda] avenue

aventar [abentar] to throw

aventón: pedir aventón [abenton] to hitch a lift

avergonzado [abairgonsado] ashamed

avería f [abairee-a] breakdown

averiarse [abair-yarseh] to break down

avión m [ab-yon] aeroplane, airplane

por avión by air

avisar [abeesar] to inform

aviso m [abeeso] advertisement; notice

aviso a los señores pasajeros passenger information

avispa f [abeespa] wasp

ayer [ī-yair] yesterday

ayer por la mañana [man-yana] yesterday morning

ayer por la tarde [tardeh] yesterday afternoon

ayuda f [ī-yooda] help

ayudar [ī-yoodar] to help

ayuntamiento m [ī-yoontam-yento] town hall

azotea f [asoteh-a] roof

azteca [asteka] Aztec
azul (m) [asool] blue
azul claro light blue
azul marino navy blue

B

baca f roof rack
bache m [bacheh] hole in the
  road
bahía f [ba-ee-a] bay
bailar [bīlar] to dance
  ir a bailar to go dancing
baile m [bīleh] dance; dancing
¡bajan! [baHan] next stop
  please!, people getting off!
bajar [baHar] to go down
  bajar de [deh] to get off
  bajar la velocidad [beloseeda] to
  slow down
bajarse (de) [baHarseh (deh)] to
  get off
bajeño [baHen-yo] from/of Baja
  California
Bajío m [baHee-yo] Baja
  California
bajo [baHo] low; short; under;
  underneath
balacera f [balasaira] exchange
  of fire
balanceo m [balanseh-yo]
  wheel-balancing
balcón m balcony
balón m ball
balonmano m handball
balsa f raft
banco m bank; bench
bandeja f [bandeHa] tray

bandera f [bandaira] flag
bandido m bandit
banqueta f [banketa] pavement,
  sidewalk
bañador m [ban-yador]
  swimming costume
bañarse [ban-yarseh] to go
  swimming; to have a bath/
  shower
bañera f [ban-yaira] bathtub
baño m [ban-yo] bathroom;
  toilet, rest room; bath
baños mpl toilets, rest room
baraja f [baraHa] pack of cards
barato cheap, inexpensive
barba f chin; beard
barbacoa f barbecue;
  barbecued meat
barbería f [barbairee-a] barber's
  shop
barbero m [barbairo] barber
barco m boat
barco de remo [deh] rowing
  boat
barco de vela [bela] sailing
  boat
barcos para alquilar boats to
  rent
barra de labios f [deh lab-yos]
  lipstick
barrio m [barr-yo] district, area
básquet m [basket] basketball
bastante [bastanteh] enough;
  quite; very
  bastante más quite a lot more
basura f rubbish, garbage
bata f dressing gown
bate m [bateh] bat
batería f [batairee-a] battery;

drum kit
batería de cocina [deh ko**see**na]
  pots and pans
bautismo m [bow**tees**mo]
  christening
bebé m [beh-beh] baby
beber [beb**air**] to drink
béisbol m [**bays**bol] baseball
Belice [bel**ee**seh] Belize
bello [beh-yo] beautiful
besar to kiss
beso m kiss
betún m [bet**oon**] shoe polish
biblioteca f [beebl-yo**teka**]
  library; bookcase
bicicleta f [beesee**kleta**] bicycle
bien [b-yen] well
¡**bien**! good!
bien ... bien ... either ... or ...
o bien ... o bien ... either ...
  or ...
bienes mpl [b-yen-es]
  possessions
¡**bienvenido**! [b-yenben**eedo**]
  welcome!
bifurcación f [beefoorkas-yon]
  fork
bigote m [bee**goteh**] moustache
billete m [bee-**yeteh**] banknote,
  (US) bill
blanco (m) white
blusa f blouse
boca f mouth
boda f wedding
bodega f wine cellar
boleador m [boleh-a**dor**]
  shoeshine boy
boletería f ticket office
boleto m ticket

boleto de ida [deh **ee**da] single
  ticket, one-way ticket
boleto de ida y vuelta [ee
  b**welta**] return ticket, round-
  trip ticket
bolígrafo m ballpoint pen
bolsa f bag; stock exchange
bolsa de dormir [deh] sleeping
  bag
bolsa de plástico plastic bag
bolsa de viaje [b-ya**Heh**] travel
  bag
bolsillo m [bol**see**-yo] pocket
bolso m handbag, (US) purse
bomba f bomb
bomba de gas [deh] camping
  gas cylinder
bomberos mpl [bom**bairos**] fire
  brigade
bordado embroidered
borracho drunk
bosque m [**boskeh**] forest
bota f boot
botanas fpl snacks
botar to throw away
botella f [bo**teh**-ya] bottle
botiquín m [botee**keen**] first-
  aid kit
botón m button
botón desatascador coin
  return button
boxeo m [bok**seh**-o] boxing
boya f buoy
bracero m [bra**sairo**] migrant
  labourer from Mexico to
  the US
bragas fpl pants, panties
brazo m [**braso**] arm
bricolaje m [breekola**Heh**] DIY,

do-it-yourself
brillar [bree-yar] to shine
brincar to jump
brisa f breeze
británico British
brocha de afeitar f [deh afaytar]
  shaving brush
broche m [brocheh] brooch
bronce m [bronseh] bronze
bronceado (m) [bronseh-ado]
  suntan; suntanned
bronceador m [bronseh-ador]
  suntan oil/lotion
bronquitis f [bronkeetees]
  bronchitis
brújula f [brooHoola] compass
bruto stupid
bucear [booseh-ar] to skin-dive
buceo m [booseh-o] skin-diving
buenas noches [bwenas noch-es]
  good night
buenas tardes [tard-es] good
  evening
bueno [bweno] good; good-
  natured; hello
buenos días [dee-as] good
  morning
bufanda f scarf
bufete m [boofeteh] lawyer's
  office
bujía f [booHee-a] spark plug
bulto m package; lump,
  swelling
burro m donkey
buscar to look for
busqué [booskeh] I looked for
butacas fpl stalls
buzón [booson] letter box,
  postbox, mailbox

C

c/ street
c/c current account
caballeros mpl [kaba-yairos]
  gents, men's rest room
caballo m [kaba-yo] horse
cabaña f [kaban-ya] beach hut
cabello m [kabeh-yo] hair
cabeza f [kabesa] head
cabida ... personas capacity ...
  people
cabina telefónica f telephone
  booth, phone box
cable m [kableh] wire
cable de extensión m [deh
  ekstens-yon] extension lead
cabra f goat
cabrón m bastard
cachetada f slap in the face
cacto m cactus
cada every
cada vez (que) [bes (keh)]
  every time (that)
cadena f chain
cadera f [kadaira] hip
caduca ... expires ...
caer [ka-air] to fall
caerse [ka-airseh] to fall over,
  to fall down
café [kafeh] coffee; café
cafetera f [kafetaira] coffee pot
cafetería f [kafetairee-a] bar-
  type restaurant
caída f [ka-eeda] fall
caimán m [kiman] alligator
caja f [kaHa] cash desk, till;
  cashier

caja de ahorros [deh a-**o**rros]
savings bank

caja de cambios [kamb-yos]
gearbox

cajera f [kaнaira], cajero m
cashier

cajero automático
[owtomateeko] cashpoint,
automatic teller, ATM

cajeta f [kaнeta] fudge

cajetilla f [kaнetee-ya] packet,
(US) pack

cajuela f [kaнwela] boot (of car),
(US) trunk

calambre m [kalambreh] cramp

calcetines mpl [kalseteen-es]
socks

calculadora f calculator

calefacción f [kalefaks-yon]
heating

calefacción central [sentral]
central heating

calendario m [–dar-yo] calendar

calidad f [kaleeda] quality

caliente [kal-yenteh] hot

calle f [ka-yeh] street

calle comercial [komairs-yal]
shopping street

calle de sentido único one-
way street

callejón m [ka-yeh-нon] lane,
alley

callejón sin salida cul-de-sac,
dead end

calle peatonal [peh-atonal]
pedestrianized street

calle principal [preenseepal]
main street

callo m [ka-yo] corn (on foot)

calmante m [kalmanteh]
tranquillizer

calor m heat

hace calor [aseh] it's warm/
hot

calvo [kalbo] bald

calza: ¿qué número calza? [keh
n**oo**mairo kalsa] what is your
shoe size?

calzada f [kalsada] street

calzada deteriorada poor road
surface

calzada irregular uneven
surface

calzados shoe shop

calzones mpl [kalson-es]
underpants

cama f bed

cama de campaña [deh kampan-
ya] campbed

cama individual [eendeebeedwal]
single bed

cama matrimonial [matreemon-
yal] double bed

cámara f camera; inner tube

cámara fotográfica camera

camarín m sleeping berth

camarote m [kamaroteh] cabin

cambiar [kamb-yar] to change

cambiarse (de ropa) [kamb-
yarseh (deh)] to get changed

cambio m [kamb-yo] change;
exchange; exchange rate

cambio de divisas [deh
deeb**ee**sas] currency
exchange

cambio de moneda currency
exchange

cambio de sentido take filter

lane to exit and cross flow
of traffic

camellón m [kameh-yon] central
reservation

caminar to walk; to work

camino m path

camino cerrado (al tráfico) road
closed to (traffic)

camino privado private road

camión m [kam-yon] bus

camioneta f [kam-yoneta] van

camisa f shirt

camiseta f T-shirt; vest

camisón m nightdress

campana f bell

campechano from/of
Campeche

campesino m peasant farmer

camping m camping;
campsite; caravan site, trailer
park

campo m countryside; pitch;
court; field

campo de deportes [deh deportes] sports field

campo de futból football
ground

campo de golf golf course

canadiense (m/f) [kanad-yenseh]
Canadian

cancelado [kanselado]
cancelled; stamped

cancelar [kanselar] to cancel;
to stamp

cancha f court; pitch

canción f [kans-yon] song

canguro m/f baby-sitter

canoa f canoe; skiff

canoso greying; grey

cansado tired

cantar to sing

cantina f bar

canto m song; singing

caña f [kan-ya] sugar cane;
sugar cane liquor

caña de pescar [deh] fishing
rod

cañería f [kan-yairee-a] pipes

cañon m [kan-yon] canyon

capaz: ser capaz (de) [sair kapas
(deh)] to be able (to); to be
capable (of)

capazo m [kapaso] carry-cot

capilla f [kapee-ya] chapel

capitalina f, capitalino m
person who lives in the
capital city

capitán m captain

capó(t) m bonnet (of car), (US)
hood

cara f face

carácter m [karaktair] character;
nature

tiene mal carácter [t-yeneh]
he's got a bad temper

¡carajo! [karaHo] Christ!, shit!

¿dónde carajos? [dondeh]
where in hell?

caravana f caravan, (US) trailer

carburador m carburettor

cárcel f [karsel] prison

carey m [karay] tortoiseshell

Caribe: el Caribe [kareebeh] the
Caribbean

caricaturas fpl cartoons

cariño m [kareen-yo] love;
affection

carnet de identidad m [deh

eedenteeda] identity card

carnet de chofer m [chofair] driving licence

carnicería f [karneesairee-a] butcher's

caro expensive

carpa f large tent, marquee

carpintería f [karpeentairee-a] joiner's, carpenter's

carrera f [karraira] race; career

carreras de caballos mpl [deh kaba-yos] horse racing

carrete m [karreteh] film (for camera)

carretera f [karretaira] main road

carretera cortada road blocked, road closed

carretera de circunvalación by-pass

carretera de doble carril two-lane road

carril m lane

carrito m trolley; cart; pushchair

carrito de niño [deh neen-yo] pushchair

carrito portaequipajes [porta-ekeepaн-es] baggage trolley

carro m car

carrocería f [karrosairee-a] bodywork

carro-comedor m buffet car, restaurant car

carro rentado m rented car

carta f letter; menu

cartel m poster

cartelera de espectáculos f [kartelaira deh] entertainments guide

cartera f [kartaira] briefcase; wallet

carterista m pickpocket

cartero m postman, mailman

cartón m cardboard; carton

casa f house

en casa at home

en casa de Juan [deh] at Juan's

está en su casa make yourself at home

casa de cambio f [kamb-yo] bureau de change

casa de huéspedes [deh wesped-es] guesthouse

casa de socorro emergency first-aid centre

casado married

casarse [kasarseh] to get married

cascada f waterfall

caseta telefónica phone box, phone booth

casete f [kaset] cassette

casi almost

caso m case

en caso de que [deh keh] in case

caso urgente [oorнenteh] emergency

caspa f dandruff

castaño (m) [kastan-yo] sweet chestnut; brown

castigar to punish

castigo m punishment

castillo m [kastee-yo] castle

casualidad: de casualidad [deh kaswaleeda] by chance

catarro: tengo catarro I've got a cold

católico (**m**) Catholic

catorce [katorseh] fourteen

causa f [kowsa] cause

cauteloso [kowteloso] cautious; careful

cayó [kī-yo] he/she fell

caza f [kasa] hunting

cazadora f [kasadora] bomber jacket, blouson jacket

cazar [kasar] to hunt

cazuela f [kaswela] casserole; saucepan

ceda el paso give way

ceja f [seнa] eyebrow

celos: tener celos [tenair selos] to be jealous

celoso [seloso] jealous

cementerio m [sementair-yo] cemetery

cena f [sena] dinner

cenar to have dinner

cenicero m [seneesairo] ashtray

cenote m [senoteh] deep pool used for ceremonial purposes by the Mayas

central camionera f [sentral kam-yonaira] main bus station

central de autobuses [deh owtoboos-es] main bus station

central telefónica telephone exchange

centro m [sentro] centre

centro ciudad [s-yooda] city/town centre

centro comercial [komairs-yal] shopping centre

centro deportivo sports centre

centro de salud [deh saloo] health centre

centro urbano city/town centre

ceñido [sen-yeedo] tight-fitting

cepillo m [sepee-yo] brush

cepillo de dientes [deh d-yent-es] toothbrush

cepillo de pelo hairbrush

cera f [saira] wax

cerámica f [sairameeka] pottery; ceramics

cerca de [sairka deh] near

cerilla f [sairee-ya] match

cero [sairo] zero

cerrada f [sairrada] cul-de-sac

cerrado [sairrado] closed

cerrado por defunción closed due to bereavement

cerrado por descanso del personal closed for staff holidays

cerrado por obras/reforma/vacaciones closed for alterations/renovation/holidays

cerradura f [sairradoora] lock

cerramos los ... we close on ...

cerrar [sairrar] to close

cerrar con llave [yabeh] to lock

cerrojo m [sairroнo] bolt

certificado m [sairteefeekado] certificate; registered letter

cervecería f [sairbesairee-a] bar specializing in beer

césped m [sesped] lawn

cesta f [sesta] basket

cesto de la compra m [sesto deh] shopping basket

chabacano m apricot

chaleco m [chaleko] waistcoat, (US) vest

chaleco salvavidas [salbabeedas] life-jacket

chalet m [chaleh] villa

chalupa f dugout

chamarra f woollen jacket; waistcoat, (US) vest

champú m shampoo

changarro m small store

chapapote m [chapapoteh] tar; pitch

chaparro very small

chaparrón m shower; downpour

chaqueta f [chaketa] cardigan; jacket

charcutería f [charkootairee-a] delicatessen

charlar to chat

charreada f [charreh-ada] horse-riding display, rodeo

charro m horseman

chato snub-nosed

chava f [chaba] girl

chavo m boy

checar to check

cheque de viajero m [chekeh deh b-yaHairo] traveller's cheque

chequera f [chekaira] cheque book

chiapaneco [ch-yapaneko] from/of Chiapas

chica f girl

chicle m [cheekleh] chewing gum

chico m boy

chiflar to whistle

chilango from/of Mexico City

chileno (m) Chilean

chillar [chee-yar] to shout, to scream

chinampa f man-made island

chinche m drawing pin, (US) thumbtack; bug

chingadera: ¡qué chingadera! [keh cheengadaira] what a fuck-up!

chingar to fuck

chingo: un chingo de [deh] loads of

chino (m) Chinese

chiste m [cheesteh] joke

chocar con to run into

chocolate con leche m [chokolateh kon lecheh] milk chocolate

chofer m [chofair] driver

choque m [chokeh] crash; clash

chorros: a chorros loads

chubasco m sudden short shower

chubasquero m [choobaskairo] cagoule

churrasco m roast meat

Cía. company

cicatriz f [seekatrees] scar

ciclismo m [seekleesmo] cycling

ciclista m/f [seekleesta] cyclist

ciego (m) [s-yego] blind

cielo m [s-yelo] sky

cien [s-yen] hundred

ciencia f [s-yens-ya] science

ciento ... [s-yento] a hundred and ...

cierre m [s-yairreh] zip, zipper

cierren las puertas close the doors

cierro [s-yairro] I close

cigarro m [seegarro] cigarette

cinco [seenko] five

cincuenta [seen-kwenta] fifty

cine m [seeneh] cinema, movie theater

cinta f [seenta] tape; ribbon

cintura f [seentoora] waist; waist measurement

cinturón m [seentooron] belt

cinturón de seguridad [deh segooreeda] seat belt

circo m [seerko] circus

circulación f [seerkoolas-yon] traffic; circulation

circule despacio drive slowly

circule por la derecha keep to your right

círculo m [seerkoolo] circle

circunvalación f [seerkoonbalas-yon] ring road

cita f [seeta] appointment

ciudad f [s-yooda] town, city

claro clear; light

¡claro! of course!

clase f [klaseh] class

clausurar [klowsoorar] to close down

clavado de acantilado m [klabado] cliff-diving

clavo m [klabo] nail; clove

claxon m [klakson] horn

clima m climate

climatizado [kleemateesado] air-conditioned

clínica f hospital; clinic

cobija f [kobeeHa] rug, blanket

cobrar to charge; to earn

cobre m [kobreh] copper

cocer [kosair] to boil

coche-cama m sleeper, sleeping car

cochecito m [kocheseeto] pram

coche-comedor m [kocheh komedor] dining car

cocina f [koseena] kitchen

cocinar [koseenar] to cook

cocinera f [koseenaira], cocinero m cook

código de la circulación m highway code

código postal m [pos-tal] postcode, zip code

codo m elbow

coger [koHair] to fuck

cojo m [koHo] person with a limp

cola f tail; queue

hacer cola to queue

colcha f bedspread

colchón m mattress

colchoneta inflable f [eenflableh] air mattress

colección f [koleks-yon] collection

colectivo m [kolekteebo] collective taxi

colegio m [koleH-yo] school

collar m [ko-yar] necklace

colocar to place, to put

colonia f [kolon-ya] urban district

color m colour

columna vertebral f spine

comadre f [komadreh] godmother

combi **m** collective taxi, minibus

combustible **m** [komboost**ee**bleh] fuel

comedor **m** dining room

comenzar [komen**sar**] to begin

comer [ko**mair**] to eat

comerciante **m** [komairs-**yan**teh] shopkeeper; dealer

comicios **mpl** [ko**mees**-yos] elections

comida **f** lunch; food; meal

comidas para llevar [ye**var**] take-away meals, meals to go

comienzo (**m**) [kom-**yen**so] I begin; beginning

comisaría **f** police station

como as; like

¿cómo está? how are you?

¿cómo le va? [leh ba] how are things?

como quieras [k-y**ai**ras] it's up to you

compact **m** compact disc

compadre **m** [kom**pad**reh] godfather

compañera **f** [kompan-y**ai**ra] girlfriend

compañero **m** mate; boyfriend

compañía **f** [kompan-y**ee**-a] company

compañía aérea [a-**ai**reh-a] airline

comparar to compare

compartir to share

completamente [–**men**teh] completely

completo full; no vacancies

complicado complicated

compra: hacer la compra [a**sair**] to do the shopping

compramos a ... buying rate ...

comprar to buy

compras: ir de compras [eer deh] to go shopping

compresa **m** sanitary towel, sanitary napkin

comprimido efervescente **m** soluble tablet

comprimidos **mpl** tablets

computadora **f** computer

comunicando engaged, busy, occupied

con with

concha **f** shell

concierto **m** [kons-y**air**to] concert

condenar to sentence

condición: a condición de que [kondees-yon deh keh] on condition that

condón **m** condom

confección **f** [konfeks-yon] clothing industry

confecciones **fpl** [konfeks-yon-es] ready-to-wear clothes

conferencia internacional **f** [konf**ai**rens-ya eentairnas-yo**nal**] international call

conferencia interurbana long-distance call

confesar to admit; to confess

confirmar to confirm

confitería **f** [konfeetai**ree**-a] sweetshop, candy store

conforme [kon**for**meh] as

estar conforme to agree

congelado [konHelado] frozen

congelador m [konHelador] freezer

congelados mpl [konHelados] frozen foods

conjunto m [konHoonto] group; band

conmigo with me

conmoción cerebral f [konmos-yon sairebral] concussion

conmover [konmobair] to move

conmutadora f switchboard

conocer [konosair] to know

conozco [konosko] I know

conque [konkeh] so, so then

consentido spoiled

consérvese en lugar fresco store in a cool place

consigna f [konseegna] left luggage, baggage check

consigna automática [owtomateeka] left luggage lockers, baggage lockers

consigo with himself; with herself; with yourself; with themselves; with yourselves

constar: me consta I can confirm

consulado m consulate

consulta médica surgery, doctor's office

consúmase antes de ... best before ...

contacto: ponerse en contacto con to contact

contado: pagar al contado to pay cash

contador m, contadora f accountant

contagioso [kontaH-yoso] contagious

contaminado polluted

contar to count; to tell

contener [kontenair] to contain

contenido m contents

contento happy

contestar to reply, to answer

contigo with you

continuación: a continuación [konteenwas-yon] then, next; below

continuar [konteenwar] to continue

contra against

contradecir [kontradeseer] to contradict

contraindicaciones fpl contraindications

contraventanas fpl [kontrabentanas] shutters

control de pasaportes m passport control

convalecencia f [konbalesens-ya] convalescence

convencer [konbensair] to persuade

copa f wine glass

coquetear [koketeh-ar] to flirt

corazón m [korason] heart

corbata f tie, necktie

cordillera f [kordee-yaira] mountain range

cordones mpl [kordon-es] shoelaces

correa del ventilador f [korreh-a del benteelador] fan belt

correo m [korreh-o] post, mail; post office

correo aéreo [a-**ai**reh-o] airmail

correo central [sen-**tra**l] main
post office

correo terrestre [tair**rest**reh]
surface mail

correo urgente [oor**Hen**teh]
express (mail)

correr [kor**rair**] to run

correspondencia f [–**dens**-ya]
transfer, change

  hacer correspondencia en ...
to change (trains/buses) at ...

corrida de toros f [deh]
bullfight

corriente peligrosa dangerous
current

corrimiento de tierras danger:
landslides

cortadura f cut

cortar to cut

cortarse [kor**tar**seh] to cut
oneself

cortauñas m [korta-**oo**n-yas] nail
clippers

corte de pelo m [**kor**teh deh]
haircut

corte y confección [ee konfeks-
yon] dressmaking

cortina f curtain

corto short; short of money

cosa f thing

coser [ko**sair**] to sew

costa f coast

costar to cost

costilla f [kos**tee**-ya] rib

costumbre f [kos**toom**breh]
custom

costurera f [kostoo**rai**ra]
seamstress

cráneo m [**kra**neh-o] skull

crédito m credit; unit(s)

creer [kreh-**air**] to believe

crema f cream

crema base [**ba**seh] foundation
cream

crema de belleza [deh beh-**ye**sa]
cold cream

crema hidratante [eedra**tan**teh]
moisturizer

crema limpiadora [leemp-**ya**dora]
cleansing cream

creyó [kreh-**yo**] he/she believed

criticar to criticize

cruce m [**kroo**seh] crossroads;
junction, intersection;
crossing

cruce de ciclistas danger:
cyclists crossing

cruce de ganado danger: cattle
crossing

crucero m [kroo**sai**ro] cruise

cruda f hangover

cruzar [kroo**sar**] to cross

Cruz Roja f [kroos **ro**Ha] Red
Cross

cuaderno m [kwa**dair**no]
notebook

cuadra f [**kwa**dra] block

  está a dos cuadros it's two
blocks away

cuadrado [kwa**dra**do] square

cuadro m [**kwa**dro] painting

  de cuadros [deh] checked

cual [kwal] which; who;

¿cuál? which?

¿cuándo? [**kwan**do] when?

¿cuánto? [**kwan**to] how much?

  en cuanto ... as soon as ...

¡cuánto lo lamento! I'm so sorry!

¿cuántos? how many?

cuarenta [kwarenta] forty

cuartel m [kwartel] barracks

cuartilla f [kwartee-ya] writing paper

cuarto (m) [kwarto] quarter; fourth; room

cuarto con dos camas twin room

cuarto de baño [ban-yo] bathroom

cuarto de estar sitting room

cuarto de hora [deh ora] quarter of an hour

cuarto doble [dobleh] double room

cuarto individual [eendeebeedwal] single room

cuarto piso fourth floor, (US) fifth floor

cuate m [kwateh] friend, pal; twin

cuatro [kwatro] four

cuatrocientos [kwatros-yentos] four hundred

cubierta f [koob-yairta] deck

cubierto (m) covered; overcast; menu

cubiertos mpl cutlery

cubo m [koobo] bucket; cube

cubo de la basura [deh] dustbin, trashcan

cucaracha f cockroach

cuchara f spoon

cucharilla f [koocharee-ya] teaspoon

cuchillería f [koochee-yairee-a]

cutlery

cuchillo m [koochee-yo] knife

cuelgue, espere y retire la tarjeta hang up, wait and remove card

cuello m [kweh-yo] neck; collar

cuenta f [kwenta] bill, (US) check; account

cuenta corriente [korr-yenteh] current account

cuentas fpl beads

cuento m [kwento] tale

cuerda f [kwairda] rope; string

cuero m [kwairo] leather

cuerpo m [kwairpo] body

cuesta (f) [kwesta] it costs; slope

cuesta abajo/arriba [abaнo] downhill/uphill

cueva f [kweba] cave

cuidado (m) [kweedado] take care; look out; care

cuidado con ... caution ...

cuidado con el escalón mind the step

cuidado con el perro beware of the dog

cuidar [kweedar] to look after; to nurse

culebra f snake

culpa f fault, blame; guilt

es culpa mía it's my fault

culturismo m body building

cumplas: ¡que cumplas muchos más! many happy returns!

cumpleaños m [koompleh-an-yos] birthday

cuna f cot, (US) crib

cuneta f gutter

cuñada f [koon-yada] sister-in-law

cuñado m [koon-yado] brother-in-law

cuota m [kwota] contribution; membership fee; motorway toll

cura m priest

curado cured; drunk; smoked

curar to cure; to heal

curarse [koorarseh] to heal up

curva f [koorba] bend; curve

curva peligrosa dangerous bend

cuyo [koo-yo] whose; of which

D

D. (Don) Mr.

damas fpl draughts, (US) checkers; ladies' toilet, ladies' room

danés [dan-es] Danish

danza f [dansa] dancing; dance

danzón m [danson] popular Mexican dance

dañar [dan-yar] to damage

dañarse la espalda [dan-yarseh] to hurt one's back

daños mpl [dan-yos] damage(s)

dar to give

dar el visto bueno a [bweno] to approve

dcha. (derecha) right

de [deh] of; from

de dos metros de alto two metres high

debajo de [debaHo deh] under

deber (m) [debair] to have to; to owe; duty

deberes mpl [debair-es] homework

débil weak

decepción f [deseps-yon] disappointment

decepcionado [deseps-yonado] disappointed

decidir [deseedeer] to decide

décimo [deseemo] tenth

decir [deseer] to say; to tell

declaración f [deklaras-yon] declaration; statement

declarar to declare, to state

dedo m finger

dedo del pie [p-yeh] toe

defectuoso [defektwoso] faulty

dejar [deh-Har] to leave; to let

dejar de beber [deh bebair] to stop drinking

delante de [delanteh] in front of

delantera f [delantaira] front (part)

delantero front; foward

la parte delantera [parteh] the front (part)

Delegación de Servicios Migratorios f Immigration Department

demás: los demás the others, the rest

demasiado [demas-yado] too much

demasiados too many

democracia f [demokras-ya] democracy

demora **f** delay

demorar: ¿cuánto demora? [kwanto] how long does it take?

dentadura postiza **f** [posteesa] dentures

dentista **m/f** dentist

dentro (de) [deh] inside

dentro de dos semanas in two weeks' time

dentro de poco soon

departamento **m** apartment

departamento amueblado [amweblado] furnished apartment

departamento sin amueblar [amweblar] unfurnished apartment

depende [dependeh] it depends

dependienta **f** [–yenta], dependiente **m** [–yenteh] shop assistant

deporte **m** [deporteh] sport

deportista **m/f** sportsman/ sportswoman

deportivo [deporteebo] sports

deportivos **mpl** trainers

depósito **m** tank; deposit

deprimido depressed

derecha **f** right

a la derecha (de) on the right (of)

derecho: todo derecho straight ahead

derribar to pull down, to demolish

derrota **f** defeat

desacuerdo **m** [desakwairdo] disagreement

desagradable [–dableh] unpleasant

desaparecer [–resair] to disappear

desaparecido **m** victim of illegal arrest

desarmador **m** screwdriver

desastre **m** [desastreh] disaster

desayunar [desī-yoonar] to have breakfast

desayuno **m** [desī-yoono] breakfast

descansar to rest

descanso **m** interval

descarado cheeky

descarrilarse to be derailed

descolgar el aparato lift receiver

descomponerse [deskomponairseh] to break down

descompostura breakdown, mechanical problem

descompuesto [deskompwesto] broken; broken down

descubierto [deskoob-yairto] discovered; uncovered

descubrir to discover; to uncover

descuelgue el auricular lift the receiver

descuento [deskwento] discount

descuidado [deskweedado] careless

¡descuide! [deskweedeh] don't worry about it!

desde [desdeh] since

desde luego [lwego] of course

desde que [keh] since

desear [deseh-**ar**] to want; to wish

¿qué desea? [keh des**eh**-a] what can I do for you?

desembarcadero m [desembarkad**ai**ro] quay

desempleado (m) [desempleh-**a**do] unemployed person; unemployed

desempleo m [desempl**eh**-o] unemployment

desfile m [desf**ee**leh] procession

desfile de modas fashion show

desgracia: por desgracia [desgr**a**s-ya] unfortunately

desgraciadamente [–d**a**menteh] unfortunately

deshacer las maletas [des-as**air**] to unpack

desierto m [des-y**ai**rto] desert

desinfectante m [–t**a**nteh] disinfectant

desmadre m [desm**a**dreh] chaos; mess

¡qué desmadre! [keh desm**a**dreh] what a bloody mess!

desmaquillarse [desmakee-y**a**rseh] to remove one's make-up

desmayarse [desmī-y**a**rseh] to faint

desnudo naked

desnutrición f [desnootrees-y**o**n] malnutrition

desobediente [desobed-y**e**nteh] disobedient

desodorante m [–r**a**nteh] deodorant

desordenado untidy

desorientarse [desor-yent**a**rseh] to lose one's way

despachador automático m [owtom**a**teeka] ticket machine

despacho de petróleo m [deh petr**o**leh-o] store selling paraffin and oil for heating

despacio [desp**a**s-yo] slowly

despedida f farewell

despedirse [desped**ee**rseh] to say goodbye

despegar to take off

despegue m [desp**eh**-geh] take-off

despejado [despe**н**ado] clear

despertador m [despairtad**o**r] alarm clock

despertar to wake

despertarse [–t**a**rseh] to wake up

despierto [desp-y**ai**rto] awake

desprendimiento de terreno danger: landslides

despreocupado [despreh-okoop**a**do] thoughtless

después [despw**es**] afterwards

después de [deh] after

destinatario m addressee

destino m destination

el avión con destino a ... the plane for ...

destornillador m [destornee-yad**o**r] screwdriver

destruir [destrw**ee**r] to destroy

desvestirse [desbest**ee**rseh] to undress

desviación f [desb-yas-y**o**n] diversion

desvío m [desbee-o] detour, diversion

desvío provisional temporary diversion

detener [detenair] to arrest; to stop

detergente en polvo m [detairHenteh] washing powder

detergente lavavajillas [lababaHee-yas] washing-up liquid

detrás (de) [deh] behind

devolver [debolbair] to give back; to vomit

D.F. m [deh efeh] Mexico City

di I gave; tell me

día m [dee-a] day

día de Año Nuevo [deh an-yo nwebo] New Year's Day

Día de los Muertos [deh los mwairtos] Day of the Dead, All Souls' Day

día feriado [fer-yado] public holiday

diamante m [d-yamanteh] diamond

diapositiva f [d-yaposeeteeba] slide

diario (m) [d-yar-yo] diary; daily newspaper; daily

diarrea f [d-yarreh-a] diarrhoea

días feriados public holidays

días laborables [laborab-les] weekdays; working days

dibujar [deebooHar] to draw

dibujos animados mpl [deebooHos] cartoons

diccionario m [deeks-yonar-yo] dictionary

dice [deeseh] he/she says; you say

dicho [deecho] said

diciembre m [dees-yembreh] December

diecinueve [d-yeseenwebeh] nineteen

dieciocho [d-yesee-ocho] eighteen

dieciséis [d-yeseesays] sixteen

diecisiete [d-yesees-yeteh] seventeen

diente m [d-yenteh] tooth

dieron [d-yairon] they gave; you gave

diesel m [deesel] diesel

dieta f [d-yeta] diet

a dieta on a diet

diez [d-yes] ten

difícil [deefeeseel] difficult

dificultad f [deefeekoolta] difficulty

diga tell me

digo I say

dije [deeHeh] I said

dijeron [deeHairon] they said; you said

dijiste [deeHeesteh] you said

dijo [deeHo] he/she said; you said

¿qué dijo? what did you say?; what did he/she say?

dilatar to delay; to be late

diminuto tiny

Dinamarca f Denmark

dinero m [deenairo] money

Dios m [d-yos] God

¡Dios mío! [mee-o] my God!

dirección f [deereks-yon]

direction; address; steering; management

director m, directora f manager; director; headteacher

directorio m telephone directory

dirigir [deereeHeer] to direct; to lead

disco m record

disconformidad f [deeskonformeeda] disagreement

discoteca f record shop; disco

disculparse [deeskoolparseh] to apologize

disculpe [deeskoolpeh] excuse me

disculpen las molestias we apologize for any inconvenience

discurso m speech

discusión f [deeskoos-yon] discussion; argument

discutir to argue

diseñador de modas m [deesen-yador deh] fashion designer

disimular [deeseemoolar] to pretend

disqueta f [deesketa] diskette

distancia f [deestans-ya] distance

distinto different

distraído [deestra-eedo] absent-minded; distracted

distribuidor m [deestreebweedor] distributor

Distrito Federal m [fedairal] Federal District, Mexico City

distrito postal m postcode, zip code

disuélvase en agua dissolve in water

divertido [deebairteedo] entertaining; funny

divertirse [deebairteerseh] to have a good time

divisas fpl [deebeesas] foreign currency

divorciado [deebors-yado] divorced

divorciarse [deebors-yarseh] to divorce

divorcio m [deebors-yo] divorce

divulgar [deeboolgar] to publicize

doble [dobleh] double

doble sentido two-way

doce [doseh] twelve

docena (de) f [dosena] dozen

dólar m dollar

doler [dolair] to hurt

dolor m pain

dolor de garganta [deh] sore throat

dolor de cabeza [kabesa] headache

dolor de muelas [mwelas] toothache

dolor de oídos [o-eedos] earache

doloroso painful

domicilio m [domeeseel-yo] place of residence

domingo m Sunday

domingos y feriados Sundays and public holidays

donativa f donations

donde [**don**deh] where

¿dónde? where?

dorado (m) gold, golden; type of fish

dormido asleep

dormir to sleep

dormitorio m [dormee**to**r-yo] bedroom; dormitory

dos two

doscientos [dos-**y**entos] two hundred

doy I give

droga f drug

drogadicto m [drogad**eek**to] drug addict

drogado in debt

drogarse [dro**gar**seh] to take drugs; to get into debt

droguería f [drogair**ee**-a] drugstore

ducha f shower

ducharse [doo**char**seh] to have a shower

dudar to doubt; to hesitate

duele [**dweh**leh] it hurts

dulce [**dool**seh] sweet; gentle

dulces mpl [**dool**s-es] sweets, candies

dunas fpl sand dunes

durante [doo**ran**teh] during

Durex® m Sellotape®, Scotch tape®

duro hard

E

Do

E parking

e [eh] and

echar to throw; to throw away

echar a faltar to miss

echo de menos a mi ... [deh] I miss my ...

echar al buzón [boo**son**] to post, to mail

echar al correo [kor**reh**-o] to post, to mail

echar el cerrojo [sairro**Ho**] to bolt

echar sangre [**sang**reh] to bleed

echarse la siesta [e**char**seh] to have a nap

ecológico [ekolo**Hee**ko] ecological

ecologista m/f environmentalist, Green

economía f economy

económico cheap, inexpensive; economic; economical

ecuatoriano (m) [ekwator-**ya**no] Ecuadorean

edad f [**eda**] age

¿qué edad tienes? [keh – t-**yen**-es] how old are you?

edificio m [edee**fees**-yo] building

edredón m quilt, eiderdown; duvet

educado polite

EE.UU. (Estados Unidos) USA

efectivo: en efectivo [efek**tee**bo] in cash

eje m [**e**Heh] axle

eje del cigüeñal [seegwen-**yal**] crankshaft

ejemplo m [e**Hem**plo] example

por ejemplo for example

ejidatario m [eнeedatar-yo] member of an agricultural community

ejido m [eнeedo] communal land

el the

él he; him

elástico elastic

elecciones fpl [eleks-yon-es] elections

electricidad f [elektreeseeda] electricity

electricista m [elektreeseesta] electrician

eléctrico electric

electrodomésticos mpl electrical appliances

elegir [eleh-нeer] to choose

ella [eh-ya] she; her

ellas [eh-yas] they; them

ellos [eh-yos] they; them

embajada f [embaнada] embassy

embalse m [embalseh] reservoir

embarazada [embarasada] pregnant

embotellamiento m [emboteh-yam-yento] traffic jam

embrague m [embrageh] clutch

emergencia f [emairнens-ya] emergency

emisión f [emees-yon] programme; emission; distribution date; issue

emocionante [emos-yonanteh] exciting

empacar to pack

empalme m [empalmeh] junction

empaquetado m [empaketado] packing

empaste m [empasteh] filling

empeorar [empeh-orar] to get worse

empezar [empesar] to begin

empieza a las ocho [emp-yesa] it starts at eight

empinado steep

empleada f [empleh-ada], empleado m white collar worker, employee

empresa f firm, enterprise

empresario m businessman

empujar [empooнar] to push

en in; at; on; by

enamorados: día de los enamorados m [dee-a deh] St Valentine's Day

encantado delighted

¡encantado! pleased to meet you!

encantador lovely

encantar to please

encendedor m [ensendedor] lighter

encerrar [ensairrar] to lock in; to lock up

enchufe m [enchoofeh] plug; socket

encima [enseema] above

encima de [deh] on top of

encontrar to find

encontrarse (con/a) [–trarseh] to meet

encuentra: se encuentra [seh enkwentra] is located

encuentro (m) [enkwentro] meeting, encounter; I find

endrogarse [–garseh] to get into debt

enemigo m enemy

enero m [enairo] January

enfermarse [–marseh] to become ill, to get sick

enfermedad f [enfairmeda] disease

enfermedad venérea [benaireh-a] VD

enfermera f [enfairmaira], enfermero m nurse

enfermo [enfairmo] ill, sick

enfrente de [enfrenteh deh] opposite

enganche [engancheh] deposit

engañar [engan-yar] to cheat; to trick

enmicado m [enmeekado] plastic covering (for documents)

enojado [enoHado] angry

enojarse [–Harseh] to get angry

enorme [enormeh] enormous

enseñar [ensen-yar] to teach

entender [entendair] to understand
no entiendo I don't understand

entero [entairo] whole; in one piece

entiendo [ent-yendo] I understand

entierro m [ent-yairro] funeral

entonces [entons-es] then; therefore

entrada f entrance, way in; ticket

entrada gratis admission free

entrada libre [leebreh]
admission free

entrar to go in, to enter

entre [entreh] among; between

entretanto meanwhile

entrevista f [entrebeesta] interview

enviar [emb-yar] to send

envolver [embolbair] to wrap up; to involve

equipaje m [ekeepaHeh] luggage, baggage

equipaje de mano [deh] hand luggage

equipajes mpl [ekeepaH-es] left-luggage office, (US) baggage check

equipo m [ekeepo] team; equipment, tools

equivocado [ekeebokado] wrong

equivocarse [ekeebokarseh] to make a mistake

equivocarse de número [deh noomairo] to dial the wrong number

era [aira] I/he/she/it was; you were

éramos [airamos] we were

eran [airan] they were; you were

eras [airas] you were

eres [air-es] you are

erupción f [airoops-yon] rash; eruption

es he is; you are

esa that

ésa that (one)

esas those

ésas those (ones)

escala f intermediate stop; scale; ladder

escalera automática f escalator

escaleras fpl stairs

escarcha f frost

escayola f [eskī-yola] plaster cast

escocés [eskos-es] Scottish

Escocia f [eskos-ya] Scotland

escoger [eskoHair] to choose

esconder [eskondair] to hide

escorpión m [eskorp-yon] scorpion

escribir to write

escrito written

por escrito in writing

escritura f deed; document

escuchar to hear

escuela f [eskwela] school

escuela de párvulos [deh parboolos] kindergarten

escuincle m/f [eskweenkleh] kid, nipper; runt

escurrir a mano to wring by hand

ese [eseh] that

ése that (one)

esencial [esens-yal] essential

esfuerzo m [esfwairso] effort

esmalte de uñas m [esmalteh deh oon-yas] nail polish

esmeralda f emerald

eso that

eso es that's it, that's right

esos those

ésos those (ones)

espalda f back

espantoso dreadful; frightening

España f [espan-ya] Spain

español (m) [espan-yol], española (f) Spanish; Spaniard

especialista m/f [espes-yaleesta] specialist

especialmente [espes-yalmenteh] especially

espectáculo m show, spectacle

espejo m [espeHo] mirror

esperar [espairar] to wait; to hope

espere [espaireh] please wait

¡espéreme! [espairemeh] wait for me!

espero que sí I hope so

espeso thick

esponja f [esponHa] sponge

esposa f wife

esposo m husband

espuma de afeitar f [deh afaytar] shaving foam

esquí acuático [eskee akwateeko] waterski; waterskiing

esquina f [eskeena] corner

esta this

ésta this one

estación f [estas-yon] station; season

estacionamiento m [estas-yonam-yento] car park, parking lot

estacionamiento limitado restricted parking

estacionamiento privado private parking

estacionamiento reservado this parking place reserved

estacionamiento subterráneo underground parking

estacionamiento vigilado
supervised parking

estacionarse [estas-yonarseh]
to park

estación de autobuses [deh
owtoboos-es] bus station

estación de ferrocarril train
station

estación de servicio [sairbees-
yo] service station

estadio de fútbol m [estad-yo
deh] football stadium

Estados Unidos mpl [ooneedos]
United States

estallar [esta-yar] to explode

estampilla f [estampee-ya] stamp

estaño m [estan-yo] tin; pewter

estar to be

estas these

éstas these ones

estatua f [estatwa] statue

este m [esteh] east

este this

éste this (one)

esterilizado [estaireeleesado]
sterilized

esto this

estómago m stomach

estornudar to sneeze

estos these

éstos these (ones)

estoy I am

estrecho narrow; tight

estrella f [estreh-ya] star

estrellarse contra [estreh-yarseh]
to run into; to crash into

estreno m new film/movie
release

estreñido [estren-yeedo]

constipated

estreñimiento m [estren-yeem-
yento] constipation

estropear [estropeh-ar] to
damage

estudiante m/f [estood-yanteh]
student

estudiar [estood-yar] to study

estupefaciente m [−fas-yenteh]
hallucinogenic drug

estupendo wonderful, great

estúpido stupid

etiqueta f [eteeketa] label

... de etiqueta [deh] formal ...

europeo [eh-ooropeh-o]
European

evidente [ebeedenteh] obvious

exactamente [−menteh] exactly

¡exacto! exactly!

excelente [eselenteh] excellent

excepto [esepto] except

excepto domingos y feriados
except Sundays and holidays

excepto sábados except
Saturdays

exceso de equipaje m [eseso
deh ekeepaнeh] excess baggage

exceso de velocidad [beloseeda]
speeding

excursión f [eskoors-yon] trip

excusados mpl [eskoosados]
toilets, rest rooms

expedir [espedeer] to despatch

expendio m [ekspend-yo] stall;
kiosk; shop, store

explicación f [espleekas-yon]
explanation

explicar to explain

exportación f [esportas-yon]

export

exposición f [esposees-**yon**] exhibition

exprés m [espres] fast train; special delivery

exterior (m) [estair-**yor**] exterior, outer; foreign; overseas

Secretaría de Asuntos Exteriores Ministry of Foreign Affairs

extintor (de incendios) m [deh eensend-yos] fire extinguisher

extra four-star petrol, (US) premium gas

extranjera (f) [estranHaira], **extranjero** (m) [estranHairo] foreign; foreigner

en el extranjero abroad, overseas

extrañar [estranyar] to miss

extraño [estran-yo] strange

F

fábrica f factory

fabricado por ... made by ...

fácil [faseel] easy

facilidad: con facilidades payment by instalments

factura f bill, (US) check; invoice

facturación f [faktooras-yon] check-in

facturar el equipaje [ekeepaHeh] to check in luggage/baggage

falda f skirt; hillside

fallar [fa-yar] to fail; to break down

falso false

falta f lack; mistake; defect; fault

no hace falta ... [aseh] it's not necessary to ...

faltaba más don't mention it

falta de visibilidad poor visibility

faltar to be missing; to be absent

faltan tres there are three missing

faltan seis kilómetros para llegar there are six kilometres to go before we get there

¿cuánto falta (para) ...? how much further is it (to) ...?

echar a faltar to miss

familia f [fameel-ya] family

famoso famous

farmacia f [farmas-ya] chemist's, pharmacy

farmacia de turno [deh toorno] emergency chemist's/ pharmacy, duty chemist

faro m light; headlight; lighthouse

faro antiniebla [anteen-yebla] fog lamp

favor: a favor de [fabor deh] in favour of

por favor please

si hace favor [aseh] if you don't mind

fayuca f [fi-yooka] contraband goods

fayuquero m [fi-yookairo] seller of contraband goods

febrero m [febrairo] February

fecha f date

fecha de caducación, fecha de caducidad expiry date

fecha de nacimiento [deh naseem-yento] date of birth

fecha límite de venta sell-by date

¡Felices Pascuas y Próspero Año Nuevo! [felees-es paskwas ee prospairo an-yo nwebo] Merry Christmas and a Happy New Year!

felicidad f [feleeseeda] happiness

¡felicidades! [feleeseedad-es] happy birthday!; congratulations!

felicitar [feleeseetar] to congratulate

feliz [felees] happy

¡feliz cumpleaños! [koompleh-an-yos] happy birthday!

feo [feh-o] ugly

feria f [fair-ya] fair; loose change

feriado: días feriados [fair-yados] public holidays

ferretería f [fairretairee-a] hardware store

ferrocarril m railway, railroad

festividad f [festeebeeda] celebration

festivos bank holidays, public holidays

fibras naturales natural fibres

fiebre f [f-yebreh] fever; high temperature

fiebre del heno [eno] hay fever

fierro m [f-yairo] iron

fiesta f public holiday; party

fiesta de ... [deh] feast of ...

fila f row

fila india single file

filmar [feelmar] to film

filtro m filter

filtro solar sunblock

fin m [feen] end; purpose

por fin at last, finally

a fin de que [deh keh] so that

final m [feenal] end

final de autopista end of motorway/highway

fin de semana [deh] weekend

fin de serie discontinued articles

fingir [feenHeer] to pretend

fino fine; delicate

firma f signature; company

firmar to sign

flaco thin, skinny

flequillo m [flekee-yo] fringe

flete m [fleteh] carriage, transport cost

flojera: me da flojera [floHaira] I can't be bothered

flojo [floHo] lazy

flor f flower

florería f [florairee-a] florist

florero m [florairo] vase

flotadores mpl lifebelts

flotar to float

FMT [efemeteh] tourist card

foco m light bulb

folleto m [fo-yeto] pamphlet

Folleto de Migración Turística [deh meegras-yon] tourist card

fonda f simple restaurant; boarding house

fondo m bottom; background
al fondo (de) at the bottom
(of)
fondos mpl funds, money
fontanero m [fontanairo]
plumber
footing m jogging
forma f form
en forma fit
fósforo m match
foto f photograph
sacar fotos to take
photographs
fotografía f photograph;
photography
fotografiar [fotograf-yar] to
photograph
fotógrafo m photographer
fotómetro m light meter
fraccionamiento m [fraks-yonam-
yento] housing estate
francamente [–menteh] frankly
francés [frans-es] French
Francia f [frans-ya] France
franqueado [frankeh-ado]
franked
franqueo m [frankeh-o] postage
frazada f [frasada] blanket, rug
frecuencia: con frecuencia
[frekwens-ya] often
fregadero m [fregadairo] sink
fregar to keep on at; to annoy
fregarlo to screw up
fregar los platos to do the
washing up
freír [freh-eer] to fry
frenar to brake
freno m brake
freno de mano [deh] handbrake

frente f [frenteh] forehead
hacer frente a ... [asair] to face
up to ...
fresco fresh
frigorífico m fridge
frío [free-o] cold
hace frío [aseh] it's cold
frontera f [frontaira] border
la Frontera the Mexican-US
border
frutería f [frootairee-a] fruit
shop; greengrocer's
fue [fweh] he/she/it went;
he/she/it was; you went; you
were
fuego m [fwego] fire
¿tiene fuego? have you got a
light?
fuegos artificiales [arteefees-yal-
es] fireworks
fuente f [fwenteh] fountain;
source; font
fuera [fwaira] outside; he/she/it
was; he/she/it went; you
were; you went
fuera de [deh] apart from
fuera de horas pico off-peak
hours
fuera de servicio [deh sairbees-
yo] out of order
fuéramos [fwairamos] we were;
we went
fueran [fwairan] they were;
they went; you were; you
went
fueron [fwairon] they were;
they went; you were; you
went
fuerte [fwairteh] strong; loud

fuerza f [fwairsa] force; strength

fui [fwee] I was; I went

fuimos [fweemos] we were; we went

fuiste [fweesteh] you were; you went

fumadores [foomador-es] smoking

fumar to smoke

funcionar [foons-yonar] to work

funcionario m [foons-yonar-yo] civil servant

función de noche late showing

función de tarde early showing

funeraria f [foonairar-ya] undertaker's

funicular m [fooneekoolar] cable car

furioso [foor-yoso] furious

furúnculo m abscess; boil

fusible m [fooseebleh] fuse

fútbol m football

futuro (m) [footooro] future

G

gachupín m [gachoopeen] Spaniard

gafas fpl glasses, (US) eyeglasses

gafas de bucear [deh booseh-ar] goggles

gafas de sol sunglasses

galería f [galairee-a] gallery; enclosed balcony

galería de arte [deh arteh] art gallery

Gales m [gal-es] Wales

galés [gal-es] Welsh

gama: toda la gama the whole range

gamuza f [gamoosa] suede

ganadería f [–dairee-a] cattle farming

ganadero m [–dairo] (cattle) rancher

ganado m cattle

ganar to win; to earn

ganga f bargain

ganso m goose

garaje m [garaHeh] garage

garantía f guarantee

garantizar [–teesar] to guarantee

garganta f throat

gasolina f petrol, (US) gas

gasolina normal two-star petrol, (US) regular (gas)

gasolina super [soopair] four-star petrol, (US) premium (gas)

gasolinera f [gasoleenaira] petrol/gas station, filling station

gastar to spend

gato m cat; jack

gemelos mpl [Hemelos] twins; cufflinks

general: por lo general [Henairal] usually

en general generally, in general

genio m [Hen-yo] genius

gente f [Henteh] people

una gente a person

gerente m/f [Hairenteh] manager; manageress

gestionar [Hest-yonar] to

negotiate

gimnasia f [Heemnas-ya] gymnastics

gimnasio m gymnasium

ginecólogo m [Heenekologo] gynaecologist

gira f [Heera] tour

girar [Heerar] to turn

 gire a la izquierda [Heereh] turn left

giro [Heero] money order

gis m [Hees] chalk

gitano m [Heetano] gypsy

globo m balloon

glorieta f [glor-yeta] roundabout

gobierno m [gob-yairno] government

gol m goal

Golfo (de México) m Gulf of Mexico

golpe m [golpeh] blow

 de golpe all of a sudden

golpear [golpeh-ar] to hit; to beat up

golpiza f [golpeesa] beating

goma f glue

gomita f rubber band

gordo fat

gorra f cap

gorro m bonnet, cap

gorro de baño [deh ban-yo] bathing cap

gorro de ducha shower cap

gota f drop

gotera f [gotaira] leak

gozar [gosar] to enjoy

grabadora f tape recorder

gracias [gras-yas] thank you

gracias a Usted [oosteh] thank

you (more emphatic)

gracioso [gras-yoso] funny

grado m degree

grafitos mpl graffiti

gramática f grammar

gramo m gramme

Gran Bretaña f [bretan-ya] Great Britain

grande [grandeh] big, large; old

grandes almacenes mpl [grand-es almasen-es] large department store

granizo m [graneeso] hail

granja f [granHa] farm

granjero m [granHairo] farmer

grano m grain; spot

grapa f paper clip

grasa f fat

grasiento [gras-yento] greasy

grasoso greasy

gratis free

grave [grabeh] serious; very ill/sick

gravilla loose chippings

Grecia f [gres-ya] Greece

gremio m trade union

grifo m tap, (US) faucet

gripe f [greepeh] flu

gris grey

gritar to shout

Grito: el Grito the Declaration of Independence by Miguel Hidalgo on 16 Sept 1810, repeated by the President every Independence Day

grosería [grosairee-a] swearword, oath

 decir groserías [deseer] to swear

grosero [grosairo] rude
grúa f [groo-a] tow truck,
  breakdown lorry; crane
grueso [grweso] thick
grupo m group
grupo sanguíneo [sangeeneh-o]
  blood group
guacamayo m [gwakamī-yo]
  parrot
guajolote m [gwaнoloteh] turkey
guante m [gwanteh] glove
guapo [gwapo] handsome
guardacostas m/f [gwardakostas]
  coastguard
guardar [gwardar] to keep; to
  put away
guardarropa m [gwardarropa]
  cloakroom, (US) checkroom
guardería (infantil) f [gwar-dairee-
  a (infanteel)] crèche; nursery
  school
guárdese en lugar fresco keep
  in a cool place
guardia m/f [gward-ya] guard
guarura m/f [gwaroora] thug,
  hood
guata f [gwata] belly
guatemalteco (m) [gwatemalteko]
  Guatemalan
guayabera f [gwī-yabaira]
  embroidered shirt
güero [gwairo] blond, light
  skinned
guerra f [gairra] war
guerra civil civil war
guía m/f [gee-a] guide
guía telefónica f phone book,
  telephone directory
guía turístico m tourist guide

guisar [geesar] to cook
guitarra f [geetarra] guitar
gusano m worm
gustar to please
  me gusta ... [meh] I like ..
  (si) gusta pasar would you
  like to go in?
  me gustaría ... I'd like to ...
gusto: mucho gusto [moocho]
  pleased to meet you
  con mucho gusto certainly,
  with great pleasure
  el gusto es mío how do you
  do; it is a pleasure
  ¡qué gusto de verte! [keh – deh
  bairteh] it's good to see you!

H

h is not pronounced in Spanish

ha he/she/it has; you have
hábil [abeel] skilful
  días hábiles working days
habitante m/f [abeetanteh]
  inhabitant
habitar to live
hablador talkative
hablar to speak
hable aquí speak here
habrá there will be; he/she/it
  will have; you will have
habrán they will have; you
  will have
habrás you will have
habré [abreh] I will have
habremos we will have
habría [abree-a] I would have;

he/she/it would have; you
  would have
habríamos [abree-amos] we
  would have
habrían [abree-an] they would
  have; you would have
habrías [abree-as] you would
  have
hacer [asair] to make; to do
  hace tres días [aseh] three
  days ago
  hace calor/sol it is hot/sunny
  se me hace que ... [seh meh
  – keh] I believe that ...
  no le hace [leh] don't worry
  about it
  ¿cuánto se hace de México
  a Veracruz? how long does
  it take from Mexico to
  Veracruz?
hacerse [asairseh] to
  become
hacia [as-ya] towards
haga: ¡hágalo ahora! do it
  now!
hago I do; I make
hallar [a-yar] to find
hamaca f [amaka] hammock
hambre: tengo hambre
  [ambreh] I'm hungry
han they have; you have
haré [areh] I will do
harto full, stuffed
  estar harto de (de) [deh] to be fed
  up (with)
  es harto difícil [deefeeseel] it's
  very difficult
has you have
hasta even; until

hasta que [keh] until
hasta luego [lwego] goodbye,
  cheerio, see you later
¡hasta mañana! [man-yana] see
  you tomorrow!
¡hasta pronto! see you soon!
hay [i] there is; there are
haz [as] do; make
  ¡hazlo tú! you do it!
he [eh] I have
hecho (m) made; done; fact
hecho a la medida made-to-
  measure
helada f frost
heladería f [eladairee-a] ice-
  cream parlour
helado m ice cream
helar to freeze
hembra f female
hemos we have
henequén m [eneken] sisal-type
  fibre from the henequen
  plant, used for making rope
  and fabrics
herida f [aireeda] wound
herido injured
hermana f [airmana] sister
hermano m [airmano] brother
hermoso [airmoso] beautiful
herramientas fpl [airram-yentas]
  tools
hervir [airbeer] to boil
hice [eeseh] I made; I did
hidratante: crema hidratante f
  [eedratanteh] moisturizer
hielo m [yelo] ice
hierba f [yairba] grass
hierro m [yairro] iron
hija f [eeHa] daughter

h is not pronounced in Spanish

hijo m [eeHo] son

¡hijo de la chingada! son of a bitch!

¡híjole! [eeHoleh] hell!, damn!

hilo m thread

hipermercado [eepairmairkado] hypermarket

hipo m hiccups

hipódromo m horse-racing track

historia f [eestor-ya] history; story

hizo [eeso] he/she made; he/ she did; you made; you did

hogar m home; household goods

hoja f [oHa] leaf; sheet of paper

hoja de afeitar [deh afaytar] razor blade

hojalata f [oHalata] tin plate

¡hola! hello!, hi!

hombre m [ombreh] man

hombre de negocios [deh negos-yos] businessman

hombro m shoulder

hondo deep

hondureño (m) [ondooren-yo] Honduran

honrado honest

hora f hour

¿qué hora es/qué hora tiene/ me da su hora? what time is it?

hora local local time

horario m [orar-yo] timetable, (US) schedule

horario de camiones [deh kam-

yon-es] bus timetable/schedule

horario de invierno [eemb-yairno] winter timetable/ schedule

horario de recogidas [rekoHeedas] collection times

horario de trenes [tren-es] train timetable/schedule

horario de verano [bairano] summer timetable/schedule

horas de consulta surgery hours, (US) office hours

horas de oficina [ofeeseena] opening hours

horas de visita [beeseeta] visiting hours

horas pico rush hour

hormiga f ant

horno m oven

horquilla m [orkee-ya] hairslide, hairpin

hospedarse [ospedarseh] to stay

hotel-garaje m [–garaHeh] hotel where rooms are rented by the hour

hoy [oy] today

hoyo m [o-yo] hole

huaraches mpl [warach-es] leather sandals

hube [oobeh] I had

hubieron [oob-yairon] they had; you had

hubimos [oobeemos] we had

hubiste [oobeesteh] you had

hubo [oobo] he/she/it had; you had; there was/were

húbole: ¿qué húbole? [keh ooboleh] how's it going?

huele: huele a ... [weleh] it

smells of ...

huelga f [welga] strike

huella f [weya] print; trace

huellas digitales [deeHeetal-es] fingerprints

hueso m [weso] bone; stone (of fruit etc)

huésped m/f [wesped] guest

huipil m [weepil] short, embroidered blouse

hule m [ooleh] rubber

humedad f [oomeda] humidity, dampness

húmedo damp

humo m smoke

humor m humour

hundirse [oondeerseh] to sink

huracán m hurricane

I

idéntico (a/que) [keh] identical (to)

idioma m [eed-yoma] language

idiota m/f [eed-yota] idiot

iglesia f [eegles-ya] church

ignorar: ignoro si ... I don't know whether ...

igual [eegwal] equal; like

me da igual [meh] it's all the same to me

imbécil (m) [eembeseel] idiot; stupid

impaciente [eempas-yenteh] impatient

impactante [eempaktanteh] striking; shocking

impermeable (m) [eempairmeh-ableh] waterproof; raincoat

importación f [eemportas-yon] import; importing

artículos de importación imported goods

importante [eemportanteh] important

importar: no importa it doesn't matter

¿le importa si ...? [leh] do you mind if ...?

importe m [eemporteh] amount, sum

importe total total due

imposible [eemposeebleh] impossible

impreso m [eempreso] form

impuesto m [eempwesto] tax

incendiar [eensend-yar] to set fire to

incendio m [eensend-yo] fire (blaze)

incluido [eenkloo-eedo] included

incluso even

inconsciente [eenkons-yenteh] unconscious; unaware

increíble [eenkreh-eebleh] incredible

indemnizar [eendemneesar] to compensate

independiente [eendepend-yenteh] independent

indicaciones fpl [eendeekas-yon-es] instructions

indicador m indicator

indicador de nivel [deh neebel] gauge

indicar to indicate

indígena (m/f) [eendeeHena]

Indian; native inhabitant
indignado indignant
indispuesto [eendeespwesto]
  unwell
industria f industry; factory
infantil children's
infarto m heart attack
infección f [eenfeks-yon]
  infection
infectarse [eenfektarseh] to
  become infected
inflamado swollen
inflamarse [eenflamarseh] to
  swell
influenciar [eenflwens-yar] to
  influence
información f [eenformas-yon]
  information
información de vuelos flight
  information
información turística tourist
  information
información y turismo tourist
  information office
informar to inform
informarse (de/sobre)
  [–marseh (deh/sobreh)] to get
  information (on/about)
informe m [informeh] report
infracción f [eenfraks-yon]
  offence
ingeniero m [eenHen-yairo]
  engineer
Inglaterra f [eenglatairra]
  England
inglés (m) [eeng-les] English;
  Englishman
inglesa f Englishwoman
ingresar to enter

ingreso m [eengreso] income;
  entry
ingresos mpl income; deposits
iniciales fpl [eenees-yal-es]
  initials
inmediatamente [eenmed-
  yatamenteh] immediately
inocente [eenosenteh] innocent
inscribirse [–beerseh] to
  register, to enrol
insistir to insist
insolación f [eensolas-yon]
  sunstroke
instrucciones fpl [eenstrooks-
  yon-es] instructions
instrucciones de lavado
  washing instructions
íntegro [eentegro] complete;
  intact
inteligente [eenteleeHenteh]
  intelligent
intentar to try
interés m [eentair-es] interest
interesante [eentairesanteh]
  interesting
intereses mpl [eentaires-es]
  interest
interino: en el interino
  [eentaireeno] meanwhile
interior (m) [eentairee-or]
  interior, inner; domestic,
  home
intermedio (m) [eentairmed-
  yo] intermission, interval;
  intermediate
intermitente m [eentairmeetenteh]
  indicator
intérprete m/f [eentairpreteh]
  interpreter

interruptor m [eentairrooptor] switch

interurbano long-distance

intoxicación alimenticia f [eentokseekas-yon aleementees-ya] food poisoning

introduzca el dinero exacto insert exact amount

introduzca la tarjeta y marque insert card and dial

introduzca moneda insert coin

inundación f [eenoondas-yon] flood

inundar to flood

inútil useless, pointless

inversión f [eenbairs-yon] investment

invierno m [eemb-yairno] winter

invitada f [eembeetada], invitado m guest

invitar [eenbeetar] to invite

inyección f [een-yeks-yon] injection

ir [eer] to go

ir de paseo [deh paseh-o] to go for a walk

Irlanda f [eerlanda] Ireland

Irlanda del Norte [norteh] Northern Ireland

irlandés (m) [eerland-es] Irish; Irishman

irlandesa f Irishwoman

irse [eerseh] to leave, to go away

isla f [eesla] island

itinerario m [eeteenairar-yo] itinerary

IVA (impuesto sobre el valor añadido) [eeba] VAT

izq. (izquierda) left

izquierda f [eesk-yairda] left

a la izquierda (de) [deh] on the left (of)

J

jabón m [Habon] soap

jabón de afeitar [deh afaytar] shaving soap

jacal m [Hakal] straw hut; shack

jaiba f [Hiba] crab

jalar [Halar] to pull

jaliscense [Haleesenseh] from/ of Jalisco

jamás [Hamas] ever; never

jardín m [Hardeen] garden

jardín de niños [deh neen-yos] kindergarten

jardines públicos mpl [Hardeen-es] park, public gardens

jarocho [Harocho] from/of Veracruz

jarra f [Harra] jug

jarrón m [Harron] vase

jefe m [Hefeh] boss; chief

jefe de tren [deh] guard

jícara f [Heekara] gourd

joder [Hodair] to irritate, to annoy; to mess about; to screw up

¡lo jodiste! [Hodeesteh] you screwed up!

jodido [Hodeedo] annoying, a nuisance; knackered

jornada f [Hornada] working day

jorocho [Horocho] from/of

Veracruz
jorongo m [Horongo] poncho
joropo m [Horopo] dance from
  Veracruz
joven (m/f) [Hoben] young;
  young man; young woman
joyas fpl [Hoyas] jewellery
joyería f [Hoyairee-a] jewellery;
  jeweller's
jubilación f [Hoobeelas-yon]
  pension
jubilada f [Hoobeelada], **jubilado**
  m retired person, pensioner
jubilarse [Hoobeelarseh] to retire
judío [Hoodee-o] Jewish
juego (m) [Hwego] game; I play
  el juego gambling
jueves m [Hweb-es] Thursday
jugar [Hoogar] to play
jugos y licuados juices and
  milkshakes
juguete m [Hoogeteh] toy
juguetería f [Hoogetairee-a]
  toyshop
juicio m [Hwees-yo] judgement;
  opinion; trial
  llevar una persona al juicio to
  take someone to court
julio m [Hool-yo] July
junio m [Hoon-yo] June
juntar [Hoontar] to collect, to
  gather
junto (a) [Hoonto] next (to)
juntos together
justo [Hoosto] just; exact,
  precise
juventud f [Hoobentoo] youth;
  the young
juzgar [Hoosgar] to judge

K

kínder m [keendair]
  kindergarten
klaxon m [klakson] horn

L

la the; her; it
labios mpl [lab-yos] lips
laborables weekdays, working
  days
laca f hair spray
LADA national telephone
  system
Ladatel long-distance phone
lado m side
  al lado de [deh] beside, next
  to
ladrar to bark
ladridos mpl barking
ladrillo m [ladree-yo] tile
ladrón m thief
lagartija f [lagarteeHa] lizard
lagarto m alligator
lago m lake
lágrimas fpl tears
lámpara f lamp
lana f wool; money
lana pura pure wool
lanzar [lansar] to throw
lápiz m [lapees] pencil
lápiz de ojos [deh oHos] eyeliner
lapizlabios m [lapees-lab-yos]
  lipstick
larga distancia [deestans-ya]
  long-distance

largo (**m**) length; long
 a lo largo de [deh] along
¡lárguese! [lárgeseh] go away!
las the; them; you
 las que ... the ones that ...
lata **f** tin; can
 dar lata to be a nuisance
latinoamericana (**f**),
 latinoamericano (**m**) Latin
 American
latón **m** brass
lavabo **m** [lababo] washbasin
lavado **m** [labado] washing
lavado de carros [deh] carwash
lavadora **f** [labadora] washing
 machine
lavandería **f** [labandairee-a]
 laundry
lavandería automática
 [owtomateeka] launderette,
 laundromat
lavar [labar] to wash
lavar a mano wash by hand
lavar en seco dry clean
lavar la ropa to do the washing
lavarse [labarseh] to wash
 lavarse la cara to wash one's
 face
lavar separado wash separately
lavavajillas **m** [labababaHee-yas]
 dishwasher
laxante **m** [laksanteh] laxative
le [leh] him; her; you
lección **f** [leks-yon] lesson
leche limpiadora **f** [leemp-
 yadora] skin cleanser
lechería **f** [lechairee-a] dairy;
 dairy shop
lectura **f** [lektoora] reading

leer [leh-air] to read
lejano [leh-Hano] distant,
 faraway
lejía **f** [leHee-a] bleach
lejos [leHos] far away
 lejos de [deh] far from
lengua **f** [lengwa] tongue;
 language
lenguaje **m** [lengwaHeh]
 language
lentes de contacto **fpl** [lent-es
 deh] contact lenses
lentillas **fpl** [lentee-yas] contact
 lenses
lentillas blandas soft lenses
lentillas duras hard lenses
lentillas porosas gas permeable
 lenses
lento slow
les them; you
letra **f** letter; banker's draft
levantar [lebantar] to raise, to
 lift
levantarse [lebantarseh] to get up
ley **f** [lay] law
libra **f** [leebreh] pound
libre [leebreh] free; vacant
libre de impuestos [deh
 eempwestos] duty-free
librería **f** [leebrairee-a]
 bookshop, bookstore
librero **m** [leebrairo] bookshelves
libreta de ahorros **f** [deh a-orros]
 savings account book
libreta de direcciones [deereks-
 yon-es] address book
libro **m** book
libro de bolsillo [deh bolsee-yo]
 paperback

169

libro de frases [fras-es] phrasebook

licenciado m [leesens-yado] graduate

líder m [leedair] leader

liga f elastic band; suspender

ligero [leeHairo] light

lima de uñas f [deh oon-yas] nailfile

límite f [leemeeteh] limit

límite de altura maximum height

límite de peso weight limit

límite de velocidad [deh beloseedad] speed limit

limpiaparabrisas m [–breesas] windscreen wiper

limpiar [leemp-yar] to clean

limpieza f [leemp-yesa] cleanliness; cleaning

limpieza en seco dry-cleaning

limpio [leemp-yo] clean

lindo [leendo] beautiful, lovely

línea f [leeneh-a] line

linterna f [leentairna] torch

lío m [lee-o] mess

liquidación f [leekeedas-yon] sale; redundancy pay

liquidación total clearance sale

liso flat; plain; straight

lista f list

lista de correos [deh korreh-os] poste restante, (US) general delivery

lista de espera [espaira] standby; waiting list

listo clever; ready

litera f [leetaira] couchette

litro m litre

llamada f [yamada] call

llamada por cobrar reverse charge call

llamar [yamar] to call; to name

llamar por teléfono to call, to phone

llamarse [yamarseh] to be called

¿cómo te llamas? [teh yamas] what's your name?

llame a la puerta please knock

llame al timbre please ring

llame antes de entrar knock before entering

llamo: me llamo ... [meh yamo] my name is ...

llanos mpl [yanos] plains

llanta f [yanta] tyre, (US) tire

llantero m [yantairo] tyre repairs

llave f [yabeh] key; spanner, (US) wrench; tap, (US) faucet

llave inglesa [eenglesa] spanner, (US) wrench

llegada f [yegada] arrival

llegadas internacionales [eentairnas-yonal-es] international arrivals

llegadas nacionales [nas-yonal-es] domestic arrivals

llegar [yegar] to arrive; to get to

llegué [yegeh] I arrived

llenar [yenar] to fill

llenar el depósito to fill up

lleno [yeno] full

llevar [yebar] to carry; to take; to bring

llevo dos años trabajando aquí I've been working here for two years

llevar a juicio [Hwees-yo] to take to court

llevarse [yebarseh] to take away; to remove

llorar [yorar] to cry

llover [yobair] to rain

lloviendo: está lloviendo [yob-yendo] it's raining

llovizna f [yobeesna] drizzle

llueve [yweh-beh] it is raining

lluvia f [yoob-ya] rain

lo it; the

localidad f [lokaleeda] place; seat

localidades fpl [lokaleedad-es] ticket office

loción antimosquitos f [los-yon anteemoskeetos] insect repellent

loción bronceadora [bronseh-adora] suntan lotion

loción para después del afeitado [despwes del afaytado] aftershave

loco (m) mad; madman

locomotora f engine

locutor m [lokootor], **locutora f** television presenter

lodo m mud

loma f hill

lonchería f lunch counter

Londres [lond-res] London

longitud f [lonHeetoo] length

los the

los que ... the ones that ...

loza f [losa] crockery

luces de cruce [loos-es deh krooseh] dipped headlights

luces de posición fpl [posees-yon] sidelights

luces traseras [trasairas] rear lights

lucha f [loocha] fight, struggle

lucha libre [leebreh] all-in wrestling

luchar to fight

luego [lwego] then; afterwards; soon

luego luego right away, immediately

lugar m place

en lugar de [deh] instead of

lugar de veraneo [bairaneh-o] summer resort

lugares de interés [loogar-es deh eentair-es] places of interest

lujo m [looHo] luxury

lujoso [looHoso] luxurious

luna f moon

lunes m [loon-es] Monday

luto m mourning

luz f [loos] light

luz de carretera full beam

M

machista m male chauvinist, sexist

macho m male; large banana

machete m [macheteh] long, broad knife

madera f [madaira] wood

madrazo m [madraso] beating

madre f [madreh] mother

dar en la madre a uno to give someone a good beating

¡me vale madre! [meh baleh] I don't give a shit!

madrina f [madreena] godmother

madrugada f small hours

las cuatro de la madrugada four o'clock in the morning

madrugador m someone who stays up very late/gets up very early, early riser

madrugar to stay up very late; to get up very early

madurar to mature, to ripen; to come to term

maduro ripe

maestra f [ma-estra], **maestro m** teacher; primary school teacher

magna sin [seen] unleaded

maguey m [magay] agave cactus

maíz m [maees] maize, (US) corn

mal (m) wrong; evil; bad; badly

maleducado rude

malentendido m misunderstanding

maleta f suitcase

hacer las maletas to pack

maletero m [maletairo] boot (of car), (US) trunk

mal genio m [Hen-yo] bad temper

mal humor m [oomor] bad mood; bad temper; anger

Malinche f [maleencheh] Cortés' interpreter who later became his lover

malinchismo m betrayal of one's country

malo bad; sick, ill, unwell

mamá f mum

mamón! idiot!

manantial m [manant-yal] spring

mancha f stain

manchar to stain, to dirty

mandar to send; to order

mandatario: el primer mandatario [mandator-yo] leader; President; Prime Minister

mandato m period in government

¿mande? [mandeh] sorry?, pardon (me)?

mandíbula f jaw

manejar [maneHar] to drive

maneje con cuidado drive with care

manejo [maneHo] I drive

manera: de esta manera [deh – manaira] in this way

de manera que so (that)

manga f sleeve

sin manga sleeveless

manglar m mangrove swamp

mango m handle; mango

manifestación f [maneefestas-yon] demonstration; manifestation

mano f hand; pal, mate, buddy

manoplas fpl mittens

manta f blanket, rug

mantel m tablecloth

mantelerías fpl [mantelairee-as] table linen

mantenga limpia la ciudad keep our city tidy

manténgase en lugar fresco store in a cool place

manténgase fuera del alcance de los niños keep out of the reach of children

mantenimiento **m** [manteneem-yento] maintenance

manzana **f** [mansana] apple; city block

mañana (**f**) [man-yana] morning; tomorrow

por la mañana/de mañana in the morning

¡hasta mañana! see you tomorrow!

pasado mañana the day after tomorrow

mañana por la mañana tomorrow morning

mañana por la tarde [tardeh] tomorrow afternoon; tomorrow evening

mañanitas: cantar las mañanitas [man-yaneetas] to serenade someone for their birthday

mapa **m** map

mapa de carreteras [deh karretairas] road map

mapa de recorrido network map

maquiladora **f** [makeeladora] foreign-owned assembly plant located in Mexico

maquillaje **m** [makee-ya**H**eh] make-up

maquillarse [makee-yarseh] to put one's make-up on

máquina de afeitar eléctrica **f** [makeena deh afaytar] electric shaver

máquina de escribir typewriter

máquina de fotos camera

maquinaria **f** [makeenar-ya] machinery

máquina tragaperras slot machine

maquinilla de afeitar **f** [makeenee-ya deh afaytar] electric shaver

mar **m** sea

maravilloso [marabee-yoso] marvellous

marcar to dial; to mark

marca registrada **f** [re**H**eestrada] registered trade mark

marcar el número dial the number

marcha **f** gear

marcha atrás reverse gear

marcharse [marcharseh] to go away

marea **f** [mareh-a] tide

mareado [mareh-ado] dizzy; sick; drunk

mareo **m** [mareh-o] sickness; faintness

marica **m**, maricón **m** queer

marido **m** husband

marina **f** navy

mariposa **f** butterfly; fairy, pansy

marisquería **f** [mareeskairee-a] shellfish restaurant

marque ... dial ...

martes **m** [mart-es] Tuesday

martes de carnaval [deh karnabal] Shrove Tuesday

martillo **m** [martee-yo] hammer

marzo **m** [marso] March

173

más more
  más de/que [deh/keh] more than
  más pequeño smaller
  el más caro the most expensive
  ya no más that's enough
  más o menos more or less
matar to kill
matrícula f licence plate; registration; registration fees
máximo personas maximum number of people
maya (m/f) [mī-ya] Maya; Mayan
mayo m [mī-yo] May
mayor [mī-yor] adult; bigger; older; biggest; oldest
  la mayor parte (de) [parteh (deh)] most (of)
  mayor de edad of age (18), adult
mayoría: la mayoría [mī-yoree-a] most; the majority
me me; myself
  me duele aquí [dweleh] I have a pain here
mecánico m mechanic
mecate m [mekateh] string; rope; cord
media docena (de) f [med-ya dosena (deh)] half a dozen
media hora f [ora] half an hour
mediano [med-yano] medium; average
medianoche f [med-yanocheh] midnight
media pensión f [pens-yon] half board

medias fpl [med-yas] stockings; tights, pantyhose
  ir/pagar a medias to go Dutch, to share the costs
medicina f [medeeseena] medicine
médico m [medeeko] doctor
médico general [Henairal] GP
medida f size; measure
medida del cuello f [kweh-yo] collar size
medio m [med-yo] middle
  por medio de [deh] by (means of)
  de tamaño medio [taman-yo] medium-sized
medio boleto m half fare
mediodía m [med-yodee-a] midday
medio litro m half a litre
medir to measure
medusa f jellyfish
mejor [meHor] better; best
mejorar [meHorar] to improve
  se está mejorando [seh] he's getting better
mencionar [mens-yonar] to mention
menor smaller; younger; smallest; youngest
  menor de edad minor, under-age
menos less; least; fewer; fewest
  a menos que [keh] unless
mensual [menswal] monthly
mentar: mentarle la madre a uno [mentarleh la madreh] to insult someone, to swear at

someone

menú turístico m set menu

menudo tiny, minute

a menudo often

mercado m [mairkado] market

mercado cubierto [koob-yairto] indoor market

mercado de divisas [deh deebeesas] exchange rates

mercería f [mairsairee-a] haberdashery

merendar to have an afternoon snack

merendero m [mairendairo] open-air café

merienda f [mair-yenda] tea, afternoon snack

mero [mairo] exact; almost, nearly

ya mero any minute now, right away

el mero mero the big cheese

está aquí mero it's just near here

mes m month

mesa f table

mesera f [mesaira] waitress; chambermaid

mesero m waiter

mesón m restaurant specializing in regional dishes

mestizo [mesteeso] mixed race, interracial

meta f goal

metate m [metateh] mortar and pestle

metro m metre; underground, (US) subway

mexicana (f), [meHeekana]

mexicano (m) Mexican

México m [meHeeko] Mexico; Mexico City

mezquita f [meskeeta] mosque

mi my

mí me

mía [mee-a] mine

microondas: horno microondas [orno meekro-ondas] microwave oven

miedo m [m-yedo] fear

tengo miedo (de/a) [deh] I'm afraid (of)

miel f [m-yel] honey

mientras [m-yentras] while

mientras que [keh] whereas

mientras tanto meanwhile

miércoles m [m-yairkol-es] Wednesday

miércoles de ceniza [deh seneesa] Ash Wednesday

¡mierda! [m-yairda] shit!

mil [meel] thousand

militar m soldier, serviceman

millón m [mee-yon] million

un millón de ... [deh] a million ...

milpa f maize field

mina f mine

minifalda f mini-skirt

minúsculo tiny

minusválido (m) [meenoosbaleedo] disabled; disabled person

minuto m minute

mío [mee-o] mine

miope [m-yopeh] short-sighted

mirador m scenic view; vantage point

mirar to look (at); to see
mis my
misa f mass
mismo same
mitad f [meeta] half
mitad de precio [deh pres-yo] half price
mixteca (f) [meesteka] from/ of the Mixtec region; indigenous language of Southern Mexico
M.N. (moneda nacional) f national currency
mochila f rucksack
moda f fashion
  de moda fashionable
moda juvenil [Hoobeneel] young fashions
modas caballeros fpl [kaba-yairos] men's fashions
modas niños/niñas [neen-yos] children's fashions
modas pre-mamá maternity fashions
modas señora [sen-yora] ladies' fashions
modelo m model; design; style
moderno [modairno] modern
modista f dressmaker; fashion designer
modisto m fashion designer
modo: de modo que [deh – keh] so (that)
  ni modo that's how it is, what can you do?
modo de empleo instructions for use
mojado [moHado] wet
molcajete m [molkaHeteh]

mortar and pestle
moldeado con secador de mano [moldeh-ado – deh] blow-dry
molestar to disturb; to bother
molesto annoying
monasterio m [monastair-yo] monastery
moneda nacional f [nas-yonal] national currency
monedas fpl coins
monedero m [monedairo] purse
montacargas m service lift, service elevator
montaje m [montaHeh] assembly
montaña f [montan-ya] mountain
montaña rusa f big dipper, roller coaster
montañismo m [montan-yeesmo] climbing
montar to get in; to ride; to assemble
montar a caballo [kaba-yo] to go horse-riding
montar en bicicleta [beeseekleta] to cycle
morado purple
morbo m morbid interest
mordedura f bite
morder [mordair] to bite
mordida f bribe
moreno dark-haired; dark-skinned
moretón m bruise
morir to die
mosca f fly
mostrador m counter
mostrar to show

motel-garaje m [garaHeh] hotel where rooms are rented by the hour

moto f motorbike

motora f motorboat

mover [mobair] to move

mucha [moocha] much; a lot; a lot of

muchacha f girl

muchacho m boy

muchas a lot; a lot of; many

muchas gracias [gras-yas] thank you very much

muchísimas gracias thank you very much indeed

muchísimo enormously, a great deal

mucho [moochos] much; a lot; a lot of

  mucho más a lot more

  mucho menos a lot less

  mucho gusto a pleasure to meet you

muchos a lot; a lot of; many

muebles mpl [mwebl-es] furniture

muela f [mwela] tooth

  sacarse una muela [sakarseh] to have a tooth taken out

muela del juicio [Hwees-yo] wisdom tooth

muelle m [mweh-yeh] spring; quay

muerte f [mwairteh] death

muerto (m) [mwairto] dead; dead person

mugriento [moogr-yento] filthy

mujer f [mooHair] woman; wife

muletas fpl crutches

multa f fine; parking ticket

multa por uso indebido penalty for misuse

mundo m world

muñeca f [moon-yeka] wrist; doll

muro m wall

músculo m muscle

museo m [mooseh-o] museum

museo de arte [deh arteh] art gallery

música f music

muslo m thigh

musulmán Muslim

muy [mwee] very

  muy bien [b-yen] very well

N

N$ m new peso

nácar m mother-of-pearl

nacer [nasair] to be born

nacido [naseedo] born

nacimiento m [naseem-yento] birth; Nativity

nacional [nas-yonal] domestic

  el turismo nacional Mexican tourism, local tourism

nacionalidad f [nas-yonaleeda] nationality

nacionalismo m [nas-yonaleesmo] nationalism

nacionalización f [nas-yonaleesas-yon] nationalization

nada nothing

  de nada [deh] you're welcome, don't mention it

  antes que nada [ant-es keh]

first of all

nada que declarar nothing to declare

nadar to swim

nadie [nad-yeh] nobody

náhuatl (**m**) [nawatl] Aztec; language of the Aztecs

narcotraficante m/f [–kanteh] drug trafficker

narcotráfico m drug trade, drug traffic

nariz f [narees] nose

natación f [natas-yon] swimming

natural [natooral] natural

al natural at room temperature

naturaleza f [natooralesa] nature

naturalmente [–menteh] naturally; of course

náusea: siento náuseas [s-yento nowseh-as] I feel sick

navaja f [nabaнa] penknife; flick knife

Navidad f [nabeeda] Christmas

¡feliz Navidad! [felees] merry Christmas!

nayarita [nī-yareeta] from/of Nayarit

neblina f mist

necesario [nesesar-yo] necessary

necesitar [neseseetar] to need

negar to deny

negativa f [negateeba] denial; refusal

negativo m negative

negocio m [negos-yo] business

negro (**m**) black; furious; black man

nena f baby girl; little girl

nene m [neneh] baby boy; little boy

nervioso [nairb-yoso] nervous

me pone nervioso [meh poneh] it makes me nervous

neurótico [neh-ooroteeko] neurotic

nevar [nebar] to snow

nevería f [neberee-a] ice cream parlour

ni neither; nor

¡ni modo! what can you do!

ni ... ni ... neither ... nor ...

nica m/f Nigaraguan

nicaraguense (**m/f**) [neekaragwenseh] Nicaraguan

niebla f [n-yebla] fog

nieta f [n-yeta] granddaughter

nieto m [n-yeto] grandson

nieva [n-yeba] it is snowing

nieve f [n-yebeh] snow; ice cream; sorbet

ningún none; not one; no ...

en ningún sitio [seet-yo] nowhere

ninguno nobody; none; not one

niña f [neen-ya] child

niñera f [neen-yaira] nanny

niño m [neen-yo] child

nivel del aceite m [neebel del asayteh] oil level

no no; not

noche f [nocheh] night

de noche at night

buenas noches [bwenas noches] good night

esta noche tonight

por la noche at night

pasar la noche to spend the
night

Nochebuena **f** [nocheh-bwena]
Christmas Eve

Nochevieja **f** [nocheh-b-yeHa]
New Year's Eve

no contiene alcohol does not
contain alcohol

nocturno [noktoorno] night

no estacionarse no parking

no estacionarse, se usa grúa
illegally parked vehicles will
be towed away

no exceda la dosis indicada do
not exceed the stated dose

no fumadores [foomador-es] no
smoking

no fumar no smoking

no funciona [foons-yona] out
of order

no hay de qué [i deh keh] you
are welcome

no hay localidades sold out

no le hace [leh aseh] don't
worry about it

nomás just, only

díselo nomás [deeselo] just tell
him/her

nombre **m** [nombreh] name

nombre de pila [deh] first name

nombre de soltera [soltaira]
maiden name

no molestar do not disturb

nopal **m** cactus leaf

no para en ... does not stop
in ...

no pisar el pasto keep off the
grass

nordeste **m** [nordesteh] northeast

no rebasar no overtaking, no
passing

no recomendada para menores
de 18 años not recommended
for those under 18 years of
age

normal (**m**) [nor-mal] normal;
lower grade petrol, (US)
regular (gas)

normalmente [–menteh] usually

noroeste **m** [noro-esteh] northwest

norte **m** [norteh] north

al norte de la ciudad [deh la
s-yooda] north of the city

norteamericana (**f**) [norteh-
amaireekana], norteamericano
(**m**) North American

norteño [norten-yo] from the
north of Mexico

Noruega **f** [norwega] Norway

nos us; ourselves

no se admiten devoluciones no
refunds given

no se admiten perros no dogs
allowed

no ... sino ... not ... but ...

nosotras, nosotros we; us

nota **f** note

nota de consumo [deh] receipt

noticias **fpl** [notees-yas] news

noticiero **m** [notees-yairo] news
bulletin

no tocar please do not touch

no utilizar lejía do not bleach

nova **f** [noba] two-star petrol,
(US) regular gas

novaplus four-star petrol, (US) premium gas

novecientos [nobes-yentos] nine hundred

novecito [nobeseeto] very new

novela f [nobela] novel

noveno [nobeno] ninth

noventa [nobenta] ninety

novia f [nob-ya] girlfriend; fiancée; bride

noviembre m [nob-yembreh] November

novillada f [nobee-yada] bullfight featuring young bulls

novio m [nob-yo] boyfriend; fiancé; groom

Nte. north

nube f [noobeh] cloud

nublado cloudy

nuboso cloudy

nuera f [nwaira] daughter-in-law

nuestra [nwestra], nuestras, nuestro, nuestros our

Nueva York [nweba] New York

nueve [nwebeh] nine

nuevo [nwebo] new

nuevoleonés [nweboleh-on-es] from/of Nuevo Leon

nuevo peso m new peso

número m [noomairo] number; size

número de calzado [deh kalsado] shoe size

número de teléfono phone number

nunca never

nutritivo [nootreeteebo] nutritious

O

o or

o ... o ... either ... or ...

oaxaqueño [waHaken-yo] from/ of Oaxaca

obispo m [obeespo] bishop

objeción f [obHes-yon] objection

objetar [obHetar] to object

objetivo m [obHeteebo] lens; objective

objetos de escritorio [obHetos deh eskreetor-yo] office supplies

objetos perdidos lost property, lost and found

obra f work; play

obras fpl roadworks

obrero m [obrairo] worker

obsequio m [obsek-yo] gift

obstruido [obstroo-eedo] blocked

obturador m shutter

ocasión f [okas-yon] occasion; opportunity; bargain

de ocasión [deh] second hand

occidental [okseedental] Western

occidente m [okseedenteh] West

Océano Pacífico m [oseh-ano] Pacific Ocean

ochenta eighty

ocho eight

ochocientos [ochos-yentos] eight hundred

ocho días mpl [dee-as] week

ocote **m** [okoteh] resinous pine used for burning

octavo [oktabo] eighth

octubre **m** [oktoobreh] October

oculista **m/f** optician

ocultar to hide

oculto hidden

ocupado engaged; occupied; busy

ocupar to occupy

ocurrir [okooreer] to occur, happen

 ocurre que [okoorreh keh] it so happens that

odiar [od-yar] to hate

odio (**m**) [od-yo] hate, hatred; I hate

odioso odious, revolting; horrible

oeste **m** [o-esteh] west

 al oeste de la ciudad [deh la s-yooda] west of the city

ofender [ofendair] to offend

oferta **f** [ofairta] special offer

oficial (**m/f**) [ofees-yal] officer; official

oficina **f** [ofeeseena] office

oficina de correos [deh korreh-os] post office

oficina de correos y telégrafos post office and telegrams

oficina de información y turismo [eenformas-yon] tourist information office

oficina de objetos perdidos [obHetos] lost property office, lost and found

oficina de reclamaciones [reklamas-yon-es] complaints

department

oficina de registros [reHeestros] registrar's office

oficina de turismo tourist information office

oficinista **m/f** [ofeeseeneesta] office worker

oficio **m** [ofees-yo] job; trade

ofrecer [ofresair] to offer

oído (**m**) [o-eedo] ear; hearing; heard

¡oiga! [oyga] listen here!; excuse me!

oigo I am listening

oír [o-eer] to listen

ojo **m** [oHo] eye

 ¡ojo! watch out!

ola **f** wave

ola de calor [deh] heatwave

oler [olair] to smell

olfato **m** sense of smell

olmeca from/of ancient Olmec culture

olor **m** smell

olvidar [olbeedar] to forget

once [onseh] eleven

ONU **f** [o eneh oo] UN

operación **f** [opairas-yon] operation

operadora **f** operator

operarse [opairarseh] to have an operation

oportunidad **f** [oportooneeda] chance, opportunity

oposición **f** [oposees-yon] opposition

óptica **f** optician's

óptico **m** optician

optimista optimistic

¡órale! [oraleh] go on then!, get on with it!

orden f order, instruction
  a sus órdenes at your service

orden m order
  en orden in order

organización f [organeesas-yon] organization

organizar [organeesar] to organize

orgulloso [orgoo-yoso] proud

oriental east, eastern

orientar to direct, to guide

oriente m [or-yenteh] east

orilla f [oree-ya] shore; side

oro m gold

orquesta f [orkesta] orchestra

oscuro dark

Ote. east

otoño m [oton-yo] autumn, (US) fall

otorrinolaringólogo m ear, nose and throat specialist

otra vez [bes] again

otro another (one); other

oveja f [obeHa] sheep

overol m [obairol] overall

oye [o-yeh] he/she listens; you listen; he/she hears; you hear

P

pabellón m [pabeh-yon] (hospital) ward

pachanga f party; partying

paciente m/f [pas-yenteh] patient

padecer [padesair] to suffer

padecer del corazón [korason] to have a heart condition

padre m [padreh] father
  ¡está padre! it's great!

padres mpl [pad-res] parents

padrino m [padreeno] godfather

pagadero [pagadairo] payable

pagar to pay

página f [paHeena] page

páginas amarillas [amaree-yas] yellow pages

pago m payment

país m [pa-ees] country

paisaje m [pīsaHeh] landscape; scenery

pájaro m [paHaro] bird

pala f spade

palabra f word

palacio m [palas-yo] palace

Palacio de Justicia [deh Hoostees-ya] Law Courts

palanca de velocidades f [beloseedad-es] gear lever

palco m box (at theatre)

paleta f ice lolly

paliacate m [pal-yakateh] headscarf

palmera f [palmaira] palm tree

palo m stick; tree

palomitas fpl popcorn

palos de golf mpl [deh] golf clubs

paludismo m [paloodeesmo] malaria

PAN (Partido de Acción Nacional) m National Action Party (centre-right party)

panadería f [panadairee-a] baker's

panal m honeycomb

panameño (m) [panamen-yo] Panamanian

pantalla f [panta-ya] screen

pantalón corto m shorts

pantalones mpl [pantalon-es] trousers, (US) pants

panteón m [panteh-on] cemetery

pantimedias fpl tights, pantyhose

panza f [pansa] belly

pañal m [pan-yal] nappy, diaper

pañuelo m [panwelo] handkerchief; scarf

papa f [papa] potato

papá m dad

papalote m [–loteh] kite

papel m [papel] paper; rôle

papel de envolver [deh embolbair] wrapping paper

papel de escribir writing paper

papel de plata silver foil

papelera f [papelaira] litter; litter bin

papelería f [papelairee-a] stationery, stationer's

papel sanitario [saneetar-yo] toilet paper

papel tapiz [tapees] wallpaper

paquete m [paketeh] packet; package holiday

paquetería f [paketairee-a] left luggage office, baggage check

par m pair

para for; in order to

cuarto para las tres quarter to three

parabrisas m windscreen

paracaidismo m [parakideesmo] parachuting; squatting

paracaidista m/f parachutist; squatter

parachoques m [parachok-es] bumper, (US) fender

parada f stop

parada de camión [deh] bus stop

paradero f [paradairo] stop

paraguas m [paragwas] umbrella

para que [keh] in order that

parar to stop

pararse to stand (up)

para uso del personal staff only

para uso externo not to be taken internally

parcela f [parsela] plot (of land)

parecer [paresair] to seem; to resemble

parece que sí/no it seems so/not

me parece (que) ... I think (that) ...

parecido [pareseedo] similar

pared f [pareh] wall

pareja f [pareHa] pair; couple; partner

parezco [paresko] I am like

pariente m/f [par-yenteh] relative

parir to give birth

parque m [parkeh] park

parque de atracciones [deh atraks-yon-es] amusement park

parque de bomberos [bombairos] fire station

parque de recreo [rekreh-o]

amusement park
parque infantil [eenfanteel]
children's park
parrilla f [parree-ya] grill
párroco m parish priest
parte m [parteh] report
parte f [parteh] part
en todas partes [part-es]
everywhere
en otra parte elsewhere
en alguna parte somewhere
¿de parte de quién? [deh –
k-yen] who's calling?
participar [parteeseepar] to take
part; to inform
particular [parteekoolar] private
un particular a private
individual
partida f game
partido m match, game, bout;
(political) party
partir to cut (into pieces); to
leave, to go
a partir de mañana from
tomorrow onwards
parto m birth
parvulario m [parboolaree-o]
nursery school
pasado last
la semana pasada last week
pasado mañana [man-yana]
the day after tomorrow
pasado de moda [deh] out of
fashion
pasaje m [pasaHeh] ticket; fare
pasajero m [pasaHairo]
passenger
pasajeros de tránsito transit
passengers

pasaporte m [pasaporteh]
passport
pasaportes passport control
pasar to pass; to overtake; to
happen
pasar la aduana [adwana] to go
through Customs
pasarlo bien [b-yen] to enjoy
oneself
pasatiempo m [pasat-yempo]
hobby
Pascua [paskwa] Easter
pase [paseh] come in
pasear [paseh-ar] to go for a
walk; to take for a walk
paseo m [paseh-o] walk; drive;
ride
paseo de ... ... avenue
pasillo m [pasee-yo] corridor
paso m passage; pass; step
estar de paso [deh] to be
passing through
pasó: ¿qué pasó? how's it
going?, what's happening?
paso a desnivel underpass
paso a nivel level crossing, (US)
grade crossing
paso de contador [deh]
(metered) unit
paso de peatones [peh-aton-es]
pedestrian crossing
paso prohibido no admittance,
no entry
paso subterráneo pedestrian
underpass
pasta de dientes f [deh d-yent-
es] toothpaste
pastelería f [pastelairee-a] cake
shop

pastilla **f** [past**ee**-ya] pill, tablet

pastillas para la garganta throat pastilles

patatas fritas crisps, (US) potato chips

patinaje **m** [pateena**Heh**] skating

patinar to skid; to skate

patria **f** [p**at**ree-a] motherland, home country

las fiestas patrias celebration of national independence

paz **f** [pas] peace

PB ground floor, (US) first floor

peatón **m** [peh-a**ton**] pedestrian

peatonal pedestrian

peatón, circula por tu izquierda pedestrians keep to the left

peatones [peh-a**ton**-es] pedestrians

pecado **m** sin

pecho **m** chest; breast

pedazo **m** [pe**das**o] piece

pediatra **m/f** [pedee-**a**tra] pediatrician

pedir to order; to ask for

pedir hora [**o**ra] to ask the time

pedir disculpas to apologize

pegar to hit; to stick

no me pega la gana I don't feel like it

peinar [pay**nar**] to comb

peinarse [pay**nar**seh] to comb one's hair

peine **m** [**pay**neh] comb

pelado cropped; bare, barren; skint, penniless

pelea **f** [pel**eh**-a] fight

peletería **f** [peletair**ee**-a] furs, furrier

película **f** film, movie

película de color [**deh**] colour film

película en versión original [bairs-yon oree**Heen**al] film/ movie in the original language

peligro **m** danger

peligro de incendio danger: fire hazard

peligro deslizamientos slippery road surface

peligroso dangerous

es peligroso bañarse danger: no swimming

es peligroso asomarse do not lean out

pelirrojo [peleerro**Ho**] redheaded

pelo **m** hair

pelón bald

pelota **f** ball

peluca **f** wig

peluquera **f** [pelook**ai**ra], peluquero **m** hairdresser

peluquería **f** [pelookair**ee**-a] hairdresser's

peluquería de caballeros [**deh** kaba-y**ai**ros] gents' hairdresser's

peluquería de señoras [sen-**yo**ras] ladies' salon

Pemex State-owned oil company

pena **f** sadness, sorrow

¡qué pena! [**keh**] what a pity!

me da mucha pena [**meh**] I'm very sorry

tener pena [ten**air**] to be shy,

embarrassed

penca f cactus leaf

pendejada f [pendeHada] (piece of) stupidity

pendejo m [pendeHo] bloody idiot, (US) jerk

pendiente m [pend-yenteh] slope

estar pendiente de [deh] to be waiting for

estar al pendiente de to watch out for

pene m [peneh] penis

penetrar [penetrar] to enter

penicilina f [peneeseeleena] penicillin

pensamiento m [pensam-yento] thought

pensar to think

pensión f [pens-yon] guesthouse, boarding house; pension

pensión completa [kompleta] full board

pensionista m [pens-yoneesta] old-age pensioner

peña f [pen-ya] rock, boulder; singing club

peón m [peh-on] labourer; pawn

peor [peh-or] worse; worst

pepenar to scavenge, to scour rubbish tips

pequeño (m) [peken-yo] small; child

perder [pairdair] to lose

echar a perder to miss

perderse [pairdairseh] to get lost

pérdida f [pairdeeda] loss

perdón [pairdon] sorry, excuse

me; pardon, pardon me

perfecto [pairfekto] perfect

perfumería f [pairfoomairee-a] perfume shop

periódico m [pair-yodeeko] newspaper

periodista m/f [pair-yodeesta] journalist

período m [pairee-odo] period

perla f [pairla] pearl

permiso m [pairmeeso] licence; permit

con permiso excuse me, may I pass

permitir [pairmeeteer] to allow

pero [pairo] but

perro m [pairro] dog

perro caliente m [kal-yenteh] hot dog

persona f [pairsona] person

persona mayor [mi-yor] elderly person, senior citizen

pesadilla f [pesadee-ya] nightmare

pesado heavy; boring, tedious

pésame: dar el pésame [pesameh] to offer one's condolences

pesar: a pesar de que [deh keh] despite the fact that

a pesar de in spite of

pesca f fishing

ir a pescar to go fishing

pescadería f [peskadairee-a] fishmonger's

pescar to fish; to catch out

pesero m [pesairo] collective taxi

peso m weight; Mexican

national currency
peso máximo maximum
  weight
peso neto net weight
pestañas fpl [pestan-yas]
  eyelashes
petate m [petateh] straw mat
petróleo para lámparas m
  [petroleh-o] paraffin oil,
  kerosene oil
pez m [pes] fish
picadura f bite
picante [peekanteh] hot, spicy
picar to sting; to itch
pico: horas pico fpl rush hour
picor m itch
picoso [peekoso] hot
pidió [peed-yo] he/she asked
  for; you asked for
pie m [p-yeh] foot
  a pie on foot
piedra f [p-yedra] stone
piedra preciosa [pres-yosa]
  precious stone
piel f [p-yel] skin
pienso [p-yenso] I think
pierna f [p-yairna] leg
pijama m [peeнama] pyjamas
pila f battery
píldora f pill
piloto m pilot
pilotos mpl rear lights
pincel m [peensel] paint brush
pinchazo m [peenchaso]
  puncture
pinche [peencheh] bloody,
  lousy
pintada f graffiti
pintar to paint

pintura f painting; paint
pinzas fpl [peensas] tweezers
piña f [peen-ya] pineapple
pipa f pipe
piragua f [peeragwa] canoe
piragüismo m [peeragweesmo]
  canoeing
pirámide f [peerameedeh]
  pyramid
piscina f [peeseena] swimming
  pool
piscina cubierta [koob-yairta]
  indoor swimming pool
piso m floor
pista f track; clue
pista de baile [deh bīleh] dance
  floor
pista de tenis tennis court
pistola f gun
placa f [plaka] number plate,
  licence plate
plancha f iron
planchar to iron
planear [planeh-ar], planificar
  [planeefeekar] to plan
plano (m) flat; map
planta f plant; floor
planta baja [baнa] ground
  floor, (US) first floor
plástico (m) plastic
plata f silver; money, (US)
  dough
plateado [plateh-ado] silver
plática [plateeka] conversation;
  talk
platicar [plateekar] to talk, to
  converse
platillo m [platee-yo] saucer
plato m plate; dish, course

playa f [plī-ya] beach
playera f [plī-yaira] T-shirt
playeras fpl [plī-yairas] trainers
plaza f [plasa] square; seat
plaza de toros [deh] bullring
plazas libres [leeb-res] seats
  available
plomero m [plomairo] plumber
pluma f pen; feather
plumón m [ploomon] felt-tip pen
población f [poblas-yon] village;
  town; population
poblano from/of Puebla
pobre [pobreh] poor
pobreza f [pobresa] poverty
pocho Americanized (used to
  refer to Americanized Mexican)
poco little; rarely
poco profundo shallow
pocos few
  unos pocos a few
poder (m) [podair] to be able
  to; power
podrido rotten
policía f [poleesee-a] police
policía m/f policeman;
  policewoman
política f politics
político (m) politician; political
póliza de seguros f [poleesa deh]
  insurance policy
polvo m [polbo] powder; dust
pólvora f [polbora] gunpowder
pomada f ointment
pon put
poner (m) [ponair] to put
ponerse de pie [ponairseh deh
  p-yeh] to stand up
ponerse en marcha to set off

pongo I put
poniente m [pon-yenteh] west
popote m [popoteh] (drinking)
  straw
poquito: un poquito [pokeeto] a
  little bit
por by; through; for
por allí [a-yee] over there
por fin [feen] at last
por lo menos at least
por qué [keh] why
por semana per week
por avión [ab-yon] airmail
porcentaje m [porsentaHeh]
  percentage
por ciento [s-yento] per cent
por correo terrestre [korreh-o
  tairrestreh]
por favor [fabor] please
porfiriato m [porfeer-yato]
  period under rule of Porfirio
  Díaz 1876-1911
por qué [keh] why
porque [porkeh] because
portada f cover
portaequipajes m [porta-
  ekeepaH-es] luggage rack
portátil [portateel] portable
portero m [portairo] porter;
  doorman; goalkeeper
portugués [portoog-es]
  Portuguese
posada f hotel
posible [poseebleh] possible
postal f [pos-tal] postcard
potosino from/of San Luis
  Potosí
PRD (Partido Revolucionario
  Democrático) m Democratic

Revolutionary Party (left-wing party)

precaución f [prekows-yon] caution

precio m [pres-yo] price

precios fijos [feeHos] fixed prices

precioso [pres-yoso] beautiful; precious

precio unidad [ooneeda] price per unit, price per item

preferencia f [prefairens-ya] right of way; preference

preferir [prefaireer] to prefer

prefijo m [prefeeHo] dialling code, area code

pregunta f question

preguntar to ask

premio m [prem-yo] prize

prenda las luces switch on your lights

prendas fpl clothing

prender [prendair] to light; to switch on

prender luces de cruce switch headlights on

prensa f press; newspapers

preocupado [preh-okoopado] worried

preocuparse [preh-okooparseh] to worry (about)

¡no te preocupes! [teh preh-okoop-es] don't worry!

preparar to prepare

prepararse [prepararseh] to get ready

prepa(ratoria) f pre-university level school

prepotente [prepotenteh] arrogant

presentar to introduce

preservativo m [presairbateebo] condom

presidencia f [preseedens-ya] presidency

presión f [pres-yon] pressure

presión de las llantas [deh las yantas] tyre pressure

prestado: pedir prestado to borrow

prestar to lend

PRI (Partido Revolucionario Institucional) m Institutional Revolutionary Party (party of government since 1920)

prieto [pree-yeto] dark-skinned; black

prima f cousin

primavera f [preemabaira] spring

primera (clase) f [klaseh] first class

primera especial [espes-yal] deluxe first-class

primero first

primeros auxilios [owk-seel-yos] first-aid post

primer piso first floor, (US) second floor

primer plato m first course

primo m cousin

principal [preenseepal] main

principiante m/f [preenseep-yanteh] beginner

principio m [preenseep-yo] beginning

prioridad a la derecha give way/yield to vehicles coming from the right

prisa: tener prisa to be in a
hurry
privado (m) [preebado] private;
cul-de-sac
privatización f [preebateesas-yon]
privatization
probablemente [probableh-
menteh] probably
probador m fitting room
probarse [probarseh] to try on
problema m problem
producto preparado con
ingredientes naturales
product prepared using
natural ingredients
productos alimenticios
[prodooktos aleementees-yos]
foodstuffs
productos de belleza [deh beh-
yesa] beauty products
profesor m, profesora f
teacher; lecturer
profundidad f [profoondeeda]
depth
profundo deep
prohibida la entrada no entry,
no admission
prohibida la entrada a menores
de ... no admission for those
under ... years of age
prohibida la vuelta en U no
U-turns
prohibida su reproducción
copyright reserved
prohibida su venta not for sale
prohibido [pro-eebeedo]
prohibited, forbidden; no
prohibido asomarse do not
lean out of the window

prohibido bañarse no
swimming
prohibido cantar no singing
prohibido echar basura no
litter
prohibido el paso no entry; no
trespassing
prohibido escupir no spitting
prohibido estacionarse no
parking
prohibido estacionarse
excepto carga y descarga no
parking except for loading
and unloading
prohibido fijar carteles stick
no bills
prohibido fumar no smoking
prohibido girar a la izquierda
no left turn
prohibido hablar con el chofer
do not speak to the driver
prohibido hacer auto-stop no
hitch-hiking
prohibido pescar no fishing
prohibido pisar el pasto keep
off the grass
prohibido prender fuego no
campfires
prohibido sacar fotografías no
photographs
prohibido tocar el claxon do
not sound your horn
prometer [prometair] to promise
prometida f fiancée
prometido (m) engaged; fiancé
pronóstico del tiempo m
[t-yempo] weather forecast
pronto early; soon
de pronto suddenly

¡hasta pronto! [asta] see you soon!

llegar pronto [yegar] to be early

pronunciar [pronoons-yar] to pronounce

propaganda f advertising; publicity; propaganda

propiedad privada [prop-yeda preebada] private property

propietario m [prop-yetar-yo] owner

propina f tip

propósito: a propósito deliberately

proteger [proteHair] to protect

provecho: ¡buen provecho! [bwen probecho] enjoy your meal!

provincia f [probeens-ya] province

en provincia in the country, in the provinces

provocar [probokar] to cause

¿te provoca un café? [teh] do you feel like a coffee?

próximo next

la semana próxima next week

prudente [proodenteh] careful

prueba de alcoholemia f [prweba deh alko-olem-ya] breath test

prueba de embarazo [embaraso] pregnancy test

Pte. west

público (m) public; audience

pueblo m [pweblo] village; people; nation; ordinary people

puede [pwedeh] he/she can; you can

puede ser [sair] maybe

puedo [pwedo] I can

puente m [pwenteh] bridge

puente aéreo [a-aireh-o] shuttle flight

puente colgante [kolganteh] rope bridge

puente de cuota [kwota] toll bridge

puerta f [pwairta] door; gate

por la otra puerta use other door

puerta de embarque [embarkeh] gate

puerta nº. gate no.

puerto m [pwairto] harbour, port

puerto de montaña [deh montan-ya] mountain pass

puerto deportivo marina

pues [pwes] since; so

puesta de sol f [pwesta deh] sunset

puesto de periódicos m [pair-yodeekos] newspaper kiosk

puesto de socorro first-aid post

puesto que [keh] since

pulga f flea

pullman m luxury bus

pulmones mpl [poolmon-es] lungs

pulmonía f [poolmonee-a] pneumonia

pulque m [poolkeh] drink made from fermented agave cactus sap pulquería f [poolkairee-a] bar specializing in pulque

pulsera f [poolsaira] bracelet

pulso m pulse

punto m dot; spot; point

hacer punto [asair] to knit

punto de vista [deh beesta] point of view

puntual: llegar puntual [yegar poontwal] to arrive on time

pura lana virgen pure new wool

puro (m) [pooro] cigar; pure

es la pura verdad [vairda] it's the absolute truth

puse [pooseh] I put

Q

que [keh] who; that; which; than

¿qué? what?; which?

quedar [kedar] to stay; to remain

quédate con él [kedateh] keep it

no me queda otra [meh keda] I've no choice

¿dónde queda? [dondeh] where is it?

queda muy cerca it's very near

quedarse [kedarseh] to stay

quedarse con to keep

quedarse sin gasolina to run out of petrol/gas

¿qué hubo? [oobo] what's happening?; how's things?

quejarse [keh-Harseh] to complain

quemadura f [kemadoora] burn

quemadura de sol [deh] sunburn

quemar [kemar] to burn

quemarse [kemarseh] to burn oneself

querer [kerair] to love; to want

querido [kaireedo] dear

queso m [keso] cheese

¿qué tal? how do you do?

¡qué va! [ba] no way!

¿quién? [k-yen] who?

quiero [k-yairo] I want; I love

no quiero I don't want to

¿quihubo? [k-yoobo] how's it going?

quince [keenseh] fifteen

quince días [dee-ás] fortnight

quinientos [keen-yentos] five hundred

quinto [keento] fifth

quiosco m [k-yosko] kiosk

quisiera [kees-yaira] I would like; he/she would like; you would like

quiso [keeso] he/she wanted; you wanted

quitaesmalte m [keeta-esmalteh] nail polish remover

quitar [keetar] to remove

quizá(s) [keesa(s)] maybe

R

rabia f [rab-ya] rage; rabies

me da rabia it makes me mad

rabioso [rab-yoso] furious

ración f [ras-yon] portion

radiador m [rad-yador] radiator

radio m [rad-yo] spoke

radio f radio

radiografía f [rad-yografee-a] X-ray

rajarse [raHarseh] to back down, to run away

ranchero m [ranchairo] small farmer

rancho m small farm, smallholding

rápidamente [–menteh] quickly

rápido fast

raro rare; strange

rascar to scratch

rasgar to tear

rasgo m feature

rasuradora f shaver

rasurarse [rasoorarseh] to shave

rata f rat

rato: espera un rato wait a minute, wait a bit
pasar buen/mal rato to have a good/bad time
cada rato every now and then

ratón m mouse

rayas: de rayas [deh rī-yas] striped

razón f [rason] reason; rate
tiene razón [t-yeneh] you're right
con razón ... so that's why ...

razonable [rasonableh] reasonable

realizar [reh-aleesar] to carry out

realmente [reh-almenteh] really; in fact

rebajado [rebaHado] reduced

rebajas fpl [rebaHas] reductions, sale

rebajas de verano [deh bairano] summer sale

rebasar to overtake, to pass

rebozo m [reboso] shawl

recado m message
¿quiere dejar recado? would you like to leave a message?

recámara f bedroom

recepción f [reseps-yon] reception

recepcionista m/f [reseps-yoneesta] receptionist

receta f [reseta] recipe; prescription
con receta médica only available on prescription

recetar [resetar] to prescribe

recibir [reseebeer] to receive

recibo m [reseebo] receipt

recién [res-yen] recently
recién salía de casa cuando ... I'd just left home when ...

recién pintado wet paint

reclamación de equipajes f [reklamas-yon deh ekeepaH-es] baggage claim

reclamaciones fpl [reklamas-yon-es] complaints

recoger [rekoHair] to collect; to pick up

recogida de equipajes f [rekoHeeda deh ekeepaH-es] baggage claim

recoja su boleto take your ticket

recomendar to recommend

reconocer [rekonosair] to recognize; to examine

reconocimiento **m** [rekonoseem-yento] examination

reconocimiento médico medical examination

recordar to remember

recorrer [rekorair] to travel; to travel through; to move along

recorrido **m** journey

recreo **m** [recreh-o] playtime, break

recto straight

   todo recto straight ahead

recuerdo **(m)** [rekwairdo] memory; souvenir; I remember

red **f** [reh] network; net

redondo round

reduzca la velocidad reduce speed now

reembolsar [reh-embolsar] to refund

reembolsos refunds

reestreno **m** [reh-estreno] re-release (of a classic movie)

refacciones **fpl** [refaks-yon-es] spare parts, spares

regadera **f** [regadaira] shower

regalo **m** present

regalón spoiled

regatear [regateh-ar] to haggle

regenta **f** [reHenta], regente **m** [reHenteh] mayor

régimen **m** [reHeemen] diet; regime

regiomontano [reH-yomontano]

from/of Monterrey

registrar [reHeestrar] to search; to register, to certify

registro de equipajes **m** [reHeestro deh ekeepaH-es] check-in

regla **f** rule; period

reglamento **m** rule

regresar to return

regresar a casa to go home

regreso **m** return

reina **f** [rayna] queen

Reino Unido **m** United Kingdom

reír [ray-eer] to laugh

relajarse [relaHarseh] to relax

relajo **m** [relaHo] disorder; noise, hubbub

rellenar [reh-yenar] to fill in; to fill

reloj **m** [reloH] watch; clock

reloj de pulsera [deh poolsaira] watch, wristwatch

relojería **f** [reloHairee-a] watches and clocks; watchmaker's shop

remar to row

remate **m** [remateh] sale, auction sale; the final detail

remitente **m/f** [remeetenteh] sender

remo **m** oar

remolque **m** [remolkeh] trailer

renta **f** rent; rental

rentado rented

rentar to rent; to hire

   se renta to rent, for hire

renunciar [renoons-yar] to resign

reparación **f** [reparas-yon]

repair(s)

reparación de calzado [deh kalsado] shoe repairs

reparaciones [reparas-yon-es] faults service

reparar to repair

repelente de mosquitos m [repelenteh deh] mosquito repellent

repente: de repente [deh repenteh] suddenly

repetir to repeat; to have a second helping

reponerse [reponairseh] to recover

representante m/f [representanteh] representative, agent

repuestos mpl [repwestos] spare parts

repugnante [repoognanteh] disgusting

requisito m [rekeeseeto] requirement, condition

res m cow, bull

resbaladizo [resbaladeeso] slippery

resbalar to slip

rescatar to rescue

reserva f [resairba] reservation

reserva de asientos [deh as-yentos] seat reservation

reservado [resairbado] reserved

reservado el derecho de admisión the management reserve the right to refuse admission

reservar [resairbar] to reserve; to book

reservas fpl reservations

resfriado m [resfree-ado] cold

respeto m respect

respirar to breathe

responder [respondair] to answer, to reply

responsable (m/f) [responsableh] the person in charge; responsible

respuesta f [respwesta] answer

restaurante m [restowranteh] restaurant

resto m rest

retar to challenge

rete: está rete lindo [reteh] it's really beautiful

reumatismo m [reh-oomateesmo] rheumatism

reunión f [reh-oon-yon] meeting

revelado m [rebelado] film processing

revelar [rebelar] to develop; to reveal

revisar [rebeesar] to check

revisor m [rebeesor] conductor; guard

revista m [rebeesta] magazine

revolución f [reboloos-yon] revolution

la Revolución Mexicana the Mexican Revolution 1910-17

rey m [ray] king

Reyes: día de los Reyes m [dee-a deh los ray-es] 6th of January, Epiphany

rico rich

ridículo ridiculous

riego: tierras de riego **fpl**
  irrigated land
rímel **m** mascara
rincón **m** corner
riñón **m** [reen-yon] kidney
río **m** [ree-o] river
risa **f** laughter
  me da risa [meh] it makes me
  laugh
rizado [reesado] curly
robar to steal
robo **m** theft
roca **f** rock
rodilla **f** [rodee-ya] knee
rogar to beg
rojo [roHo] red
rómpase en caso de
  emergencia break in case of
  emergency
romper to break
ropa **f** clothes
ropa de caballeros [deh kaba-
  yairos] men's clothes
ropa de cama bed linen
ropa de señoras [sen-yoras]
  ladies' clothes
ropa infantil [eenfanteel]
  children's clothes
ropa interior [eentair-yor]
  underwear
ropa sucia [soos-ya] laundry
rosa (f) pink; rose
roto broken
rubeola **f** [roobeh-ola] German
  measles
rubí **m** [roobee] ruby
rubio [roob-yo] blond
rueda **f** [rweda] wheel
rueda de repuesto **f** [deh

repwesto] spare wheel
ruega: se ruega ... [seh rwega]
  please ...
ruego I request
ruido **m** [rweedo] noise
ruidoso [rweedoso] noisy
ruinas **fpl** [rweenas] ruins
rural [rooral] rural, country
ruta **f** route

S

S.A. (Sociedad Anónima) PLC,
  Inc
sábado **m** Saturday
sábana **f** sheet
saber [sabair] to know
  saber a to taste of
sabor **m** taste
sabroso tasty, delicious
sacacorchos **m** corkscrew
sacar to take out; to get out
sacar una foto to take a photo
sacar un boleto to buy a ticket
saco **m** jacket
sal (f) salt; leave
sala **f** room; lounge; hall
sala climatizada [kleematisada]
  air-conditioned
sala de belleza [beh-yesa]
  beauty salon
sala de cine [deh seeneh]
  cinema, movie theater
sala de conciertos [kons-yairtos]
  concert hall
sala de embarque [embarkeh]
  departure lounge

sala de espera [espaira]
  waiting room

sala de exposiciones [esposees-yon-es] exhibition hall

sala de tránsito transit lounge

salado salty

sala X X-rated cinema, adult
  movie theater

saldar to sell at a reduced price

saldo m clearance; balance

sales de baño fpl [sal-es deh
  ban-yo] bath salts

salgo I'm leaving, I'm going
  out

salida f exit; departure

salida ciudad take this
  direction to leave the city

salida de ambulancias
  ambulance exit

salida de autopista end
  of motorway/highway;
  motorway/highway exit

salida de camiones heavy
  goods vehicle exit, works exit

salida de emergencia [deh
  emairHens-ya] emergency exit

salida de incendios [eensend-yos] fire exit

salida de socorro f emergency
  exit

salidas fpl departures

salidas internacionales
  [eentairnas-yonal-es]
  international departures

salidas nacionales [nas-yonal-es] domestic departures

salir to go out; to leave

salón de baile m [deh bīleh]
  dance hall

salón de belleza [beh-yesa]
  beauty salon

salón de demostraciones
  [demostras-yon-es] exhibition
  hall

salón de peluquería
  [pelookairee-a] hairdressing
  salon

salpicadera f [salpeekadaira]
  mudguard

saltar to jump

Salubridad f Ministry of
  Health

salud f [saloo] health

saludar to greet

saludos best wishes

salvadoreño (m) [salbadoren-yo]
  Salvadorean

salvo que [keh] except that

sangrar to bleed

sangre f [sangreh] blood

sanitarios mpl [saneetar-yos]
  toilets, rest rooms

sano healthy

sarampión m [saramp-yon]
  measles

sarape m [sarapeh] woven
  blanket

sartén f frying pan

sastre m [sastreh] tailor

scotch® m Sellotape®, Scotch
  tape®

se [seh] himself; herself;
  itself; yourself; themselves;
  yourselves; oneself

sé I know
  no sé I don't know

se aceptan tarjetas de crédito
  we accept credit cards

secador de pelo **m** [deh] hair dryer

secar to dry

secarse el pelo [sekarseh] to dry one's hair, to have a blow-dry

sección **f** [seks-yon] department

seco dry

secretaria **f**, secretario **m** secretary

secretaría **f** Ministry

Secretaría de Turismo Ministry of Tourism

secreto secret

Sectur tourist office

sed: tengo sed [seh] I'm thirsty

seda **f** silk

seda natural pure silk

sede **f** [sedeh] head office, headquarters

seguida: en seguida [segeeda] immediately, right away

seguido [segeedo] often

seguir [segeer] to follow

según according to

segunda (clase) **f** [klaseh] second class

segundo (**m**) second de segunda mano second-hand

segundo piso **m** second floor, (US) third floor

seguridad **f** [segooreeda] safety; security

seguro (**m**) safe; sure; insurance; safety pin

seguro de viaje **m** [deh b-yaheh] travel insurance

se habla inglés English spoken

se hacen fotocopias photocopying service

seis [says] six

seiscientos [says-yentos] six hundred

selva **f** [selba] jungle; rain forest

semáforo **m** traffic lights

semana **f** week

semanal weekly

Semana Santa Holy Week

senador **m** Senator

sencillo [sensee-yo] simple

se necesita ... ... needed, required

sensible [senseebleh] sensitive

sentar: sentar bien (a) [b-yen] to suit

sentarse [sentarseh] to sit down

sentido **m** direction; sense; meaning

sentir to feel; to hear

señas **fpl** [sen-yas] address

señor [sen-yor] gentleman, man; sir
  el señor López Mr López

señora **f** [sen-yora] lady, woman; madam
  la señora López Mrs López

señoras **fpl** ladies; ladies' toilet, ladies' room; ladies' department

señores **mpl** [sen-yor-es] men; gents' toilet, men's room

señorita **f** [sen-yoreeta] young lady, young woman; miss
  la señorita López Miss López

separado separate; separated

por separado separately

se precisa ... ... needed

se prohibe ... ... forbidden

se prohibe echar basura no
litter

se prohibe fumar no smoking

se prohibe hablar con el chofer
do not speak to the driver

se prohibe la entrada no entry,
no admittance

se prohibe la entrada a
mujeres, uniformados e
integrantes de la fuerzas
armadas no admittance to
women, members of the
armed forces and anyone in
uniform

septiembre **m** [set-yembreh]
September

séptimo [septeemo] seventh

sequía f [sekee-a] drought

ser [sair] to be

a no ser que [keh] unless

se renta for hire, to rent

se renta departamento flat to
let, apartment for rent

se rentan cuartos rooms to
rent

serio [sair-yo] serious

en serio seriously

serpiente f [sairp-yenteh] snake

serranía f mountains

se ruega please ...

se ruega desalojen su cuarto
antes de las doce please
vacate your room by twelve
noon

se ruega no ... please do not ...

se ruega no estacionarse no

parking please

se ruega no molestar please do
not disturb

se ruega pagar en caja please
pay at the desk

se vende for sale

servicio a través de operadora
operator-connected calls

servicio automático direct
dialling

servicio de cuarto [sairbees-yo
deh kwarto] room service

servicio de fotocopias
photocopying service

servicio estrella [estreh-ya] first
class (coach) service

servicios **mpl** [sairbees-yos]
toilets, rest rooms

servicios de rescate [deh
reskateh] mountain rescue

servicios de socorro
emergency services

servilleta f [sairbee-yeta]
serviette, napkin

servir [sairbeer] to serve

sesenta [sesenta] sixty

sesión continua continuous
showing

setecientos [setes-yentos] seven
hundred

setenta seventy

sexenio **m** six year Presidential
term

sexo **m** sex

sexto [sesto] sixth

si [see] if

sí [see] yes; oneself; herself;
itself; yourself; themselves;
yourselves; each other

SIDA **m** [seeda] AIDS

sido been

siempre [s-yempreh] always

siempre que [keh] whenever; as long as

siento [s-yento] I sit down; I feel

lo siento I'm sorry

sierra **f** [s-yairra] mountain range

siesta **f** siesta, nap

siete [s-yeteh] seven

siga recto straight ahead

siglo **m** century

significado **m** meaning

significar to mean

siguiente [seeg-yenteh] next

al día siguiente the day after

silencio **m** [seelens-yo] silence

silla **f** [see-ya] chair

silla de ruedas [deh rwedas] wheelchair

sillita de ruedas [see-yeeta] pushchair, buggy

sillón **m** [see-yon] armchair

simpático nice

sin [seen] without

sinagoga **f** synagogue

sincero [seensairo] sincere

sindicalista **m/f** trade unionist

sindicato **m** trade union, labor union

sin duda undoubtedly

sin embargo however, nevertheless

sino: no ... sino ... not ... but ...

si no otherwise

sino que [keh] but

sin plomo unleaded

siquiera [seek-yaira] even if; at least

sírvase [seerbaseh] please

sírvase frío serve cold

sírvase Usted mismo help yourself

sitio **m** [seet-yo] place

en ningún sitio [neen-goon] nowhere

smoking **m** [smokeen] dinner jacket

sobrar to be left over; to be too many

sobre (**m**) [sobreh] envelope; on; above

sobrecarga [sobrekarga] excess weight; extra charge

sobrevivir [sobrebeebeer] to survive

sobrina **f** niece

sobrino **m** nephew

sobrio [sobr-yo] sober

sociedad **f** [sos-yeda] society; company

socio **m** [sos-yo] associate; member

socorrer [sokorair] to help

socorrista **m/f** lifeguard

¡socorro! help!

sois [soys] you are

sol **m** sun

al sol in the sun

solamente [solamenteh] only

soleado [soleh-ado] sunny

solo lonely

sólo only

no sólo ... sino también ... [tamb-yen] not only ... but also ...

sólo camiones buses only

sólo carga y descarga loading and unloading only

sólo laborables weekdays only

sólo motos motorcycles only

sólo para residentes (del hotel) hotel patrons only

soltera (f) [soltaira] single; single woman

soltero (m) [soltairo] single; bachelor

solterón m [soltairon] bachelor

solterona f [soltairona] spinster

sombra f shade; shadow

sombra de ojos [deh oHos] eyeshadow

sombrero m [sombrairo] hat

sombrilla f [sombree-ya] parasol

somnífero m [somneefairo] sleeping pill

somos we are

son they are; you are

sonreír [sonreh-eer] to smile

sonrisa f smile

sordo deaf

sorprendente [sorprendenteh] surprising

sorpresa f surprise

sótano m lower floor; basement

soy I am

sport: de sport [deh] casual

Sr (Señor) Mr

Sra (Señora) Mrs

Sres (Señores) Messrs

Srta (Señorita) Miss

su [soo] his; her; its; their; your

suave [swabeh] soft; quiet

subir to go up; to get on; to get in; to take up

subtitulado sub-titled

subtítulos mpl subtitles

suburbios mpl [sooboorb-yos] suburbs; poor quarters

suceder [soosedair] to happen

sucio [soos-yo] dirty

sucursal f branch

sudamericana (f) [soodamaireekana], sudamericano (m) South American

sudar to sweat

Suecia f [swes-ya] Sweden

sueco [sweko] Swedish

suegra f [swegra] mother-in-law

suegro m [swegro] father-in-law

suela f [swela] sole

suelo (m) floor; I am used to

suelto [swelto] small change

sueño (m) [swen-yo] dream; I dream

tener sueño [tenair] to be tired/sleepy

suerte f [swairteh] luck

por suerte luckily, fortunately

¡buena suerte! [bwena] good luck!

suéter m [swetair] sweater

suficiente: es suficiente [soofees-yenteh] that's enough

sufragio efectivo, no reelección effective suffrage, no re-election (slogan on many official documents) suicidarse [sweeseedarseh] to commit suicide

Suiza f [sweesa] Switzerland

sumar to add; to add up to

supe [soopeh] I knew

súper [soopair] four-star petrol, (US) premium (gas); supermarket

supermercado m [soopairmairkado] supermarket

supuesto: por supuesto [soopwesto] of course

sur m south
 al sur de [deh] south of

sureste m [sooresteh] south-east

suroeste m [sooro-esteh] south-west

surtido m assortment

sus [soos] his; her; its; their; your

susto m shock

susurrar to whisper

sutil subtle

suya [soo-ya], suyas, suyo, suyos his; hers; its; theirs; yours

T

tabaco m tobacco; cigarettes

tabasqueño [tabasken-yo] from/ of Tabasco

tabique m [tabeekeh] brick

tabla de surf f [deh soorf] surfboard

tabla de windsurf f sailboard

tablero de instrumentos m

[tablairo deh eenstroomentos] dashboard

tablón de anuncios m [anoons-yos] notice board, bulletin board

tablón de información [deh eenformas-yon] indicator board

tacón m heel

tacones altos [takon-es] high heels

tacones planos flat heels

tal such
 con tal (de) que provided that

talco m talcum powder

talla f [ta-ya] size
 ¿qué número talla? what size are you?

tallas grandes [grand-es] large sizes

tallas sueltas [sweltas] odd sizes

taller mecánico m [ta-yair mekaneeko] garage

talón m heel

talonario (de cheques) m [talonar-yo (deh chek-es)] cheque book, checkbook

talón de equipajes [ekeepaн-es] baggage slip

tal vez [bes] maybe

tamaño m [taman-yo] size

tamaulipeco [tamowleepeko] from/of Tamaulipas

también [tamb-yen] also
 yo también me too

tampoco neither, nor
 yo tampoco me neither, nor me

tan: tan bonito so beautiful
 tan pronto como as soon as

tanque **m** [tankeh] tank

tantito: espere tantito wait a moment

tanto (**m**) so much; point

tanto ... como ... both ... and ...

tantos so many

tapa **f** lid

tapar to cover

tapas **fpl** savoury snacks, tapas

tapatío from/of Guadalajara

tapete **m** [tapeteh] rug, carpet

tapón **m** plug

taquería **f** [takairee-a] taco restaurant, taco stall

taquilla **f** [takee-ya] ticket office

tarahumara **m/f** [tara-oomara] indigenous person from northern Mexico

tarasco (**m**) indigenous person from Michoacan; from/of Tarascan culture

tardar: ¿cuánto tarda? [kwanto] how long does it take?

no tarda he/she won't be long

no tardes [tard-es] don't be long

tarde (**f**) [tardeh] afternoon; evening; late

a las tres de la tarde [deh] at 3 p.m.

esta tarde this afternoon, this evening

por la tarde in the evening

llegar tarde [yegar] to be late

tarifa **f** charge, charges

tarifa especial estudiante [espes-yal estood-yanteh] student reduced rate

tarifa normal standard rate

tarifa reducida [redooseeda] reduced rate

tarjeta **f** [tarHeta] card

tarjeta verde Green Card (tourist permit in Mexico)

tarjeta bancaria [bankar-ya] cheque card

tarjeta de crédito [deh kredeeto] credit card

tarjeta de embarque [embarkeh] boarding pass

tarjeta postal postcard

tarjeta telefónica phonecard

tauromaquia **f** [towromak-ya] bullfighting

taxista **m/f** taxi driver

taza **f** [tasa] cup

te [teh] you; yourself

té **m** tea

teatro **m** [teh-atro] theatre

techo **m** ceiling

teclado **m** keyboard

técnica **f** technique; technology

técnico technical

tecnología **f** [teknoloHee-a] technology

tecolote **m** [–loteh] owl

tejado **m** [teHado] roof

tejanos **mpl** [teHanos] jeans

tejidos **mpl** [teHeedos] materials, fabrics

tela **f** material

teleférico **m** cable car

teléfono **m** telephone

teléfono interurbano long-distance phone

teléfonos de emergencia

emergency telephone
numbers

telesilla m [telesee-ya] chairlift

Televisa largest Mexican
television corporation

televisión f [telebees-yon]
television

televisor m television (set)

temblor m earthquake

temer [temair] to fear

temor m fear

tempestad f [tempesta] storm

templo m temple; church

temporada f season

ten hold

tenedor m fork

tener [tenair] to have

tener derecho to have the
right

tener prisa to be in a hurry

tener prioridad [pree-oreeda] to
have right of way

tener que [keh] to have to

¡tenga cuidado! [kweedado] be
careful!

tengo I have

tengo que I have to, I must

tensión f [tens-yon] blood
pressure

teñirse el pelo [ten-yeerseh to
dye one's hair, to have one's
hair dyed

tepetate m [tepetateh] type of
soft stone used for building

tercera edad f [eda] old age

tercero third

tercer piso m [tairsair] third
floor, (US) fourth floor

tercio m [tairs-yo] third

terciopelo m [tairs-yopelo] velvet

terco [tairko] stubborn

terminal f [tairmeenal] terminus;
terminal

terminar to finish

termo m Thermos® flask

termómetro m thermometer

terrateniente m/f [tairra-ten-
yenteh] large landowner

terreno m [tairreno] piece/plot
of land

testigo m witness

testimonio m [testeemon-yo]
evidence; statement

tetera f [tetaira] teapot

tezontle m [tesontleh] volcanic
marble-like rock

ti [tee] you

tía f [tee-a] aunt

tianguis m [t-yangees] market

tibio [teeb-yo] lukewarm

tiburón m shark

tiempo m [t-yempo] time;
weather

a tiempo on time

al tiempo at room
temperature

tiempo de recreo [deh rekreh-o]
leisure

tiempo libre [leebreh] free time

tienda f [t-yenda] shop, store;
tent

esta tienda se traslada a ...
this business is transferred
to ...

tienda de abarrotes f [deh
abarrot-es] grocer's, dry goods
store

tienda de artículos de piel

[p-yel] leather goods shop

tienda de campaña tent

tienda de comestibles
[komesteebl-es] grocer's

tienda de deportes [deport-es]
sports shop

tienda de electrodomésticos
electrical goods shop

tienda de muebles [mwebl-es]
furniture shop

tienda de regalos gift shop

tienda de ultramarinos grocer's

tienda de vinos y licores
[beenos ee leekor-es] off-
licence, liquor store

tienda libre de impuestos
[leebreh deh eempwestos] duty-
free shop

tiene: ¿tiene ...? [t-yeneh] have
you got ...?, do you have ...?;
do you sell ...?

tiene que [keh] he/she must;
you must

tierra f [t-yairra] earth; land

tifo m typhus

tijeras fpl [teeнairas] scissors

tiliches mpl [teeleech-es] bits
and pieces

timbre m [teembreh] bell; stamp

timbre de alarma [deh] alarm
bell

tímido shy

tina f bath(tub)

tintorería f [teentorairee-a] dry-
cleaner's

tío m [tee-o] uncle

tipo de cambio m [deh kamb-yo]
exchange rate

tirita f Elastoplast®, Bandaid®

tiro m shot

tlapalería f [tlapalairee-a]
hardware store

toalla f [to-a-ya] towel

toalla de baño [deh ban-yo] bath
towel

tobillo m [tobee-yo] ankle

tocadiscos m record player

tocar to touch; to play

tocayo m [tokī-yo] namesake

todavía [todabee-a] still; yet

todavía no not yet

todo all, every; everything

todos los días every day

todo derecho straight on

todo recto straight ahead

todos everyone

tolteca from/of Toltec culture

tomado drunk

tomar to take; to drink

tomar el sol to sunbathe

tomavistas m cine-camera

tómese antes de las comidas
to be taken before meals

tómese después de las
comidas to be taken after
meals

tómese ... veces al día to be
taken ... times per day

tome Usted [tomeh oosteh] take

tonelada f tonne

tono m dialling tone; shade

tonto silly

topes mpl speed bumps,
'sleeping policemen'

torcer [torsair] to twist; to
sprain; to turn

torcerse el tobillo [tobee-yo] to
twist one's ankle

torero **m** [torairo] bullfighter

tormenta **f** storm

tormentoso stormy

tornillo **m** [tornee-yo] screw

toro **m** bull

toros **mpl** bullfighting

torpe [torpeh] clumsy

torre **f** [torreh] tower

tos **f** cough

toser [tosair] to cough

tosferina **f** [tosfaireena] whooping cough

total: en total [tot-al] altogether

totalmente [tot-almenteh] absolutely

tóxico [tokseeko] poisonous

toxicómano **m** [tokseekomano] drug addict

trabajador (**m**) [trabaHador], trabajadora (**f**) worker; industrious

trabajar [trabajar] to work

trabajo **m** [trabaHo] work; job

traducir [tradooseer] to translate

traer [tra-air] to bring

tráfico: tráfico de drogas drug traffic; drug-trafficking

tragar to swallow

traigo [trīgo] I bring

tráiler **m** [trīlair] large truck; caravan, (US) trailer

tráiners **mpl** [trīnairs] trainers

traje (**m**) [traHeh] I brought; suit; clothes

traje de baño [deh ban-yo] swimming costume

traje de noche [nocheh] evening dress

traje de señora [sen-yora] lady's suit

traje típico traditional regional costume

trámites **mpl** [tra-meet-es] bureaucracy, paperwork

tranquilizante [trankeeleesanteh] tranquillizer

tranquilizarse [trankeeleesarseh] to calm down

tranquilo [trankeelo] quiet

transar to sell out, to compromise

tránsito **m** traffic

tras after

trasbordo **m** transfer; change hacer trasbordo en ... change at ...

trasero (**m**) [trasairo] bottom; back; rear

trasladar to move se traslada under new management

trasnochar to spend the night

tratamiento **m** [–m-yento] treatment

tratar to treat; to try

trato **m** way of treating people

través: a través de [trav-es deh] across, through

travieso [trab-yeso] mischievous

trece [treseh] thirteen

treinta [traynta] thirty

tren **m** train

tren de carga [deh] goods train

tren de lavado automático [labado owtomateeko] carwash

tren de pasajeros [pasaHairos] passenger train

tren directo through train

tren tranvía [tranbee-a] stopping train

tres three

trescientos [tres-yentos] three hundred

tres cuartos de hora mpl [kwartos deh ora] three quarters of an hour

tribunal m [treeboonal] court; tribunal

tripulación f [treepoolas-yon] crew

triste [treesteh] sad

tristeza f [treestesa] sadness

tronco m body; buddy

tropezar [tropesar] to trip

trueno m [trweno] thunder

tu [too] your

tú you

tubo de escape m [deh eskapeh] exhaust

tubo de respirar snorkel

tuerce a la izquierda turn left

tuerza [twairsa] turn

tú mismo yourself

túnel m [too-nel] tunnel

turismo m tourism; luxury bus; tourist office

turista m/f tourist

turístico [tooreesteeko] tourist

turno m [toorno] turn; round; shift

es mi turno it's my turn/round

tus [toos] your

tuya [too-ya], tuyas, tuyo, tuyos yours

u [oo] or

ubicarse [oobeekarseh] to be located

¿lo ubicas? do you know the one I mean?

Ud (Usted) [oosteh] you

Uds (Ustedes) [oostedes] you

úlcera (de estómago) f [oolsaira] (stomach) ulcer

últimamente [oolteemamenteh] recently, lately

último last; latest

últimos días [dee-as] last days; last few days

ultramarinos m grocer's

un [oon] a

una [oona] a

unas some

universidad f [ooneebairseeda] university

uno one; someone

unos some; a few

uña f [oon-ya] fingernail

urbanización f [oorbaneesas-yon] housing estate

urbano urban, city

urgencias [oorHens-yas] casualty (department); emergencies

uruguayo [ooroogwī-yo] Uruguayan

usado used; secondhand

usar to use

no se usa [seh] it isn't done

uso use

el uso del tabaco es perjudicial para su salud

smoking can damage your
health
uso externo not to be taken
internally
**uso obligatorio cinturón de
seguridad** seatbelts must be
worn
Usted [oost**eh**] you
Ustedes [oosted-es] you
útil useful

V

v is pronounced more like a b than
an English v

va he/she/it goes; you go
vaca f cow
vacaciones fpl [bakas-y**o**n-es]
holiday, vacation
vacilar [bas**ee**lar] to party, to
have a good time
vacilón [bas**ee**lon] fun-loving
vacío [bas**ee**-o] empty
vacuna f vaccination
vacunarse [bak**oo**narseh] to be
vaccinated
vagón m carriage, coach
vagón de literas [deh leet**ai**ras]
sleeping car
vagón restaurante [restowr**a**nteh]
restaurant car
vajilla f [ba**Hee**-ya] dinner
service, set of crockery
vale: ¿cuánto vale? [kw**a**nto
b**a**leh] how much is it?
me vale (madre) [m**a**dreh] I
don't give a shit

valer [bal**air**] to be worth
valiente [bal-y**e**nteh] brave
valla f [ba-ya] fence
valle m [ba-yeh] valley
valores mpl [bal**o**r-es] securities
válvula f valve
vamos we go
van they go; you go
vapor m steam
vaquero m [bak**ai**ro] cowboy
vaqueros mpl jeans
variar [bar-yar] to vary
para variar for a change
varicela f [bar**ee**sela]
chickenpox
varios [bar-yos] several;
different
varón m male
varonil manly
vas you go
vasco Basque
vaso m glass
vatio m [bat-yo] watt
vaya [b**i**-ya] go; I/he/she/you
should go; I/he/she/you
might go
Vd (Usted) you
Vds (Ustedes) you
ve [beh] go; he/she sees; you
see
veces: a veces [bes-es]
sometimes
vecindad f [bese**e**nda] inner
city slum
vehículos pesados heavy
vehicles
v is pronounced more like a b than
an English v
vecino m [bese**e**no] neighbour

veinte [**baynteh**] twenty

vejez f [beH-**es**] old age

vela f candle; sail

velero m [be**lairo**] sailing boat

velocidad f [belo**seeda**] speed

velocidad controlada por radar radar speed checks

velocidades fpl [beloseed**ad-es**] gears

velocidad limitada speed limits apply

velocímetro m [belo**see**metro] speedometer

ven [ben] come; they see; you see

vena f vein

venda f bandage

vendar to dress (wound)

vendemos a ... selling rate

vender [ben**dair**] to sell

veneno m poison

venezolano [bene**solano**] Venezuelan

vengo I come

venir to come

venta f sale
  de venta aquí on sale here

venta de estampillas stamps sold here

venta de localidades tickets (on sale)

ventana f window

ventanilla f [benta**nee**-ya] window; ticket office

ventas a crédito credit terms available

ventas al contado cash sales

ventas a plazos hire purchase, (US) installment plan

ventilador m fan

ver [bair] to see; to watch

veraneante m/f [bairaneh-**anteh**] holiday-maker, vacationer

veranear [bairaneh-**ar**] to holiday, to take a vacation

veraneo: centro de veraneo [**sentro** deh bairaneh-**o**] holiday resort

verano m [bai**rano**] summer

veras: de veras [deh ba**iras**] really, honestly

verdad f [**bairda**] truth
  ¿verdad? don't you?; do you?; isn't it?; isn't he?; is he? etc

verdadero [bairda**dairo**] true

verde (m) [**bairdeh**] green

verguenza f [bairg**wensa**] shame

versión f [bairs-**yon**] version
  en versión original [oreegee**naal**] in the original language

vestido m dress

vestir to dress

vestirse [bes**teerseh**] to get dressed; to dress

vestuarios mpl [bestwar-**yos**] fitting rooms; changing rooms

vez f [bes] time
  una vez once
  en vez de [deh] instead of

vi [bee] I saw

vía f [**bee**-a] platform, (US) track

vía aérea: por vía aérea [a-**air**-eh-a] by air mail

viajar [b-ya**Har**] to travel

viaje m [b-ya**Heh**] journey
  ¡buen viaje! [bwen] have a

good trip!

viaje de negocios [deh negos-yos] business trip

viaje de novios [nob-yos] honeymoon

viaje organizado [organeesado] package tour

viajero m [b-yaHairo] traveller

vía oral orally

vía rectal per rectum

víbora f [beebora] snake

vida f life

vidrio m [beedr-yo] glass; window

viejo (m) [b-yeHo] old; mate, buddy

mi viejo my old man, my father

mis viejos my parents

viene: la semana que viene [keh b-yeneh] next week

viento m [b-yento] wind

vientre m [b-yentreh] stomach

viernes m [b-yairn-es] Friday

Viernes Santo Good Friday

vine [beeneh] I came

vinos y licores wines and spirits

viñedo [been-yedo] vineyard

violación f [b-yolas-yon] rape

violar [b-yolar] to rape

violencia f [b-yolensee-a] violence

violento [b-yolento] violent

visita f visit

visita con guía [gee-a] guided tour

visitante m/f [beeseetanteh] visitor

visitar to visit

visor m viewfinder

víspera f [beespaira] the day before

vista f view

visto seen

viuda f [b-yooda] widow

viudo m widower

vivir to live

vivo alive; I live

VO (versión original) original language

voceador m [boseador] newspaper seller

vocero m [bosairo] spokesman

volante m [bolanteh] steering wheel

volar to fly

volcán m [bolkan] volcano

volibol m [boleebol] volleyball

voltaje m [boltaHeh] voltage

voltear [bolteh-ar] to turn over; to knock over

volver [bolbair] to come back

volver a hacer algo to do something again

vomitar to vomit

v.o. subtitulada version in the original language with subtitles

voy I go

voz f [bos] voice

vuelo m [bwelo] flight

vuelo nacional [nas-yonal] domestic flight

v is pronounced more like a b than an English v

vecino m [beseeno] neighbour

vuelo regular scheduled flight

vuelta f [bwelta] tour, trip
  a la vuelta around the corner
  dar una vuelta to go for a
  walk

vuelto m [bwelto] change

vuelvo [bwelbo] I return

vulcanizadora f
  [boolkaneesadora] vulcanizer,
  tyre repairs

Y

y [ee] and

ya already; now
  ya está there you are
  ya mero [mairo] right here,
  right now

yace [ya-seh] lies

yanqui m/f [yankee] Yankee,
  North American

ya que [keh] since

yerba f [yairba] herb

yerno m [yairno] son-in-law

yo I; me

yo mismo myself

yucateco [yookateko] from/of
  Yucatán

Z

zacateco [sakateko] from/of
  Zacatecas

zafarse [safarseh] to get away,
  to escape

zancudo m [sankoodo]
  mosquito

zapatería f [sapatairee-a] shoe
  shop/store

zapatero m [sapatairo] cobbler;
  shoe repairer

zapatismo m [sapateesmo]
  peasant movement led by
  Emiliano Zapata (1911-19);
  peasant movement in Chiapas
  1994-

zapatista m/f follower of the
  above

zapatos mpl [sapatos] shoes

zapoteco [sapoteko] from/of
  Zapotec culture

zenzontle m [sensontleh]
  mockingbird

zócalo m [sokalo] central square

zona f [sona] area

zona arqueológica [arkeh-
  ologeeka] archaeological site

zona de servicios [deh sairbees-
  yos] service area

zona industrial [eendoostree-al]
  industrial estate

zona monumental historic
  monuments

zona postal [pos-tal] postcode,
  zip code

zona (reservada) para
  peatones pedestrian precinct

zopilote m [sopeeloteh] vulture

zurdo [soordo] left-handed

Menu
Reader:
Food

Essential Terms

bread el pan
butter la mantequilla [mantekee-ya]
cup la taza [tasa]
dessert el postre [postreh]
fish el pescado
fork el tenedor
glass (tumbler) el vaso [baso]
  (wine glass) la copa
knife el cuchillo [koochee-yo]
main course el plato principal
meat la carne [karneh]
menu la carta
pepper (spice) la pimienta [peem-yenta]
plate el plato
salad la ensalada
salt la sal
set menu el menú, la comida corrida
soup la sopa
spoon la cuchara
starter la entrada
table la mesa

another ..., please otro/otra ..., por favor [fabor]
waiter! ¡señor! [sen-yor]
waitress! ¡señorita! [sen-yoreeta]
could I have the bill, please? me pasa la cuenta, por favor [meh pasa la kwenta]

aceite [asayteh] oil

aceite de oliva [deh oleeba] olive oil

aceitunas [asaytoonas] olives

aceitunas aliñadas [aleenyadas] olives with salad dressing

aceitunas negras [neh-gras] black olives

aceitunas rellenas [reh-yenas] stuffed olives

achicoria [acheekor-ya] chicory, endive

achiote [achee-oteh] spicy seasoning from Yucatán

acocil [akoseel] freshwater shrimp

adobado tossed in adobo seasoning

adobo red chilli paste used for cooking, in marinades etc

aguacate [agwakateh] avocado

ahumado [a-oomado] smoked

ajo [aHo] garlic

a la brasa barbecued

a la crema creamed

a la criolla [kree-o-ya] in hot, spicy sauce

a la marinera [mareenaira] in white wine sauce with garlic

a la mexicana [meHeekana] with chilli peppers, onions and garlic

a la parrilla [parree-ya] grilled

a la plancha grilled

a la romana fried in batter

a la Tampiqueña [tampeeken-ya] with chilli sauce and black refried beans

a la Veracruzana [bairakroosana] in a tomato-based sauce with olives, capers and chillies

al carbón grilled

al mojo de ajo [moHo deh aHo] in a garlic sauce

al natural [natooral] plain

albahaca [alba-aka] basil

albóndigas meatballs

albóndigas de lomo [deh] pork meatballs

alcachofas artichokes

alcachofas a la romana artichokes in batter

alcaparras capers

al horno [orno] baked

aliñado [aleen-yado] with salad dressing

ali oli garlic mayonnaise

almejas [almeh-Has] clams

almejas a la marinera [mareenaira] clams stewed in white wine

almejas al natural [natooral] live clams

almendras almonds

almuerzo [almwairso] set menu; lunch

anchoas [ancho-as] anchovies

anchoas a la barquera [barkaira] marinated anchovies with capers

anguila [angeela] eel

antojitos [antoHeetos] snacks

apio [ap-yo] celery

arroz [arros] rice

arroz a la cubana boiled rice with fried eggs and either bananas or chillies

arroz a la mexicana
[meHeekana] rice with garlic,
tomato and coriander

arroz blanco boiled white rice

arroz con leche [lecheh] rice
pudding

arroz con mariscos rice with
seafood

arroz verde [bairdeh] rice with
olives and green peppers

asado roast; roast meat

ate [ateh] quince jelly

atún tuna

avellanas [abeh-yanas]
hazelnuts

aves [ab-es] poultry

azafrán [asafran] saffron

azúcar [asookar] sugar

bacalao a la vizcaína [bakalow
– beeska-eena] cod served with
ham, peppers and onions

bacalao al pil pil [peel] cod
cooked in olive oil

baleada [baleh-ada] corn meal
pancake filled with beans,
cheese and eggs

barbacoa barbecued meat

berenjena [bairenHena]
aubergine, eggplant

besugo sea bream

besugo al horno [orno] baked
sea bream

besugo asado baked sea
bream

besugo mechado sea bream
stuffed with ham and bacon

betabel beetroot

bien hecho [b-yen echo] well-
done

bife [beefeh] steak

birria [beer-ya] mutton stew

bistec steak

bistec de ternera [deh tairnaira]
veal steak

bizcocho [beeskocho] sponge
finger

blanquillo [blankee-yo] egg

bolillo [bolee-yo] bread roll

bollo [bo-yo] roll

bomba helada [elada] baked
Alaska

bonito tuna

bonito al horno [orno] baked
tuna

bonito con jitomate [Hitomateh]
tuna with tomato

boquerones fritos [bokairon-es]
fried fresh anchovies

borracho cake soaked in rum

botanas snacks

brazo de gitano [braso deh
Heetano] swiss roll

brochetas kebabs

budín bread pudding

buey [boo-eh] beef

buñuelos [boon-ywelos] light
fried pastries; doughnuts

burritos stuffed tortilla parcels

cabeza [kabesa] pig's head
(brains, cheeks etc)

cabrilla [kabree-ya] sea bass

cabrito kid

cabrito al pastor grilled kid

cabrito asado roast kid

cacahuates [kakawat-es]
peanuts

cajeta [kaнeta] fudge

calabacines [kalabaseen-es] courgettes, zucchini; marrow, squash

calabacitas courgettes, zucchini

calabaza [kalabasa] pumpkin, squash

calamares a la romana [kalamar-es] squid rings fried in batter

calamares en su tinta squid cooked in their ink

calamares fritos fried squid

caldeirada [kaldairada] fish soup

caldillo [kaldee-yo] stew

caldo de ... [deh] ... soup

caldo de perdiz [pairdees] partridge soup

caldo de pescado clear fish soup

caldo de pollo [po-yo] chicken soup

caldo gallego [ga-yego] clear soup with green vegetables, beans

caldo tlalpeño [tlalpen-yo] chicken broth with vegetables, chicken strips and coriander

caldo Xóchitl [socheetl] chicken broth with pumpkin blossoms

callos [ka-yos] tripe

camarones [kamaron-es] prawns

camarones al mojo de ajo

[moнo deh aнo] garlic prawns

camote [kamoteh] sweet potato

campechana de camarón [deh] spicy prawn cocktail

canela cinnamon

canelones [kanelon-es] cannelloni

capirotada bread pudding

caracoles [karakol-es] sea snails

carne [karneh] meat

carne de chancho [deh] pork

carne de puerco [pwairko] pork

carne de res beef

carne picada minced meat

carnero [karnairo] mutton

carnes [karn-es] meat; meat dishes

carnitas barbecued pork

carta menu

casero [kasairo] home-made

castañas [kastan-yas] chestnuts

caza [kasa] game

cazuela [kaswela] casserole, stew

cazuela de hígado [deh eegado] liver casserole

cazuela de mariscos seafood stew

cebolla [sebo-ya] onion

cebollitas [sebo-yeetas] spring onions

cecina [seseena] sun-dried pork

cena [sena] dinner, evening meal

cerdo [sairdo] pork, pig

cereza [sairesa] cherry

ceviche [sebeecheh] marinated

raw seafood cocktail
chabacano apricot
chalupa fried tortilla with filling
champiñones [champeen-yon-es] mushrooms
chancho pork, pig
chayote [chī-yoteh] vegetable similar to marrow or squash
chicharrón pork crackling
chícharros peas
chilaquiles [cheelakeel-es] fried tortillas in hot chilli sauce
chile [cheeleh] chilli pepper
chile de árbol [deh] dried reddish chilli pepper
chile güero [gwairo] very hot, white chilli pepper
chile habanero [abanairo] very hot red or green chilli
chile jalapeño [Halapen-yo] green chilli pepper, usually in vinegar with onions and carrots
chile Pekin small, green, very hot chilli pepper
chile poblano large green bell pepper, usually stuffed
chile rubio very hot, white chilli pepper
chiles en nogada [cheel-es] stuffed peppers with a sauce made from walnuts and pomegranate seeds
chile serrano [sairrano] very hot, thin green chilli pepper
chiles rellenos [reh-yenos] stuffed green peppers
chimichanga stuffed, fried

tortilla
chipirones [cheepeeron-es] baby squid
chipotle [cheepotleh] dark chilli sauce
chirimoya soursop (a tart-flavoured fruit)
cholgas mussels
chongos zamoranos [samoranos] curds in syrup
chorizo [choreeso] spicy red sausage
chuleta chop, cutlet
chuleta de cerdo [deh sairdo] pork chop
chuleta de cerdo empanizada [empaneesada] breaded pork chop
chuleta de chancho pork chop
chuleta de cordero [kordairo] lamb chop
chuleta de lomo ahumado [a-oomado] smoked pork chop
chuleta de ternera [tairnaira] veal chop
chuleta de ternera empanizada [empaneesada] breaded veal chop
chuleta de venado [benado] venison chop
churrasco roast or grilled meat
churros [choorros] long fritters
cigalas [seegalas] crayfish
cigalas a la parrilla [parree-ya] grilled crayfish
cilantro [seelantro] coriander
ciruela [seerwela] plum,

greengage

ciruela pasa prune

cochinillo asado [kocheenee-yo]
roast sucking pig

cochinita pibil [peebeel]
barbecued pork

cocido [koseedo] stew made
from meat, chickpeas and
vegetables

coco coconut

coctel de gambas [deh] prawn
cocktail

coctel de langostinos king
prawn cocktail

coctel de mariscos seafood
cocktail

codornices [kodornees-es]
quails

codornices estofadas braised
quails

coles de Bruselas [kol-es deh]
Brussels sprouts

corvina bass

coliflor cauliflower

coliflor con bechamel
[beshamel] cauliflower in
white sauce

comal griddle

comida set menu; meal; food

comida corrida set menu

comidas para llevar [yebar]
take-away meals

comino cumin

conejo [koneHo] rabbit

congrio [kon-gryo] conger eel

conservas [konsairbas] jams,
preserves

consomé de pollo [deh po-yo]
chicken consommé

cordero [kordairo] lamb

cordero asado roast lamb

costillas [kostee-yas] ribs

costillas de cerdo [deh sairdo]
pork rib

coyotas biscuits, cookies

crema cream

crema de espárragos [deh]
cream of asparagus soup

crema de espinacas cream of
spinach soup

cremada dessert made from
egg, sugar and milk

crepa sweet pancake

crep(e) pancake

crepes imperiales [krep-es
eempair-yal-es] crêpes suzette

criadillas [kree-adee-yas] bull's
testicles

crocante [krokanteh] ice cream
with chopped nuts

croquetas [kroketas] croquettes

croquetas de pescado [deh]
fish croquettes

crudo raw

cubierto menu

cuerno [kwairno] croissant

cuitlacoche [kweetlakocheh]
type of edible mushroom
which grows on the maize/
corn plant

damasco apricot

dátiles [dateel-es] dates

de fabricación casera [deh
fabreekas-yon kasaira] home-
made

desayuno [desĭ-yoono]
breakfast

dorado type of fish

dulce de membrillo [doolseh deh membree-yo] quince jelly

dulces [dools-es] sweets, candies

durazno [doorasno] peach

ejotes [eHot-es] green beans, runner beans

elote [eloteh] maize, corn on the cob, corncob

embutidos cured pork sausages

empanada pasty filled with meat or fish

empanizado [empaneesado] in breadcrumbs

en escabeche [eskabecheh] pickled

enchilada fried corn meal pancake filled with meat, vegetables and cheese

enchiladas rojas [roHas] stuffed tortillas in red chilli sauce

enchilada suiza [sweesa] stuffed tortilla with soured cream

enchiladas verdes [baírd-es] stuffed tortillas in green chilli sauce

endivias [endeeb-yas] endive, chicory

ensalada salad

ensalada de frutas [deh] fruit salad

ensalada de pollo [po-yo] chicken salad

ensalada mixta [meesta] mixed salad

ensalada verde [bairdeh] green salad

ensaladilla [ensaladee-ya] vegetables and chicken in mayonnaise

ensaladilla rusa Russian salad

entrecot de ternera [deh tairnaira] veal entrecôte

entremeses [entremes-es] hors d'oeuvres

entremeses variados [bar-yados] assorted hors d'œuvres

epazote [epasoteh] commonly used Mexican herb

escabeche de ... [eskabecheh deh] pickled ...

escamoles [eskamol-es] ants' eggs

escarola curly endive

espada ahumado [a-oomado] smoked swordfish

espaguetis [espagetees] spaghetti

espárragos asparagus

espárragos con mayonesa [mī-yonesa] asparagus with mayonnaise

espárragos dos salsas asparagus with mayonnaise and vinaigrette dressing

espárragos en vinagreta [beenagreta] asparagus in vinaigrette dressing

especia [espes-ya] spice

especialidad [espes-yaleeda] speciality

espinacas spinach

espinacas a la crema creamed spinach

estragón tarragon

fabada (asturiana) [astoor-yana] bean stew with red sausage

fajitas [faнeetas] soft wheat tortillas stuffed with chicken or beef, peppers and onion

faisán [fisan] pheasant

faisán con castañas [kastan-yas] pheasant with chestnuts

faisán estofado stewed pheasant

faisán trufado pheasant with truffles

fiambres [f-yamb-res] cold meats, cold cuts

fideos [feedeh-os] thin pasta; noodles; vermicelli

filete [feeleteh] meat or fish steak

filete a la parrilla [parree-ya] grilled beef steak

filete a la plancha grilled beef steak

filete de puerco [deh pwairko] pork fillet

filete de res beef steak

filete de ternera [tairnaira] veal steak

flan crème caramel

flan con nata crème caramel with whipped cream

flan de café [deh kafeh] coffee-flavoured crème caramel

flan de caramelo crème caramel

flan (quemado) al ron [kemado] crème caramel with rum

flautas [flowtas] fried tacos

flor de calabaza [deh kalabasa] pumpkin flower

frambuesas [frambwesas] raspberries

fresas strawberries

fresas con nata strawberries and cream/whipped cream

frijol [freeнol] bean

frijoles [freeнol-es] kidney beans

frijoles blancos white beans

frijoles borrachos beans cooked with beer

frijoles de olla [deh o-ya] boiled beans in gravy-type sauce

frijoles negros [neh-gros] black beans

frijoles refritos refried beans

fruta fruit

fruta variada [bar-yada] selection of fresh fruit

frutas en almíbar fruit in syrup

frutillas [frootee-yas] strawberries

galleta [ga-yeta] biscuit, cookie

gallina [ga-yeena] chicken

gamba large prawn

garbanzos [garbansos] chickpeas

garnachas tortillas with garlic sauce, typical of Veracruz

garobo iguana

gazpacho andaluz [gaspacho andaloos] cold soup made from tomatoes, onions, garlic, peppers and cucumber

gelatina [нelateena] gelatine; jelly, (US) jello

221

gorditas stuffed tortillas

granada pomegranate

granadilla [granadee-ya] passion fruit

gratinado au gratin – baked in a cream and cheese sauce

grosellas [groseh-yas] redcurrants

guacamole [gwakamoleh] avocado dip

guanábana [gwanabana] soursop

guayaba [gwi-yaba] guava

guinda [geenda] black cherry; alcoholic drink made from black cherries

guineo [geeneh-o] small banana

guisado [gweesado] stew

gusanos de maguey [deh magay] maguey worms

hamburguesa [amboorgesa] hamburger

harina [areena] flour

harina de maíz [ma-ees] cornflour

helado [elado] ice cream

helado de chocolate [deh chokolateh] chocolate ice cream

helado de fresa strawberry ice cream

helado de nata dairy ice cream

helado de vainilla [binee-ya] vanilla ice cream

hierbas [yairbas] herbs

hígado [eegado] liver

hígado con cebolla [sebo-ya] liver cooked with onion

hígado de ternera estofado [deh tairnaira] braised calves' liver

hígado encebollado [ensebo-yado] liver in an onion sauce

hígado estofado braised liver

higos [eegos] figs

higos con miel y nueces [m-yel ee nwes-es] figs with honey and nuts

higos secos dried figs

hongos [ongos] mushrooms

huachinango [wacheenango] red snapper

huachinango al ajo [aHo] red snapper with garlic butter

huevo [webo] egg

huevo duro [dooro] hard-boiled egg

huevo pasado por agua [agwa] boiled egg

huevos a la mexicana [meHeekana] scrambled eggs with peppers, onions and garlic

huevos a la oaxaqueña [waHaken-ya] eggs in chilli and tomato sauce

huevos cocidos [koseedos] hard-boiled eggs

huevos con jamón [Hamon] ham and eggs

huevos con papas fritas fried eggs and chips/French fries

huevos con tocino [toseeno] eggs and bacon

huevos escalfados poached eggs

huevos estrellados [estreh-yados] fried eggs

huevos fritos fried eggs

huevos fritos con chorizo [choreeso] fried eggs with Spanish sausage

huevos motuleños [motoolen-yos] eggs cooked in chillis and tomatoes, served on a fried tortilla and garnished with cheese, ham and chillis

huevos rancheros [ranchairos] fried eggs with hot tomato sauce and tortilla

huevos rellenos [reh-yenos] stuffed eggs

huevos revueltos [rebweltos] scrambled eggs

huevo tibio [teeb-yo] soft-boiled egg

humitas [oomeetas] sweetcorn tamales

incluye pan, postre y vino includes bread, dessert and wine

jaiba [Hība] crab

jalapeños [Halapen-yos] hot green chilli peppers

jalea [Haleh-a] gelatine; jelly, (US) jello

jamón [Hamon] ham

jamón serrano [sairrano] cured ham, similar to Parma ham

jamón York boiled ham

jarabe [Harabeh] syrup

jícama [Heekama] sweet turnip-like fruit eaten with lemon juice or chilli

jitomate [Heetomateh] tomato

langosta lobster

langosta a la americana [amaireekana] lobster with brandy and garlic

langosta fría con mayonesa [free-a kon mī-yonesa] cold lobster with mayonnaise

langosta gratinada lobster au gratin

langostinos a la plancha grilled king prawns

langostinos con mayonesa [mī-yonesa] king prawns with mayonnaise

langostinos dos salsas king prawns cooked in two sauces

laurel [lowrel] bay leaves

lechuga [lechooga] lettuce

lengua [lengwa] tongue

lengua de cordero estofada [deh kordairo] stewed lambs' tongue

lengua de res ox tongue

lenguado a la plancha [lengwado] grilled sole

lentejas [lenteHas] lentils

lima [leema] lime

limón lemon; lime

lobina sea bass

lomo pork fillet, pork loin, tenderloin

longaniza [longaneesa] cooked spicy sausage

macarrones [makarron-es] macaroni

macarrones gratinados
macaroni cheese

machaca shredded meat

macho large green banana

maduro ripe

magdalena sponge cake, (US)
muffin

maíz [ma-ees] sweetcorn,
maize, (US) corn

mamey [mamay] round, apple-
sized tropical fruit

mandarina tangerine

manitas de cerdo [deh sairdo]
pig's trotters

manitas de cordero [kordairo]
leg of lamb

mantequilla [mantekee-ya]
butter

manzana [mansana] apple

manzanas asadas baked
apples

maracuyá [marakoo-ya] passion
fruit

mariscada cold mixed
shellfish

mariscos shellfish

mariscos de temporada
seasonal shellfish

masa dough

mayonesa [mī-yonesa]
mayonnaise

mazapán [masapan]
marzipan

mazorca f [masorka] corn on
the cob, (US) corncob

medallones de anguila [meda-
yon-es deh angeela] eel steaks

medallones de merluza
[mairloosa] hake steaks

mejillones [meHee-yon-es]
mussels

mejillones a la marinera
[mareenaira] mussels in wine
sauce with garlic

mejillones con salsa mussels
with tomato and herb sauce

melón melon

membrillo [membree-yo]
quince; quince jelly

menestra de verduras [deh
bairdooras] vegetable stew

menú [menoo] set menu

menú de la casa [deh] fixed-
price menu

menú del día today's set menu

menudo tripe; sweetbreads

menú turístico set menu

merluza a la parrilla [mairloosa a
la parree-ya] grilled hake

merluza a la riojana [r-yoHana]
hake with chillies

merluza a la romana hake
steaks in batter

merluza frita fried hake

mermelada [mairmelada] jam;
marmalade

mermelada de ciruelas [deh
seerswelas] plum jam

mermelada de damasco
apricot jam

mermelada de durazno
[doorasno] peach jam

mermelada de fresas
strawberry jam

mermelada de limón lemon
marmalade

mermelada de naranja
[naranHa] orange marmalade

miel [m-yel] honey

milanesa breaded chop or escalope

milanesa de ternera [deh tairnaira] breaded veal escalope

mojarro [moHarro] type of fish

mole [moleh] sauce made with chilli peppers, chocolate and spices

mole de olla [deh o-ya] spicy meat stew

mole oaxaqueño [waHaken-yo] type of black or green mole sauce

mole poblano rich mole sauce made from nuts, prunes and bananas, a Puebla speciality

mollejas de ternera [mo-yeHas deh tairnaira] calves' sweetbreads

molletes [mo-ye-tes] toasted roll with refried beans and cheese

mondongo tripe

morcilla [morsee-ya] black pudding, blood sausage

morcilla de ternera [deh tairnaira] black pudding made from calves' blood

mortadela salami-type sausage

mostaza [mostasa] mustard

mousse de limón [deh] lemon mousse

nabo turnip

nacatamales [nakatamal-es] corn meal dough filled with meat in sauce and steamed in banana leaves

nachos tortilla chips with cheese

naranja [naranHa] orange

nata cream

natilla [natee-ya] custard

natillas [natee-yas] cold custard with cinnamon

natillas de chocolate [deh chokolateh] cold custard with chocolate

nieve [n-yeveh] sorbet; ice cream

níscalos wild mushrooms

nixtamal [neestamal] maize dough, (US) corn dough

nopalitos chopped cactus-leaf salad

nueces [nwes-es] walnuts

nuez [nwes] nut

ostión [ost-yon] oyster

paella [pa-eh-ya] fried rice with seafood and chicken

paella valenciana [balens-yana] paella with assorted shellfish

paleta ice lolly

palmito palm heart

palomitas popcorn

pan bread

pan blanco white bread

pan de cazón [kason] layered dish of tortillas, beans and dogfish with a hot sauce

pan de centeno [senteno] brown bread

pan de higos [deh eegos] dried fig cake with cinnamon

pan dulce [doolseh] buns and cakes, sweet pastries

pan integral [eentegral]
  wholemeal bread
pancita [panseeta] tripe
papa potato
papadzules [papadsul-es]
  tortillas stuffed with hard-
  boiled eggs from Yucatán
papas a la criolla [cree-o-ya]
  potatoes in hot, spicy sauce
papas asadas baked potatoes
papas bravas potatoes in
  cayenne pepper
papas fritas chips, French
  fries
papaya papaya, pawpaw
parrillada de caza [parree-yada
  deh kasa] mixed grilled game
parrillada de mariscos mixed
  grilled shellfish
pasas raisins
pasta biscuit, cookie; pastry;
  pasta
pastel cake; pie
pastel de carne [karneh]
  brawn, jellied meat
pata foot, trotter
patatas (fritas) crisps, (US)
  potato chips
pato duck
pato a la naranja [naranHa]
  duck à l'orange
pato asado roast duck
pavo [pabo] turkey
pavo relleno [reh-yeno] stuffed
  turkey
pay [pi] pie with a sweet
  filling
pay de queso [deh keso]
  cheesecake

pechuga de pollo [deh po-yo]
  breast of chicken
pepinillos [pepeenee-yos]
  gherkins
pepinillos en vinagreta
  [beenagreta] gherkins in
  vinaigrette dressing
pepino cucumber
pera [paira] pear
perdices [pairdees-es]
  partridges
perdices a la campesina
  partridges with vegetables
perdices asadas roast
  partridges
perdices con chocolate
  [chokolateh] partridges with
  chocolate
perdices encebolladas [ensebo-
  yadas] partridge with onion
perejil [paireh-Heel] parsley
perro caliente [pairro kal-yenteh]
  hot dog
pescaditos fritos fried sprats
pescado fish
pescado a la veracruzana
  [bairakroosana] seasoned sea
  bass or red snapper fillets
  fried and served with tomato
  sauce on top
pez espada ahumado
  [a-oomado] smoked swordfish
píbil cooked in a pit
picadillo [peekadee-yo] minced
  meat
picadillo de pollo [deh po-yo]
  minced chicken
picadillo de ternera [tairnaira]
  minced veal

picante hot, spicy

pichón pigeon

pichones estofados [peechon-es] stewed pigeon

picoso hot, spicy

pierna [p-yairna] leg

piloncillo [peelonsee-yo] unrefined brown sugar

pimentón paprika

pimienta [peem-yenta] black pepper

pimienta blanca white pepper

pimienta de cayena [deh ki-yena] cayenne pepper

pimiento rojo [roHo] red pepper

pimiento verde [bairdeh] green pepper

pinchitos snacks/appetizers served in bars; kebabs

pincho kebab

piña [peen-ya] pineapple

piña fresca fresh pineapple

piña gratinada pineapple au gratin

piñones [peen-yon-es] pine nuts

pipián [peep-yan] sauce of ground nuts, seeds and spices

pitahaya [peetahī-ya] red fruit of a cactus plant with soft, sweet flesh

plátano banana

plátano macho plantain

plátanos flameados [flameh-ados] flambéed bananas

platos combinados meat and vegetables, hamburgers and eggs etc

poco hecho [echo] rare

pollo [po-yo] chicken

pollo al ajillo [aHee-yo] fried chicken with garlic

pollo a la parrilla [parree-ya] grilled chicken

pollo al vino blanco [beeno] chicken in white wine

pollo asado roast chicken

pollo con verduras [bairdooras] chicken and vegetables

polvorones [polboron-es] sugar-based dessert (eaten at Christmas)

postre [postreh] dessert

pozole [posoleh] thick broth of vegetables meat and corn

primer plato [preemair] starter, appetizer

puerco [pwairko] pork

puerro [pwairo] leek

pulpitos con cebolla [sebo-ya] baby octopuses with onions

pulpo octopus

pupusa dumpling usually filled with cheese or meat

puré de papas [pooreh deh] mashed potatoes, potato purée

queque [kekeh] cake

quesadilla [kesadee-ya] fried corn meal pancake usually filled with cheese

queso [keso] cheese

queso con membrillo [membree-yo] cheese with quince jelly

queso fresco soft white cheese

queso fundido melted cheese

queso manchego hard, strong

cheese
queso Oaxaca [waHaka]
soft white cheese used for
cooking

rábanos radishes
ración [ras-yon] portion
**ración pequeña para niños
[peken-ya para neen-yos]**
children's portion
rajas [raHas] strips of pickled
green chillies; sliced green
peppers in cream
ravioles [rab-yol-es] ravioli
raya [rī-ya] skate
**raya con manteca negra
[neh-gra]** skate in butter and
vinegar sauce
rebanada slice
refritos refried beans
relleno [reh-yeno] stuffed;
stuffing
remolacha beetroot
repollo [repo-yo] cabbage
res beef
riñones [reen-yon-es] kidneys
riñones a la plancha grilled
kidneys
riñones al jerez [Hair-es]
kidneys in a sherry sauce
róbalo bass
romero [romairo] rosemary
ron rum
ropa vieja [b-yeh-Ha] shredded
meat
rosca round sponge made at
Christmas
roscas sweet pastries
rosquillas [roskee-yas] small

sweet pastries
sal salt
salbute type of filled tortilla
typical of Yucatán
salchicha sausage
salchichas de Frankfurt [deh]
frankfurters
salchichón salami-type
sausage
salmón [sal-mon] salmon
salmón a la parrilla [paree-ya]
grilled salmon
salmón ahumado [a-oomado]
smoked salmon
salmón frío [free-o] cold
salmon
salmonetes [sal-monet-es] red
mullet
**salmonetes a la parrilla [paree-
ya]** grilled red mullet
**salmonetes en papillote
[papee-yoteh]** red mullet
cooked in foil
salpicón de mariscos [deh]
shellfish with vinaigrette
dressing
salsa sauce
**salsa allioli/ali oli [a-yee-olee/
alee olee]** garlic mayonnaise
salsa bechamel [beshamel]
béchamel sauce, white sauce
**salsa de jitomate [deh
Heetomateh]** tomato sauce
salsa holandesa [olandesa]
hollandaise sauce
**salsa mexicana/pico de gallo
[meHeekana/peeko deh ga-yo]**
hot sauce made with chillies,
onions and red tomatoes

salsa romesco sauce made from peppers, tomatoes and garlic

salsa tártara tartare sauce

salsa verde [bairdeh] green sauce made from tomatillo and chillies

salsa vinagreta [beenagreta] vinaigrette dressing

salteado [salteh-ado] sautéed

sancocho vegetable soup with meat or fish

sandía [sandee-a] water melon

sandwich sandwich

sandwich mixto [meesto] cheese and ham sandwich

sardina sardine

sardinas a la brasa barbecued sardines

sardinas a la parrilla [parree-ya] grilled sardines

sardinas fritas fried sardines

segundo plato main course

servicio incluido service charge included

servicio no incluido service charge not included

sesos a la romana brains in batter

sesos rebozados [rebosados] brains in batter

solomillo [solomee-yo] fillet steak

solomillo con papas fritas fillet steak with chips/French fries

solomillo de cerdo [deh sairdo] fillet of pork

solomillo de ternera [tairnaira] fillet of veal

solomillo de vaca [baka] fillet of beef

solomillo frío [free-o] cold roast beef

sopa soup

sopa de aguacate fría [deh agwakateh] cold avocado soup

sopa de ajo [aHo] garlic soup

sopa de arroz rice soup

sopa de fideos [feedeh-os] noodle soup

sopa de frijoles negros [freeHol-es neh-gros] black bean soup

sopa de gallina [ga-yeena] chicken soup

sopa del día soup of the day

sopa de lentejas [lenteeHas] lentil soup

sopa de mariscos fish and shellfish soup

sopa de pescado fish soup

sopa de tortilla [tortee-ya] soup with corn meal pancakes

sopa de tortuga turtle soup

sopa de verduras [bairdooras] vegetable soup

sopa inglesa trifle

sopaipillas [sopipee-yas] sweet fritters

sopa seca rice or pasta dish served with a sauce on top

sopa tarasca creamy bean and tomato soup

sopes [sop-es] garnished tortillas

sorbete [sorbeteh] sorbet

soufflé soufflé

soufflé de fresas [deh]

strawberry soufflé

soufflé de naranja [naranHa] orange soufflé

soufflé de queso [keso] cheese soufflé

taco stuffed maize/corn pancake

tacos al pastor tacos with grilled meat

tacos de pollo [deh po-yo] tacos stuffed with chicken

tajadas [taHadas] fried banana strips

tallarines [ta-yareen-es] noodles

tallarines a la italiana [eetal-yana] tagliatelle with tomato sauce

tamal filled maize/corn dough cooked in banana leaf, tamale

tamarindo tamarind

tapa de ternera rellena [deh tairnaira reh-yena] stuffed veal hock

tapado stew

tapas appetizers

tarta cake

tarta Alaska baked Alaska

tarta de almendra [deh] almond tart or gâteau

tarta de arroz [arros] cake or tart containing rice

tarta de chocolate [chokolateh] chocolate gâteau

tarta de fresas strawberry tart or gâteau

tarta de la casa tart or gâteau baked on the premises

tarta de manzana [mansana]

apple tart

tarta helada [elada] ice cream gâteau

tarta mocha/moka [moka] mocha tart

tártar crudo raw minced steak, steak tartare

tejos de queso [teHos deh keso] cheese pastries

tencas tench

tencas con jamón [Hamon] tench with ham

ternera [tairnaira] veal

ternera asada roast veal

tocino [toseeno] bacon

todo incluido all inclusive

tomate [tomateh] green tomato

tomates rellenos [tomat-es reh-yenos] stuffed tomatoes

tomatillo [tomatee-yo] green tomato used for sauces

tomillo [tomee-yo] thyme

tordo thrush

tordos braseados [braseh-ados] grilled thrushes

tordos estofados braised thrushes

toronja [toronHa] grapefruit

torrejas [torreHas] French toast

torrijas [torreeHas] sweet pastries

torta filled bread roll with salad, cream and tomato garnish

tortilla [tortee-ya] maize pancake, (US) corn pancake

tortilla de harina [deh areena] wheat pancake

tortilla de huevo [webo]

omelette
tortilla española [espan-**y**ola]
Spanish omelette with
potato, onion and garlic
tostada fried corn pancake
topped with meat, vegetables
and salsa; toast
totopo thin, fried tortilla
trucha [**troo**cha] trout
trucha ahumada [a-oom**a**da]
smoked trout
trucha a la marinera
[mareen**ai**ra] trout in white
wine sauce
trucha con jamón [**Ham**on]
trout with ham
trucha escabechada
marinated trout
tuétano [t**we**tano] marrow,
squash
tuna [t**oo**na] prickly pear
turrón nougat
turrón de coco [deh] coconut
nougat
turrón de Jijona [Hee**H**ona] hard
nougat
turrón de yema [**y**ema] nougat
with egg yolk

uchepos small sweet tamales
uvas [**oo**bas] grapes

vainilla [bīn**ee**-ya] vanilla
venado [ben**a**do] venison
verduras [baird**oo**ras] vegetables
verduras capeadas [kapeh-
adas] courgettes and
cauliflower in batter served
with hot tomato sauce and

cream
vinagre [been**a**greh] vinegar
vuelvealavida [bwelbeh-a-
lab**ee**da] marinated seafood
cocktail with chilli

yema yolk
yerba [**y**airba] herb
yogur [yo-g**oo**r] yoghurt
yuca manioc

zanahoria [sana-**o**ree-a] carrot
zanahorias a la crema carrots
à la crème
zapallo [sap**a**-yo] marrow,
squash
zapote [sap**o**teh] sweet
pumpkin
zarzamoras [sarsam**o**ras]
blackberries
zarzuela de mariscos [sarsw**e**la
deh] shellfish stew

Menu
Reader:
Drink

Essential Terms

beer la cerveza [sairbesa]
bottle la botella [boteh-ya], el frasco
brandy el coñac [kon-yak]
black coffee el café americano [kafeh amaireekano]
 (strong) el café solo
coffee el café [kafeh]
cup la taza [tasa]
 a cup of ... una taza de ... [deh]
fruit juice el jugo de frutas [Hoogo deh]
gin la ginebra [Heenebra]
 a gin and tonic un gintónic [jeentoneek]
glass (tumbler) el vaso [baso]
 (wine glass) la copa
 a glass of ... un vaso de ... [deh], una copa de ...
milk la leche [lecheh]
milkshake el licuado [leekwado]
mineral water el agua mineral [agwa meenairal]
red wine el vino tinto [beeno teento]
soda (water) la soda
soft drink el refresco
sugar el azúcar [asookar]
tea el té [teh]
tonic (water) la tónica
vodka el vodka [bodka]
water el agua [agwa]
whisky el whisky
white wine el vino blanco [beeno]
wine el vino
wine list la lista de vinos [leesta deh beenos]

another ... otro/otra ...

agua [**a**gwa] water

agua de fruta fruit drink made from fruit and water

agua de granada [deh] grenadine juice

agua de jamaica [Ham**ee**ka] hibiscus blossom drink

agua de melón melon juice

agua de panela drink made from water and sugar

agua mineral [meena**ira**l] mineral water

agua mineral con gas fizzy mineral water

agua mineral sin gas [seen] still mineral water

aguardiente [agward-y**e**nteh] a clear spirit similar to brandy or white rum

al tiempo [t-y**e**mpo] at room temperature

añejo [an-y**e**h-Ho] vintage; mellow; mature

anís aniseed-flavoured spirit

aperitivo [apaireet**ee**bo] aperitif

api thick custard-like drink made from maize and cinnamon

aromáticas herb teas

atole [at**o**leh] thick drink made from maize/corn

azúcar [as**oo**kar] sugar

bebida drink

bebidas alcohólicas alcoholic drinks

Bohemia® brand of lager

cacao [kak**ow**] cocoa

café [kaf**eh**] coffee

café americano black coffee

café capuchino cappuccino

café con leche [**le**cheh] coffee with milk (large cup)

café cortado coffee with a dash of milk (small cup)

café de olla [deh **o**-ya] coffee made with cinnamon and raw sugar

café descafeinado [deskafay-een**a**do] decaffeinated coffee

café escocés [eskos-**e**s] black coffee, whisky/scotch and vanilla ice cream

café exprés [espr**e**s] strong black coffee

café instantáneo [eenstan-t**a**neh-o] instant coffee

café irlandés [eerland-**e**s] black coffee, whisky, vanilla ice cream and whipped cream

café negro [**ne**h-gro] black coffee, usually strong and often sweet

café perfumado coffee with a dash of brandy or other spirit

café solo black coffee, usually strong and often sweet

carta de vinos [deh b**ee**nos] wine list

Cava [**ka**ba] champagne

cebada [seb**a**da] drink made from fermented barley

cerveza [sairb**e**sa] beer, lager

cerveza clara light, lager-style beer

cerveza de barril draught beer
cerveza negra dark beer
cerveza oscura dark beer
champán [champan]
  champagne
chocolate caliente [chokolateh
  kal-yenteh] hot chocolate
  drink, sometimes sweetened
  with honey and flavoured
  with vanilla and spices
coctel cocktail
con azúcar [asookar] with
  sugar
con gas fizzy, sparkling
coñac [kon-yak] brandy
cosecha vintage
cubalibre [koobaleebreh] rum
  and cola
cubito de hielo [deh yelo] ice
  cube
cucaracha tequila and strong,
  alcoholic, coffee-flavoured
  drink

destornillador [destornee-yador]
  vodka and orange juice
Domecq [domek] Mexican
  wine producer
Dos Equis® [ekees] light
  Mexican beer

embotellado en ... bottled
  in ...
espumoso sparkling

gaseosa [gaseh-osa] lemonade
ginebra [Heenebra] gin
gintónic [jeentoneek] gin and
  tonic

granizada/granizado
  [graneesada] crushed ice drink
guinda [geenda] alcoholic
  drink made from black
  cherries; black cherry
guindada [geendada], guindilla
  [guindee-ya] cherry brandy

Hidalgo Mexican wine
  producer
hielo [yelo] ice
horchata [orchata] cold drink
  made from rice and water
horchata de chufas [deh] cold
  almond-flavoured milky
  drink

infusión [eenfoos-yon] herb tea

jarra de cerveza/vino [Harra
  deh sairbesa/beeno] jug of
  beer/wine
jerez [Hair-es] sherry
jerez fino light, dry sherry
jerez oloroso sweet sherry
jugo [Hoogo] juice
jugo de damasco apricot
  juice
jugo de durazno [doorasno]
  peach juice
jugo de jitomate [Heetomateh]
  tomato juice
jugo de lima lime juice
jugo de limón lemon juice
jugo de naranja [naranHa]
  orange juice
jugo de piña [peen-ya]
  pineapple juice
leche [lecheh] milk

leche de soja [deh soнa] soya milk

leche desnatada skimmed milk

licor liqueur; spirit

licor de avellana [deh abeh-yana] hazelnut-flavoured liqueur

licor de manzana [mansana] apple-flavoured liqueur

licor de durazno [doorasno] peach-flavoured liqueur

licor de melón melon-flavoured liqueur

licor de naranja [naranнa] orange-flavoured liqueur

licores [leekor-es] spirits, liqueurs

licuado [leekwado] milkshake

licuado de fresa [deh] strawberry milkshake

licuado de plátano banana milkshake

limonada fresh lemonade

lista de precios [pres-yos] price list

Málaga sweet wine

malta dark beer

malteada [malteh-ada] milkshake

manzanilla [mansanee-ya] dry sherry-type wine; camomile tea

margarita cocktail of tequila, lime juice and either grenadine, Curaçao or triple sec

mate [mateh] bitter tea made from the dried leaves of the yerba mate bush

media de agua [med-ya deh ag-wa] half-bottle of mineral water

mediana bottle of beer

mezcal [meskal] spirit distilled from the maguey cactus

Negra Modelo® dark Mexican beer

Nescafe® [neskafeh] instant coffee

Nochebuena® [nochebwena] dark Mexican beer

Oporto port

Pacífico® brand of lager

piña colada [peen-ya] rum and pineapple cocktail

posh sugar cane liquor

pozol de cacao [posol deh kaka-o] cool drink made from ground maize/corn and chocolate

pulque [poolkeh] thick alcoholic drink distilled from the pulp of the maguey cactus

puro de caña [deh kan-ya] sugar cane liquor

refresco soft drink, fizzy drink

rompope [rompopeh] egg nog, egg flip

ron rum

ron oro matured rum

sangría [sangree-a] mixture of red wine, lemon juice, spirits, sugar and fruit

sangrita orange juice, grenadine and chilli, drunk with tequila

San Miguel® [migel] type of lager

Sauza® [sowsa] brand of tequila

semidulce [semeedoolseh] medium-sweet

sidra cider

sin azúcar [seen asookar] without sugar

sin gas still

Sol® brand of lager

Superior® [soopair-yor] brand of lager

taxallate [taHa-yateh] drink from Chiapas made from maize/corn and cocoa

té [teh] tea

Tecate® [tekateh] light Mexican beer, usually served with lime and salt

té de hierbas [teh deh yairbas] herbal tea

Tehuacán® [teh-wakan] mineral water

tequila [tekeela] spirit distilled from the pulp of the agave cactus

tónica tonic

Tres Equis® [ekees] brand of lager

vino [beeno] wine

vino blanco white wine

vino de casa [deh] house wine

vino de mesa table wine

vino del país [pa-ees] local wine

vino rosado rosé wine

vino tinto red wine

yerbabuena [yairbabwena] mint tea

yerba mate [yairba mateh] bitter tea made from the dried leaves of the yerba mate bush

How the
Language
Works

Pronunciation

In this phrasebook, the Spanish has been written in a system of imitated pronunciation so that it can be read as though it were English, bearing in mind the notes on pronunciation given below:

air   as in h**air**
ay   as in m**ay**
e, eh   as in g**e**t
g   always hard as in **g**oat
H   a harsh 'ch' as in the Scottish way of pronouncing lo**ch**
ī   as the 'i' sound in m**i**ght
o   as in n**o**t
ow   as in n**ow**
s   as in mi**ss**
y   as in **y**es

Letters given in bold type indicate the part of the word to be stressed.

As i and u are always pronounced 'ee' and 'oo' in Spanish, pronunciation has not been given for all words containing these letters unless they present other problems for the learner. Thus María is pronounced 'mar**ee**-a' and fútbol is '**foo**tbol'.

Abbreviations

adj	adjective	pl	plural
f	feminine	pol	polite
fam	familiar	sing	singular
m	masculine		

Note

In the Spanish-English section and Menu Reader, the letter ñ is treated as a separate letter, as is customary in Spanish. Alphabetically, it comes after n.

Nouns

All nouns in Spanish have one of two genders: masculine or feminine. Generally speaking, those ending in **-o** are masculine:

el zapato
el sap**a**to
the shoe

Those ending in **-a**, **-d**, **-z** or **-ión** are usually feminine:

la cama	**la pensión**
la k**a**ma	la pens-y**o**n
the bed	the boarding house, the guesthouse

Nouns ending in **-or** are masculine. To form the feminine, add **-a**:

el señor	**la señora**
el sen-y**o**r	la sen-y**o**ra
the man	the woman

| **el profesor** | **la profesora** |
| the (male) teacher | the (female) teacher |

A small number of nouns ending in **-o** and **-a** (usually professions) can be either masculine or feminine:

el/la guía	**el/la violinista**
el/la g**ee**-a	el/la bee-oleen**ee**sta
the guide	the violinist

Plural Nouns

If the noun ends in a vowel, the plural is formed by adding **-s**:

el camino	**los caminos**
el kam**ee**no	los kam**ee**nos
the path	the paths

la mesera	**las meseras**
la mes**ai**ra	las mes**ai**ras
the waitress	the waitresses

If the noun ends in a consonant, the plural is formed by adding -es:

el chofer	**los choferes**
el chof**air**	los chof**air**-es
the driver	the drivers

la recepción	**las recepciones**
la reseps-y**o**n	las reseps-y**o**n-es
the reception desk	the reception desks

If the noun ends in a **-z**, change the **-z** to **-ces** to form the plural:

la luz	**las luces**
la l**oo**s	las l**oo**s-es
the light	the lights

Articles

The different articles ('the' and 'a') in Spanish vary according to the number (singular or plural) and gender of the noun they refer to.

The Definite Article

The definite article 'the' is as follows:

	singular	plural
masculine	**el**	**los**
feminine	**la**	**las**

el cuchillo/los cuchillos	**la mesa/las mesas**
el koochee-yo/los koochee-yos	la mesa/las mesas
the knife/the knives	the table/the tables

243

When the article **el** is used in combination with **a** (to) or **de** (of) it changes as follows:

a + el = al
de + el = del

vamos al museo	cerca del hotel
vamos al moos**eh**-o	s**a**irka del ot**e**l
let's go to the museum	near the hotel

The Indefinite Article

The indefinite article (a, an, some), also changes according to the gender and number of the accompanying noun:

	singular	plural
masculine	**un**	**unos**
	oon	**oo**nos
feminine	**una**	**unas**
	oona	**oo**nas

un sello	unos sellos
oon s**eh**-yo	**oo**nos s**eh**-yos
a stamp	some stamps

una chica	unas chicas
oona ch**ee**ka	**oo**nas ch**ee**kas
a girl	some girls

Adjectives and adverbs

Adjectives must agree in gender and number with the noun they refer to. Unlike English, Spanish adjectives usually follow the noun. In the English-Spanish section of this book, all adjectives are given in the masculine singular. Adjectives ending in -o change as follows for the plural:

el precio alto	los precios altos
el pr**e**s-yo **a**lto	los pr**e**s-yos **a**ltos
the high price	the high prices

The feminine singular of the adjective is formed by changing the masculine endings as follows:

masculine	feminine
-o	-a
-or	-ora
-és	-esa

un cocinero estupendo	**una cocinera estupenda**
oon koseenairo estoopendo	oona koseenaira estoopenda
a wonderful cook	a wonderful cook
un señor encantador	**una señora encantadora**
oon sen-yor enkantador	oona sen-yora enkantadora
a nice man	a nice woman
un chico inglés	**una chica inglesa**
oon cheeko eeng-les	oona cheeka eenglesa
an English boy	an English girl

For other types of adjective, the feminine forms are the same as the masculine:

un hombre agradable	**una mujer agradable**
oon hombreh agradableh	oona mooHair agradableh
a nice man	a nice woman

The plurals of adjectives are formed in the same way as the plurals of nouns, by adding an -s:

una silla roja	**dos sillas rojas**
oona see-ya roHa	dos see-yas roHas
a red chair	two red chairs

Comparatives

The comparative is formed by placing **más** (more) or **menos** (less) before the adjective or adverb:

lindo	**más lindo**
leendo	mas leendo
beautiful	more beautiful

tranquilo	menos tranquilo
trankeelo	menos trankeelo
quiet	less quiet

este hotel es más/menos caro que el otro
esteh otel es mas/menos karo keh el otro
this hotel is more/less expensive than the other one

¿tiene un cuarto más soleado?
t-yeneh oon kwarto mas soleh-ado
do you have a sunnier room?

¿podría ir más de prisa, por favor?
podree-a eer mas deh preesa por fabor
could you go faster please?

Superlatives

Superlatives are formed by placing one of the following before the adjective: **el más, la más, los más** or **las más** (depending on the noun's gender and number):

¿cuál es el más divertido?
kwal es el mas deebairteedo
which is the most entertaining?

el carro más rápido
el karro mas rapeedo
the fastest car

la casa más linda
la kasa mas leenda
the prettiest house

las mujeres más inteligentes
las mooHair-es mas eenteleeHent-es
the most intelligent women

The following adjectives have irregular comparatives and superlatives:

bueno	mejor	el mejor
bweno	meHor	el meHor
good	better	the best

grande	mayor	el mayor
grandeh	mī-yor	el mī-yor
big	bigger	the biggest
old	older	the oldest

malo	peor	el peor
malo	peh-or	el peh-or
bad	worse	the worst

pequeño	menor	el menor
peken-yo	menor	el menor
small	smaller	the smallest
	younger	the youngest

'As ... as ...' is translated as follows:

Oaxaca está tan linda como siempre!
waHaka esta tan leenda komo s-yempreh
Oaxaca is as beautiful as ever!

The superlative form ending in **-ísimo** indicates that something is 'very/extremely ...' without actually comparing it to something else:

guapo	guapísimo
gwapo	gwapeeseemo
attractive	very attractive

Adverbs

There are two ways to form an adverb. If the adjective ends in **-o**, take the feminine and add **-mente** to form the corresponding adverb:

exacto	exactamente
eksakto	eksaktamente
accurate	accurately, exactly

If the adjective ends in any other letter, add **-mente** to the basic form:

feliz	**felizmente**
fel**ee**s	fel**ee**sm**e**nteh
happy	happily

Possessive Adjectives

Possessive adjectives, like other Spanish adjectives, agree with the noun in gender and number:

	singular		plural	
	masculine	feminine	masculine	feminine
my	**mi**	**mi**	**mis**	**mis**
	mee	mee	mees	mees
your	**tu**	**tu**	**tus**	**tus**
(sing, fam)	too	too	toos	toos
his/her/its/your	**su**	**su**	**sus**	**sus**
(sing, pol)	soo	soo	soos	soos
our	**nuestro**	**nuestra**	**nuestros**	**nuestras**
	nw**e**stro	nw**e**stra	nw**e**stros	nw**e**stras
your (pl)/their	**su**	**su**	**sus**	**sus**
	soo	soo	soos	soos

tu bolsa	**sus pastillas**
too b**o**lsa	soos past**ee**-yas
your bag	his/her/your tablets

su maleta	**nuestros trajes de baño**
soo mal**e**ta	nw**e**stros tra**H**es deh b**a**n-yo
your suitcase	our swimming costumes

If when using **su/sus**, it is unclear whether you mean 'his', 'her', 'your' or 'their', you can use the following after the noun instead:

de él	his	de ellos	their (m)
deh el		deh **eh**-yos	
de ella	her	de ellas	their (f)
deh **eh**-ya		deh **eh**-yas	
de Usted	your (sing, pol)	de Ustedes	your (pl)
deh oost**eh**		deh oost**ed**-es	

el dinero de Usted   el dinero de ella
el deen**ai**ro deh oost**eh**   el deen**ai**ro deh **eh**-ya
your money   her money

el dinero de él
el deen**ai**ro deh el
his money

Possessive pronouns

To translate 'mine', 'yours', 'theirs' etc, use one of the following forms. Like possessive adjectives, possessive pronouns must agree in gender and number with the object or objects referred to:

	singular		plural	
	masculine	feminine	masculine	feminine
mine	**el mío**	**la mía**	**los míos**	**las mías**
	el **mee**-o	la **mee**-a	los **mee**-os	las **mee**-as
yours	**el tuyo**	**la tuya**	**los tuyos**	**las tuyas**
(sing, fam)	el **too**-yo	la **too**-ya	los **too**-yos	las **too**-yas
his/hers/yours	**el suyo**	**la suya**	**los suyos**	**las suyas**
(sing, pol)	el **soo**-yo	la **soo**-ya	los **soo**-yos	las **soo**-yas
ours	**el nuestro**	**la nuestra**	**los nuestros**	**las nuestras**
	el **nwe**stro	la **nwe**stra	los **nwe**stros	las **nwe**stras
yours (pl)/theirs	**el suyo**	**la suya**	**los suyos**	**las suyas**
	el **soo**-yo	la **soo**-ya	los **soo**-yos	las **soo**-yas

ésta es su llave y ésta es la mía
esta es soo y**a**beh ee **e**sta es la **mee**-a
this is your key and this is mine

no es la suya, es de sus amigos

no es la s**oo**-ya es deh soos am**ee**gos

it's not his, it's his friends'

Personal pronouns

Subject Pronouns

yo	I	**nosotros**	we (m)
yo		nos**o**tros	
tú	you (sing, fam)	**nosotras**	we (f)
too		nos**o**tras	
él	he/it	**ellos**	they (m)
el		**eh**-yos	
ella	she/it	**ellas**	they (f)
eh-ya		**eh**-yas	
Usted	you (sing, pol)	**Ustedes**	you (pl)
oost**eh**		oost**ed**-es	

Tú is used when speaking to one person and is the familiar form generally used when speaking to family, friends and children.

Usted is the polite form of address to be used when talking to someone you don't know or an older person.

Ustedes is the plural form used in Mexico whoever you are speaking to. The third person of verbs is used with **Usted** and **Ustedes**: **Usted** takes the same verb form as 'he/she/it'; **Ustedes** takes the same verb form as 'they'.

In Spanish the subject pronoun is usually omitted:

no saben	**está cansado**
no s**a**ben	esta kans**a**do
they don't know	he is tired

although it may be retained for emphasis or to avoid confusion:

¡soy yo!
soy yo
it's me!

¡somos nosotros!
somos nosotros
it's us!

yo pago los tacos, tú pagas las cervezas
yo pago los takos too pagas las sairbesas
I'll pay for the tacos, you pay for the beers

él es inglés y ella es americana
el es eeng-les ee **eh**-ya es amaireekana
he's English and she's American

Subject pronouns are also used after prepositions:

para Usted
para oost**eh**
for you

con él
kon el
with him

sin ella
seen **eh**-ya
without her

detrás de Usted
detras deh oost**eh**
behind you

después de nosotros
despw**e**s deh nos**o**tros
after us

The exceptions are **yo**, which is replaced by **mí**, and **tú** which is replaced by **tí**:

eso es para mí/tí
eso es para mee/tee
that's for me/you

After **con** (with), **mí** and **tí** change as follows:

conmigo
konm**ee**go
with me

contigo
kont**ee**go
with you

Object pronouns

me	[meh]	me		**nos**	[nos]	us
te	[teh]	you (sing, fam)		**los**	[los]	them (m), you (mpl)
lo	[lo]	him/it, you (sing, pol)		**las**	[las]	them (f), you (fpl)
la	[la]	her/it, you (sing, pol)				

Object pronouns usually precede the verb:

me la dio ayer
meh la d**ee**-o ī-y**air**
she gave it to me yesterday

las compré para ella
las kompr**eh** para **eh**-ya
I bought them for her

cada viernes la compro flores
k**a**da b-y**ai**rn-es la k**o**mpro fl**o**r-es
every Friday I buy her flowers

los vi ayer
los bee a-y**air**
I saw them yesterday

When used with infinitives, pronouns are added to the end of the infinitive:

¿puede llevarme al aeropuerto?
pw**e**deh yeb**a**rmeh al airopw**ai**rto
can you take me to the airport?

intentaré recordarlo
eententar**eh** rekordarlo
I'll try and remember it

When used with commands, pronouns are added to the end of the imperative form. See **Imperatives** page 266.

If you are using an indirect pronoun to mean 'to me', 'to you' etc (although 'to' might not always be necessarily said in English), you generally use the following:

me	[meh]	to me
te	[teh]	to you (sing, fam)
le/lo	[leh/lo]	to him, to you (sing, pol)
le/la	[leh/la]	to her, to you (sing, pol)
nos	[nos]	to us
les/los	[les/los]	to them (m), to you (mpl)
les/las	[les/las]	to them (f), to you (fpl)

me enseñó el camino
meh ensen-y**o** el kam**ee**no
he showed me the way

le pedí su dirección
leh ped**ee** soo deereks-y**o**n
I asked him/her for his/her address

Reflexive Pronouns

These are used with reflexive verbs like **lavarse** 'to wash (one-self)', that is where the subject and the object are one and the same person:

me [meh] myself (used with I)
te [teh] yourself (used with singular, familiar 'you')
se [seh] him/her/itself (used with singular, polite 'you')
nos [nos] ourselves (used with 'we')
se [seh] themselves (used with 'they' and plural 'you')

presentarse to introduce oneself
me presento: me llamo Richard
meh pres**en**to: meh **ya**mo Richard
may I introduce myself? my name's Richard

divertirse to enjoy oneself
nos divertimos mucho en la fiesta
nos deebair**tee**mos **moo**cho en la f-**ye**sta
we enjoyed ourselves a lot at the party

Demonstratives

The English demonstrative adjective 'this' is translated by the Spanish **este**. 'That' is translated by **ese** or **aquel**. **Ese** refers to something near to the person being spoken to. **Aquel** refers to something further away.

Like other adjectives, they agree with the noun they qualify in gender and number but they are placed in front of the noun. Their forms are:

masculine singular			feminine singular		
este	**ese**	**aquel**	**esta**	**esa**	**aquella**
esteh	**es**eh	a**kel**	**es**ta	**es**a	ak**eh**-ya

masculine plural			feminine plural		
estos	**esos**	**aquellos**	**estas**	**esas**	**aquellas**
estos	**es**os	ak**eh**-yos	**es**tas	**es**as	ak**eh**-yas

este restaurante	ese mesero	aquella playa
esteh resto**wr**anteh	**e**seh mes**ai**ro	ak**eh**-ya pl**ī**-ya
this restaurant	that waiter	that beach (in the distance)

'This one', 'that one', 'those', 'these' etc (as pronouns) are translated by the same words as above only they are spelt with an é:

éste	**ése**	**aquél**
esteh	**e**seh	ak**e**l
this one	that one	that one (over there)

quisiera éstos/ésos/aquéllos
kees-y**ai**ra **e**stos/**e**sos/ak**eh**-yos
I'd like these/those/those (over there)

The neuter forms **esto/eso/aquello** are used when no particular noun is being referred to:

esto	**eso**	**aquello**
esto	**e**so	ak**eh**-yo

eso no es justo	**¿qué es esto?**
eso no es H**oo**sto	keh es **e**sto
that's not fair	what is this?

Verbs

The basic form of the verb given in the **English–Spanish** and **Spanish–English** sections is the infinitive (e.g. to drive, to go etc). There are three verb types in Spanish which can be recognized by their infinitive endings: **-ar**, **-er** or **-ir**. For example:

hablar	[ab**lar**]	to talk
comer	[kom**air**]	to eat
abrir	[ab**reer**]	to open

Present Tense

The present tense corresponds to 'I leave' and 'I am leaving' in English. To form the present tense for the three main types of verb in Spanish, remove the -ar, -er or -ir and add the following endings:

hablar to speak

habl-o	[ablo]	I speak
habl-as	[ablas]	you speak (sing, fam)
habl-a	[abla]	he/she speaks, you speak (sing, pol)
habl-amos	[ablamos]	we speak
habl-an	[ablan]	they speak, you speak (pl)

comer to eat

com-o	[komo]	I eat
com-es	[kom-es]	you eat (sing, fam)
com-e	[komeh]	he/she eats, you eat (sing, pol)
com-emos	[komemos]	we eat
com-en	[komen]	they eat, you eat (pl)

abrir to open

abr-o	[abro]	I open
abr-es	[ab-res]	you open (sing, fam)
abr-e	[abreh]	he/she opens, you open (sing, pol)
abr-imos	[abreemos]	we open
abr-en	[abren]	they open, you open (pl)

Some common verbs are irregular:

dar to give

doy	[doy]	I give
das	[das]	you give (sing, fam)
da	[da]	he/she gives, you give (sing, pol)
damos	[damos]	we give
dan	[dan]	they give, you give (pl)

ir to go

voy	[boy]	I go
vas	[bas]	you go (sing, fam)
va	[ba]	he/she goes, you go (sing, pol)
vamos	[bamos]	we go
van	[ban]	they go, you go (pl)

poder can, to be able

puedo	[pwedo]	I can
puedes	[pwed-es]	you can (sing, fam)
puede	[pwedeh]	he/she can, you can (sing, pol)
podemos	[podemos]	we can
pueden	[pweden]	they can, you can (pl)

querer to want

quiero	[k-yairo]	I want
quieres	[k-yair-es]	you want (sing, fam)
quiere	[k-yaireh]	he/she wants, you want (sing, pol)
queremos	[kairemos]	we want
quieren	[k-yairen]	they want, you want (pl)

tener to have

tengo	[tengo]	I have
tienes	[t-yen-es]	you have (sing, fam)
tiene	[t-yeneh]	he/she has, you have (sing, pol)
tenemos	[tenemos]	we have
tienen	[t-yenen]	they have, you have (pl)

venir to come

vengo	[bengo]	I come
vienes	[b-yen-es]	you come (sing, fam)
viene	[b-yeneh]	he/she comes, you come (sing, pol)
venimos	[beneemos]	we come
vienen	[b-yenen]	they come, you come (pl)

The first person singular (the 'I' form) of the following verbs is irregular in some verbs:

decir to say	digo	[deego]
hacer to do, to make	hago	[a-go]
poner to put	pongo	[pongo]
saber to know	sé	[seh]
salir to go out	salgo	[salgo]

See page 263 for the present tense of the verbs **ser** and **estar** 'to be'.

Past Tense:

Preterite

The preterite is the tense normally used to talk about the past:

habl-é	[ableh]	I spoke
habl-aste	[ablasteh]	you spoke (sing, fam)
habl-ó	[ablo]	he/she spoke, you spoke (sing, pol)
habl-amos	[ablamos]	we spoke
habl-aron	[ablaron]	they spoke, you spoke (pl)

com-í	[komee]	I ate
com-iste	[komeesteh]	you ate (sing, fam)
com-ió	[komee-o]	he/she ate, you ate (sing, pol)
com-imos	[komeemos]	we ate
com-ieron	[kom-yairon]	they ate, you ate (pl)

abr-í	[abree]	I opened
abr-iste	[abreesteh]	you opened (sing, fam)
abr-ió	[abree-o]	he/she opened, you opened (sing, pol)
abr-imos	[abreemos]	we opened
abr-ieron	[abr-yairon]	they opened, you opened (pl)

¿quién te dijo eso?
k-yen teh deeHo eso
who told you that?

nos conocimos en Mérida
nos konoseemos en mereeda
we met each other in Mérida

lo compramos el año pasado
lo kompramos el an-yo pasado
we bought it last year

The verbs **ser** (to be) and **ir** (to go) are irregular and have the same form in the preterite:

fui	[fwee]	I was; I went
fuiste	[fweesteh]	you were; you went (sing, fam)
fue	[fweh]	he/she/it was; you were (sing, pol);
		he/she/it went; you went (sing, pol)
fuimos	[fweemos]	we were; we went
fueron	[fwairon]	they were; you were (pl);
		they went; you went (pl)

Perfect Tense

The perfect tense corresponds to the English past tense using 'have' – i.e. 'I have seen', 'he has said' etc. It is formed by combining the appropriate person of the present tense of **haber** with the past participle of the other verb. The present tense of **haber** is as follows:

he	[eh]	I have
has	[as]	you have (sing, fam)
ha	[a]	he/she/it has; you have (sing, pol)
hemos	[emos]	we have
han	[an]	they have; you have (pl)

The past participle is formed by removing the infinitive ending (-ar, -er or -ir) and adding -**ado** or -**ido** as follows:

infinitive	past participle	
hablar	**hablado**	[ablado]
comer	**comido**	[komeedo]
vivir	**vivido**	[beebeedo]

hemos dado una propina
emos dado oona propeena
 we have given a tip

hemos comido bien
emos komeedo b-yen
we've eaten well, we've had a
 good meal

he encendido la luz
eh ensendeedo la loos
I (have) put the light on

Some verbs have irregular past participles:

hacer to do, to make	hecho	[echo]
abrir to open	abierto	[ab-yairto]
decir to say	dicho	[deecho]
volver to return	vuelto	[bwelto]
poner to put	puesto	[pwesto]
ver to see	visto	[beesto]

Imperfect Tense

This tense is used to describe something or someone in the past, or to describe activities that were habitual in the past. It is also the tense you would use to talk about something that was going on over a period of time. It is formed as follows:

hablar to talk
habl-aba	[ablaba]	I was speaking
habl-abas	[ablabas]	you were speaking (sing, fam)
habl-aba	[ablaba]	he/she was speaking, you were speaking (sing, pol)
habl-ábamos	[ablabamos]	we were speaking
habl-aban	[ablaban]	they were speaking, you were speaking (pl)

comer to eat
com-ía	[komee-a]	I was eating
com-ías	[komee-as]	you were eating (sing, fam)
com-ía	[komee-a]	he/she/it was eating, you were eating (sing, pol)
com-íamos	[komee-amos]	we were eating
com-ían	[komee-an]	they were eating, you were eating (pl)

abrir to open

abr-ía	[abr**ee**-a]	I was opening
abr-ías	[abr**ee**-as]	you were opening (sing, fam)
abr-ía	[abr**ee**-a]	he/she/it was opening, you were opening (sing, pol)
abr-íamos	[abr**ee**-amos]	we were opening
abr-ían	[abr**ee**-an]	they were opening, you were opening (pl)

Other useful verbs in the imperfect tense are:

estar to be

estaba	[est**a**ba]	I was
estabas	[est**a**bas]	you were (sing, fam)
estaba	[est**a**ba]	he/she/it was, you were (sing, pol)
estábamos	[est**a**bamos]	we were
estaban	[est**a**ban]	they were, you were (pl)

tener to have

tenía	[ten**ee**-a]	I had
tenías	[ten**ee**-as]	you had (sing, fam)
tenía	[ten**ee**-a]	he/she/it had, you had (sing, pol)
teníamos	[ten**ee**-amos]	we had
tenían	[ten**ee**-an]	they had, you had (pl)

The following are irregular in the imperfect tense:

ir to go

iba	[**ee**ba]	I was going
ibas	[**ee**bas]	you were going (sing, fam)
iba	[**ee**ba]	he/she/it was going, you were going (sing, pol)
íbamos	[**ee**bamos]	we were going
iban	[**ee**ban]	they were going, you were going (pl)

ser to be (see page 263 for more on this)

era	[**ai**ra]	I was
eras	[**ai**ras]	you were (sing, fam)
era	[**ai**ra]	he/she/it was, you were (sing, pol)
éramos	[**ai**ramos]	we were
eran	[**ai**ran]	they were, you were (pl)

todos los viernes salíamos a dar un paseo
t**o**dos los b-y**ai**rn-es sal**ee**-amos a dar oon pas**eh**-o
every Friday we used to go for a walk, every Friday we
   went for a walk

era alto y delgado
aira **a**lto ee delg**a**do
he was tall and slim

viajaban de México a Veracruz
bee-a**H**aban deh me**H**eeko a bairakr**oo**s
they were travelling from Mexico to Veracruz

Future Tense

To form the future tense in Spanish (I will do, you will do etc)
add the following endings to the infinitive. The same endings
are used whether verbs end in **-ar**, **-er** or **-ir**:

hablar-**é**	[ablar**eh**]	I will speak
hablar-**ás**	[ablar**as**]	you will speak (sing, fam)
hablar-**á**	[ablar**a**]	he/she/you will speak (sing, pol)
hablar-**emos**	[ablar**emos**]	we will speak
hablar-**án**	[ablar**an**]	they/you will speak (pl)

llamaré más tarde
yamar**eh** mas t**a**rdeh
I'll call later

The immediate future can also be translated by **ir** + **a** + infinitive:

vamos a comprar una botella de vino tinto
bamos a komprar **oo**na bote**h**-ya deh **vee**no **tee**nto
we're going to buy a bottle of red wine

iré a recogerlo
eer**eh** a reko**H**airlo
I'll fetch him, I'll go and fetch him

In Spanish, as in English, the future can sometimes be expressed by the present tense:

tu avión sale a la una
too ab-**yo**n s**a**leh a la **oo**na
your plane takes off at one o'clock

However, Spanish often uses the present tense where the future would be used in English:

le doy ochocientos pesos
leh doy ochos-**ye**ntos **pe**sos
I'll give you 800 pesos

The following verbs are irregular in the future tense:

decir	to say	diré	I will say
hacer	to do	haré	I will do
poder	to be able	podré	I will be able
poner	to put	pondré	I will put
querer	to want	querré	I will want
saber	to know	sabré	I will know
salir	to leave	saldré	I will leave
tener	to have	tendré	I will have
venir	to come	vendré	I will come

The Verb 'To Be'

There are two verbs 'to be' in Spanish: **ser** and **estar**. The present tense is as follows:

ser

soy	[soy]	I am
eres	[**air**-es]	you are (sing, fam)
es	[es]	he/she/it is, you are (sing, pol)
somos	[**so**mos]	we are
son	[son]	they are, you are (pl)

estar

estoy	[est**oy**]	I am
estás	[est**as**]	you are (sing, fam)
está	[est**a**]	he/she/it is, you are (sing, pol)
estamos	[est**a**mos]	we are
están	[est**an**]	they are, you are (pl)

Ser

Ser is generally used to describe a permanent state, for example, what something or someone looks like or what their nature is:

> **la nieve es blanca**
> la n-y**e**beh es bl**a**nka
> snow is white

Ser is also used with occupations, nationalities, the time and to indicate possession:

somos escoceses	**mi madre es profesora**
s**o**mos esk**o**ses-es	mi m**a**dreh es profes**o**ra
we are Scottish	my mother is a teacher

éste es nuestro carro	**son las cinco de la tarde**
esteh es nw**e**stro k**a**rro	son las s**ee**nko deh la t**a**rdeh
this is our car	it's five o'clock in the afternoon

Estar

Estar, on the other hand, is used above all to answer the question 'where?':

el libro está en la mesa
el l**ee**bro est**a** en la m**e**sa
the book is on the table

Nuevo Laredo está en el norte del país
nw**e**vo lar**e**do est**a** en el n**o**rteh del pa-**ee**s
Nuevo Laredo is in the north of the country

It also describes the temporary or passing qualities of something or someone:

estoy enojado
est**oy** enoH**a**do
I'm angry

estoy cansado
est**oy** kans**a**do
I'm tired

este filete está frío
esteh feel**e**teh est**a** fr**ee**-o
this steak is cold

Note the difference between the following two phrases:

Isabel es muy guapa
Isabel es mw**ee** gw**a**pa
Isabel is very pretty

Isabel está muy guapa (esta noche)
Isabel est**a** mw**ee** gw**a**pa **e**sta n**o**cheh
Isabel looks pretty (tonight)

soy inglés
soy eeng-l**e**s
I am English

estoy en México
est**oy** en meH**ee**ko
I am in Mexico

Negatives

To express a negative in Spanish, to say 'I don't want', 'it's not here' etc, place the word **no** in front of the verb:

entiendo
ent-y**e**ndo
I understand

no entiendo
no ent-y**e**ndo
I don't understand

me gusta este helado
meh g**oo**sta **e**steh el**a**do
I like this ice cream

no me gusta este helado
no meh g**oo**sta **e**steh el**a**do
I don't like this ice cream

lo alquilé aquí	no lo alquilé aquí
lo alkeel**eh** ak**ee**	no lo alkeel**eh** ak**ee**
I rented it here	I didn't rent it here

van a cantar	no van a cantar
ban a kantar	no ban a kantar
they're going to sing	they're not going to sing

To use negative words like:

nadie	nada	nunca
n**a**d-yeh	n**a**da	n**oo**nka
no-one, nobody	nothing	never

you can either place them before the verb, or put them after the verb with **no** in front, thus:

no llegó nadie/nadie llegó	no hay nadie ahí
no yeg**o** n**a**d-yeh/n**a**d-yeh yeg**o**	no ī n**a**d-yeh a-**ee**
nobody came	there's no-one there

no compramos nada	no sabemos nada de ella
no kompr**a**mos n**a**da	no sab**e**mos n**a**da deh **eh**-ya
we didn't buy anything	we don't know anything about her

To say 'there's no ...', 'I've no ...' etc, make the accompanying verb negative:

no hay vino	no tengo cerillas
no ī b**ee**no	no t**e**ngo sair**ee**-yas
there's no wine	I've no matches

To say 'not him', 'not her' etc just use the personal pronoun followed by **no**:

nosotros, no	ella, no	yo, no
nos**o**tros no	**eh**-ya no	yo no
not us	not her	not me

265

Imperatives

When giving a command to people you would normally address with **Usted** or **Ustedes**, you form the imperative by taking the first person singular of the present tense and changing the endings as follows:

	first person singular	singular	plural
hablar to speak	**hablo**	**habl-e**	**habl-en**
		ableh	**a**blen
comer to eat	**como**	**com-a**	**com-an**
		koma	**ko**man
abrir to open	**abro**	**abr-a**	**abr-an**
		abra	**a**bran
venir to come	**vengo**	**ven-ga**	**ven-gan**
		benga	**be**ngan

coma despacio
koma despa**s**-yo
eat slowly

When you are telling someone not to do something, use the forms above and place **no** in front of the verb:

no me moleste, por favor	**¡no beba alcohol!**
no meh mole**ste**h por fa**bo**r	no **be**ba alk**o**l
please don't disturb me	don't drink alcohol!

¡no venga esta noche!
no **be**nga **e**sta **no**cheh
don't come tonight!

To give a command to people you would normally address as **tú**, remove the endings **-ar**, **-er**, and **-ir** from the verb and add these endings:

hablar to speak	**habl-a**	[**a**bla]
comer to eat	**com-e**	[**ko**meh]
abrir to open	**abr-e**	[**a**breh]

To form a negative imperative to people addressed as **tú**, **no** is placed in front of the verb and the endings change:

habla	no habl-es	[no **ab**-les]
come	no com-as	[no **ko**mas]
abre	no abras	[no **a**bras]

por favor, no hables tan rápido (to one person)
por fab**or** no **ab**-les tan ra**pee**do
please don't speak so quickly

Pronouns are added to the end of the imperative form:

despiérteme a las ocho, por favor
desp-y**air**temeh a las **o**cho por fab**or**
wake me up at eight o'clock, please

bébelo	**ciérralas**	**ayúdeme, por favor**
b**e**belo	s-y**air**alas	a-y**oo**demeh por fab**or**
drink it	close them	help me please

but when the imperative is negative, they are placed in front of it:

no lo bebas	**no las cierres**
no lo b**e**bas	no las s-y**air**-res
don't drink it	don't close them

The imperatives of the verb **ir** 'to go' are irregular:

forms	Usted	Ustedes	tú
	vaya	vayan	ve
	b**ī**-a	b**ī**-an	beh

Questions

Often the word order remains the same in a question, but the intonation changes, the voice rising at the end of the question:

¿quieres bailar?   ¿quieres ir al cine?
k-yair-es bilar   k-yair-es eer al seeneh
do you want to dance?   do you want to go to the cinema?

Dates

Use the numbers on page 270 to express the date:

el uno de septiembre [el **oo**no deh set-yembreh] the first of
  September
el dos de diciembre [dos deh dees-yembreh] the second of
  December
el treinta de mayo [traynta deh mī-yo] the thirtieth of May
el treinta y uno de mayo [traynti **oo**no deh mī-yo] the thirty-first of
  May

Days

Sunday domingo
Monday lunes [**loo**n-es]
Tuesday martes [mart-es]
Wednesday miércoles [m-yairkol-es]
Thursday jueves [Hweb-es]
Friday viernes [b-yairn-es]
Saturday sábado

Months

January enero [enairo]
February febrero [febrairo]
March marzo [marso]
April abril
May mayo [mī-yo]
June junio [Hoon-yo]
July julio [Hool-yo]
August agosto

September septiembre [set-yembreh]
October octubre [oktoobreh]
November noviembre [nob-yembreh]
December diciembre [dees-yembreh]

Time

what time is it? ¿qué hora es? [keh ora]
one o'clock la una
two o'clock las dos
it's one o'clock es la una
it's two o'clock son las dos
it's ten o'clock son las diez [d-yes]
five past one la una y cinco [ee seenko]
ten past two las dos y diez
quarter past one la una y cuarto [ee kwarto]
quarter past two las dos y cuarto
half past ten las diez y media [d-yes ee med-ya]
twenty to ten veinte para las diez [baynteh]
quarter to ten cuarto para las diez
at eight o'clock a las ocho [ocho]
at half past four a las cuatro y media [kwatro ee med-ya]
2 a.m. las dos de la mañana [deh la man-yana]
2 p.m. las dos de la tarde [tardeh]
6 a.m. las seis de la mañana [seh-ees deh la man-yana]
6 p.m. las seis de la tarde
noon mediodía [med-yo-dee-a]
midnight medianoche [med-ya-nocheh]
an hour una hora [ora]
a minute un minuto
two minutes dos minutos
a second un segundo
a quarter of an hour un cuarto de hora [kwarto deh ora]
half an hour media hora [med-ya]
three quarters of an hour tres cuartos de hora [kwartos deh ora]

Numbers

0	cero [sairo]	
1	uno, una	
2	dos	
3	tres	
4	cuatro [kwatro]	
5	cinco [seenko]	
6	seis [says]	
7	siete [s-yeteh]	
8	ocho [ocho]	
9	nueve [nwebeh]	
10	diez [d-yes]	
11	once [onseh]	
12	doce [doseh]	
13	trece [treseh]	
14	catorce [katorseh]	
15	quince [keenseh]	
16	dieciséis [d-yeseese-ees]	
17	diecisiete [d-yesees-yeteh]	
18	dieciocho [d-yesee-ocho]	
19	diecinueve [d-yeseenwebeh]	
20	veinte [baynteh]	
21	veintiuno [bayntee-oono]	
22	veintidós [baynteedos]	
23	veintitrés [baynteetres]	
30	treinta [traynta]	
31	treinta y uno [traynti oono]	
40	cuarenta [kwarenta]	
50	cincuenta [seenkwenta]	
60	sesenta	
70	setenta	
80	ochenta [ochenta]	
90	noventa [nobenta]	
100	cien [s-yen]	

120	ciento veinte [s-yento baynteh]	
200	doscientos, doscientas [dos-yentos]	
300	trescientos, trescientas [tres-yentos]	
400	cuatrocientos, cuatrocientas [kwatros-yentos]	
500	quinientos, quinientas [keen-yentos]	
600	seiscientos, seiscientas [says-yentos]	
700	setecientos, setecientas [setes-yentos]	
800	ochocientos, ochocientas [ochos-yentos]	
900	novecientos, novecientas [nobes-yentos]	
1,000	mil	
2,000	dos mil	
5,000	cinco mil [seenko]	
10,000	diez mil [d-yes]	
1,000,000	un millón [meel-yon]	

When **uno** is used with a masculine noun, the final **-o** is dropped:

> **un carro**
> oon karo
> a/one car

una is used with feminine nouns:

> **una bicicleta**
> oona beeseekleta
> a/one bike

With multiples of a hundred, the **-as** ending is used with feminine nouns:

trescientos hombres	**quinientas mujeres**
tres-yentos omb-res	keen-yentas mooHair-es
300 men	500 women

Ordinals

1st primero [preemairo]
2nd segundo
3rd tercero [tairsairo]
4th cuarto [kwarto]
5th quinto [keento]
6th sexto [sesto]
7th séptimo
8th octavo [oktabo]
9th noveno [nobeno]
10th décimo [deseemo]

Conversion Tables

1 centimetre = 0.39 inches   1 inch = 2.54 cm

1 metre = 39.37 inches = 1.09 yards   1 foot = 30.48 cm

1 kilometre = 0.62 miles = 5/8 mile   1 yard = 0.91 m

1 mile = 1.61 km

km	1	2	3	4	5	10	20	30	40	50	100
miles	0.6	1.2	1.9	2.5	3.1	6.2	12.4	18.6	24.8	31.0	62.1

miles	1	2	3	4	5	10	20	30	40	50	100
km	1.6	3.2	4.8	6.4	8.0	16.1	32.2	48.3	64.4	80.5	161

1 gram = 0.035 ounces   1 kilo = 1000 g = 2.2 pounds

g	100	250	500	1 oz = 28.35 g
oz	3.5	8.75	17.5	1 lb = 0.45 kg

kg	0.5	1	2	3	4	5	6	7	8	9	10
lb	1.1	2.2	4.4	6.6	8.8	11.0	13.2	15.4	17.6	19.8	22.0

kg	20	30	40	50	60	70	80	90	100
lb	44	66	88	110	132	154	176	198	220

lb	0.5	1	2	3	4	5	6	7	8	9	10	20
kg	0.2	0.5	0.9	1.4	1.8	2.3	2.7	3.2	3.6	4.1	4.5	9.0

1 litre = 1.75 UK pints / 2.13 US pints

1 UK pint = 0.57 l   1 UK gallon = 4.55 l
1 US pint = 0.47 l   1 US gallon = 3.79 l

centigrade / Celsius   °C = (°F - 32) x 5/9

°C	-5	0	5	10	15	18	20	25	30	36.8	38
°F	23	32	41	50	59	64	68	77	86	98.4	100.4

Fahrenheit   °F = (°C x 9/5) + 32

°F	23	32	40	50	60	65	70	80	85	98.4	101
°C	-5	0	4	10	16	18	21	27	29	36.8	38.3